Russian
A Self-Teaching Guide

Kathryn Szczepanska

WILEY

John Wiley & Sons, Inc.

Published by John Wiley & Sons, Inc., Hoboken, New Jersey
Published simultaneously in Canada

For general information about our other products and services, please contact our Customer Care Department within the United States at (800) 762-2974, outside the United States at (317) 572-3993 or fax (317) 572-4002.

Wiley also publishes its books in a variety of electronic formats. Some content that appears in print may not be available in electronic books. For more information about Wiley products, visit our web site at www.wiley.com.

ISBN-13 978-0-471-26989-2 (paper)
ISBN-10 0-471-26989-1 (paper)

Printed in the United States of America

10 9 8 7 6 5 4 3 2 1

In memory of
Bruce Everett Fritch
(1936–1985)

Contents

Acknowledgments

I hereby acknowledge publicly to my former professors at Stanford University—Joseph A. Van Campen and Dina B. Crockett—that they were right about everything. I am grateful to the editors at John Wiley & Sons for their unstinting generosity of time and labor, especially to John Simko for his attention to detail, Jeff Golick for his patience, and copy editor Dobrochna Dyrcz-Freeman for her sharp eye and mind. To Stan and Nancy, the *sine qua non* of my existence, a big fat punch in the nose. And to my Muse and herself a future author, Pamela Rose Machado, thanks for keeping me up at all hours of the day and night, and for simply being you.

1 The Russian Alphabet

Русский алфавит

The Russian alphabet, also called Cyrillic, consists of thirty-three letters representing thirty-one sounds and two signs that have no phonetic value of their own. It is attributed to the Greek monks Cyrill and Methodius, who came as missionaries to Christianize the Slavic countries and left their mark on the language as well. Modified forms of this alphabet are still in use today in countries other than Russia, including Bulgaria and some of the new nations of the former Yugoslavia.

Approximately one-third of the Cyrillic alphabet consists of letters that are identical to the Roman alphabet, with a phonetic value that is either almost equal or similar. Another third of the letters are recognizable to Westerners because of their Greek origin: п is the Greek *pi,* р is the Greek *rho,* and so forth. The final third consists of letters that were created to represent sounds in the Slavic languages that had no counterpart in the original Greek of the missionary monks. Some of these letters have a Hebrew origin, such as the letter ш [sh].[1]

Although there are visual and phonetic similarities, almost no Russian letter is pronounced in quite the same way as its English counterpart. Russian vowels are purer and more clear than English vowels, and, except for combinations with the consonant-glide й, do not form diphthongs. Many Russian consonants form "hard" and "soft" pairs, which are not easy to represent in English. Consonants that are plosive in English (*p, b, t, d*) are not plosive in Russian, which makes their

---

[1]Brackets will be used throughout the text to indicate pronunciation.

pronunciation for English speakers difficult. And last, the famous Russian fricatives ш [sh], ж [zh], ч [ch], щ [sh'], ц [ts] pose challenges all their own.

You will find a complete list of the Russian alphabet on page 13.

Sounds and Spelling

Vowels

There are ten Russian letters for five vowel sounds:

Hard		Soft	
Letter	Pronunciation	Letter	Pronunciation
а	*a* as in *father*	я	*ya* as in *yard*
э	*e* as in *fed*	е	*ye* as in *yet*
ы	*i* as in *sit*	и	*ee* as in *feet*
о	*o* as in *home*	ё	*yo* as in *yore*
у	*oo* as in *food*	ю	*yu* as in *Yukon*

The vowels in the first column are called hard and are written at the beginning of a word and after hard consonants. The vowels in the second column are the soft vowels. They are written after soft consonants and when the word begins with an iotated vowel (the sound [y]). Compare the following: а́лто (alto)—Я́лта (Yalta); Эми́лия (Emilia)—Еле́на (Yelena); О́льга (Olga)—ёжик (hedgehog); Ура́л (Urals)—Ю́рий (Yuri). The letters representing the sound [i] do not quite fit this paradigm, since their pure sounds are not quite the same. Nonetheless, they obey the rule above: the ы is written after hard consonants and the и after soft consonants.

Consonants

Hard or Soft

Russian consonants may be either hard or soft.[2] Most English consonants are pronounced with a hard articulation, but most Russian consonants can be pronounced either way. By far the best example for English speakers of the difference between a hard and a soft consonant is the Spanish consonant ñ and the English letter *n*. The sound also occurs occasionally in English words, such as

---

[2]They are also called palatalized and nonpalatalized.

onion and *poignant*. As a device to assist in the pronunciation of Russian soft consonants, some textbooks suggest the insertion of the glide [y] between the consonant and the following vowel so that a hard **n** plus **a** would be transcribed as [na] and a soft **n** plus **a** as [nya]. This device is not quite correct, but it can be useful to help the student achieve a correct pronunciation.

The following list of consonants shows the hard and soft pairs possible in modern Russian. For ease in pronunciation, they are shown with the vowel letters **э** and **e**.

Hard	Soft	Hard	Soft
бэ	бе	нэ	не
вэ	ве	пэ	пе
гэ	ге	рэ	ре
дэ	де	сэ	се
зэ	зе	тэ	те
кэ	ке	фэ	фе
лэ	ле	хэ	хе
мэ	ме		

There are six consonants in Russian that are either hard or soft, but not both. The three always-hard consonants are **ж** [zh], **ц** [ts], and **ш** [sh]. No matter which vowel follows them, they will always be pronounced hard. The three consonants that are always pronounced soft are **ч** [ch], **щ** [sh'], and **й** ([y] as in *boy*). These facts have various consequences for the writing system. None of these consonants may be followed by the vowel **ы** (the vowel **и** is written instead). In addition, the vowels **я** and **ю** appear as **a** and **y**. The result is the all-important seven-letter spelling rule:

> After the fricatives **ж, ч, ш, щ,** and the velars **к, г, х,** do not write **ы, я,** or **ю;** instead, write **и, a,** or **y.**

The letter **ц** is not part of this spelling rule. The full explanation for this spelling rule can be appreciated only with an understanding of the historical morphology of Russian.

The pronunciations of the consonants **ж, ч, ш,** and **щ** differ from their transliterated values [zh], [ch], [sh], and [sh']. In fact, their articulation in terms of hardness and softness is opposite to their sounds in English. In Russian, the consonants **ж** and **ш** are always hard, whereas they are soft in English. The reverse is true for the consonants **ч** and **щ.** This will explain the English transliteration of the name of the composer **Чайко́вский** as *Tchaikovsky,* which attempts to move the articulation of the sound [ch] to the front of the mouth, toward the teeth, to more accurately reflect the correct pronunciation. In other words, start to pronounce [t] and then immediately follow with [ch].

As for the hard consonants, there is no way to represent on paper the *whooshing* sound of the letters ж and ш in the mouth of a native speaker. Focus your attention on passing the air past your molars, in the back or your mouth, rather than at your front teeth. But by all means, find a Russian who can produce for your ear the true sound of these letters.

One further fact must be mentioned regarding the fricatives ш and щ. In the Moscow (or Standard) pronunciation, the first is pronounced as a hard [sh], which does not appear in English. But the second, the Russian щ, is pronounced as a soft [sh], which corresponds exactly to the English. In the Petersburg pronunciation, however, the letter щ is pronounced with a further articulation as [shch]. This pronunciation is actively discouraged not only by the faculty of the Language Department of Moscow State University but also by teachers of Russian abroad, who find that students have a most difficult time with this letter. The sound itself occurs in English within a word (for instance, *question*) or between words (*fresh cheese*) but does not occur in initial position.

Voiced or Devoiced

Russian consonants may be either voiced or devoiced. This phenomenon is observed only in the pronunciation of Russian words but serves to explain one of the peculiarities of the Russian accent that is occasionally encountered in English. Voiced consonants are pronounced with the vocal cords, and devoiced consonants without. The following six pairs comprise the voiced/devoiced consonants of Russian: б/п, д/т, в/ф, з/с, г/к, and ж/ш.

The environment in which devoicing operates is word-final position. (Consonants may also be devoiced within a word in consonant clusters, but this is not of great significance for introductory remarks on phonetics.) Thus, to Russian speakers, the English words *bank* and *bang* are pronounced absolutely identically, as are the pairs *mob* and *mop, have* and *half, mad* and *mat, raze* and *race.* If you cannot remember to devoice consonants, you will have an accent in Russian similar to the Russian who says in English, "*Fife bucks,*" when he wants to say, "*Five bugs.*"

There are several letters that represent voiced or devoiced sounds in Russian that do not have corresponding letters to depict their counterparts. One such example is the devoiced sound represented by the letter ч. The voiced counterpart phonetically would be the sound represented in English by the letter *j,* but this sound has no letter in Cyrillic. Nonetheless, the sound exists in certain environments. In order to represent this sound in the transcription of foreign words, the combination **дж** is used: **Джон** (John), **Джо́рджия** (Georgia), **Нью-Джéрси** (New Jersey). Similarly, the letters **х, ц,** and **щ** are devoiced only. Russians resort to various means to represent voiced variants for foreign words that contain these sounds. The voiced variant of **ц,** for instance, which occurs in surnames from Georgia, is represented by the letters **дз: Шевардна́дзе, Орждоники́дзе.** The voiced variant of **щ** appears only rarely in spoken Russian and is usually spelled by the letter combination **зж** or a double **ж: éзжу** (I drive), **дро́жжи** (yeast), **уезжа́ть** (to depart).

The letters **м, н, р, л** are voiced only.

Pronunciation Rules for Vowels

Whereas there are ten letters in the Cyrillic alphabet that represent vowels, there are a different number of actual vowel sounds because of the following pronunciation rules.

1. The letters **a** and **o** are pronounced as **a** and **o** when under stress. When not stressed, they are reduced to the following values:

a: Whenever the vowel **a** occurs after a stressed syllable or more than one syllable before the stressed syllable, except for initial position, it is pronounced as the *u* in *but* or the *a* in *about* or *sofa*. Sometimes books use the symbol ǝ (also called a schwa) to represent this reduced sound.

Thus, a multisyllabic word with the letter **a** in all vowel positions would be phonetically represented as **a_ǝ_a_á_ǝ_ǝ.**

o: The vowel **o** is pronounced as **a** in the first pretonic position (the syllable immediately before the stressed syllable) and at the beginning of a word. In all other positions it is pronounced as ǝ (see above).

The same theoretical multisyllabic word with the letter **o** in all positions would be shown as **a_ǝ_a_ó_ǝ_ǝ.**

Examples

хорошо́	[kherasho] (three distinct vowel sounds, but one vowel letter!)
борода́	[berada]
окно́	[akno]
обстано́вка	[abstanofke]
отстоя́ть	[atstayat']
погово́рка	[pegavorke]

Examples

отро́сток	[astrostek]
отвороти́ть	[atveratit']
достопримеча́тельность	[desteprimichatil'nest']

2. The letters **е** and **я** are pronounced with their full value only under stress. In all other positions their value is reduced to a sound approaching the vowel **и.**

Examples

язы́к	[yizyk]
де́сять	[desyit']
пятьдеся́т	[pyit'disyat']
интерпрета́ция	[intirpritatsiye]
беспоко́иться	[bispakoyitse]

Transliteration

When a Russian word is written in the Roman alphabet, it is said to be transliterated. This is an attempt not to reproduce the correct pronunciation but rather to render the letters from one alphabet into another. The system of transliteration used in this book is close to the phonetic value of the letters, with a few exceptions.

1. The soft vowels **я, ё,** and **ю** are written *ya, yo,* and *yu* in all positions. The soft vowel **е** is written *ye* initially and after vowels but *e* after consonants. There is no special symbol for the vowel **э,** which is written in all positions as *e.*

2. The vowels **и** and **ы** are transliterated respectively as *i* and *y* in all positions.

3. To avoid needless punctuation, the consonant **ш** is written as *sh* and the consonant **щ** as *shch.*

4. The soft sign is indicated by a single apostrophe; the relatively rare hard sign by a double apostrophe.

NOTE: In the reverse process when Russian adopts foreign names that begin with an *h,* which does not exist in Russian, the *h* is replaced by the letter **г.** Thus, the following proper names are the correct transliteration into Russian: **Гава́йи** (Hawaii), **Гомер** (Homer), **Галифакс** (Halifax), **Голландия** (Holland), and **Голливуд** (Hollywood).

Practice

In the following tables, you will see words of varying degrees of familiarity. Try to pronounce them aloud before you scan your eye to the English version.

Typical Russian Names for Women

Full Name	Nickname	English
А́нна	А́ня	Anna
Алекса́ндра	Са́ша, Шу́ра	Alexandra
Анастаси́я	А́ся, На́стя	Anastasia
Ве́ра	—	Vera
Валенти́на	Ва́ля	Valentina
Викто́рия	Ви́ка	Victoria
Гали́на	Га́ля	Galina
Евге́ния	Же́ня	Eugenia
Екатери́на	Ка́тя	Katherine
Еле́на	Ле́на	Yelena, Ellen, Helen
Елизаве́та	Ли́за	Elizabeth
Зо́я	—	Zoya, Zoë
Ири́на	И́ра	Irene
Лари́са	Ла́ра	Larisa
Любо́вь	Лю́ба	Lyubov, Amy
Ли́дия	Ли́да	Lydia
Мари́на	(various)	Marina
Мари́я	Ма́ша	Maria, Mary
Наде́жда	На́дя	Nadezhda, Hope
Ната́лья	Ната́ша	Natalie, Natasha
Ни́на	—	Nina
О́льга	О́ля	Olga
Раи́са	Ра́я	Raisa
Светла́на	Све́та	Svetlana
Софи́я	Со́ня	Sophia, Sonia, Sophie
Тама́ра	То́ма	Tamara
Татья́на	Та́ня	Tatiana, Tania
Ю́лия	Ю́ля	Julia, Julie

Unusual names for both men and women in Russian are most often associated with the names of obscure saints from the Russian Orthodox calendar or are borrowings from exotic, non-Slavic languages.

Some Unusual Russian Names for Women

Full Name	Nickname	English
Авдо́тья	Ду́ня	—
Ага́фья	Ага́ша	—
Васили́са	Ва́ся	Vasilisa
Владле́на[3]	Ле́ня	—
Да́рья	Да́ша	Daria
Евдо́кия	(various)	—
Евфроси́нья	Фро́ся	—
Зинаи́да	Зи́на	Zinaida
Ки́ра	—	Kira
Ксе́ния	Кса́на	—
Луке́рья	Лу́ся	—
Матрёна	Матрёша	—
Нине́ль[4]	Не́ля	—
Праско́вья	(various)	—
Серафи́ма	Си́ма	—
Фёкла	—	—

Most of these names have no direct counterpart in Modern English. Many were popular in the nineteenth century, especially among the peasantry. Thus, **Тётя Даша** sounds to the Russian ear something like *Auntie Millie*. They are widely encountered throughout Russian literature.

Some Typical Russian Names for Men

Full Name	Nickname	English
Алекса́ндр	Са́ша	Alexander
Алексе́й	Алёша	Aleksei
Анато́лий	То́лик	Anatoly
Андре́й	Андрю́ша	Andrei, Andrew
Анто́н	Анто́ша	Anton
Бори́с	Бо́ря	Boris
Вади́м	Ди́ма	Vadim
Васи́лий	Ва́ся	Vasily

---

[3]Contracted from *Vlad*imir *Len*in.
[4]"Lenin" backward.

Full Name	Nickname	English
Ви́ктор	Ви́тя	Victor
Влади́мир	Воло́дя	Vladimir
Вячесла́в	Сла́ва	Vyacheslav
Глеб	—	Gleb
Григо́рий	Гри́ша	Gregory
Дави́д	—	David
Дми́трий	Ди́ма	Dmitry
Евге́ний	Же́ня	Eugene
Ива́н	Ва́ня	Ivan, John
И́горь	—	Igor
Илья́	Илью́ша	Ilya
Константи́н	Ко́стя	Constantine
Лев	Лёва	Leo
Макси́м	Макс	Maxim
Михаи́л	Ми́ша	Michael
Никола́й	Ко́ля	Nicholas
Оле́г	—	Oleg
Па́вел	Па́ша	Paul
Пётр	Пе́тя	Peter
Семён	Се́ня	Simon
Серге́й	Серёжа	Sergei
Степа́н	Стёпа	Steven
Фёдор	Фе́дя	Theodore
Ю́рий	Ю́ра	Yuri
Я́ков	Я́ша	Jacob

Some Less Frequently Encountered Russian Names for Men

Full Name	Nickname	English
Авра́м	Авра́ша	Abraham
Аполло́н	Аполло́ша	Apollo
Арка́дий	Арка́ша	Arcady
Артём	Тёма	—
Афана́сий	Афо́н	Athanasius
Виссарио́н	Ви́ся	Vissarion
Владле́н	Вла́дя	—
Все́волод	Воло́дя	—

Full Name	Nickname	English
Гаврии́л	Га́ня	Gabriel
Гена́дий	Ге́на	—
Гераси́м	Ге́ра	—
Дании́л	Да́ня	Daniel
Демья́н	Дёма	—
Евдоки́м	Евдо́ша	—
Емелья́н	Еме́ля	—
Ермола́й	Ермо́ша	—
Заха́р	—	—
Ипполи́т	По́ля	Hippolytus
Кири́лл	Ки́ра	Cyril
Кузьма́	Ку́зя	—
Лавре́нтий	Ла́врик	Laurence
Лука́	Лука́ша	Luke
Мака́р	—	—
Ники́та	Ни́ка	—
Плато́н	То́ша	Plato
Порфи́рий	Фи́рик	Porfiry
Родио́н	Ро́дя	—
Тере́нтий	Терёха	—
Тимофе́й	Ти́ма	Timothy
Тихо́н	Ти́ша	—
Трофи́м	Тро́ша	—
Филли́п	Фи́ля	Philip
Фома́	—	Thomas
Харито́н	—	—

Typical American Names in Russian

Russian	English	Russian	English
Джон	John	Пол	Paul
Дже́ннифер	Jennifer	Мэ́ри	Mary
Бе́тти	Betty	Кэ́трин	Catherine
Шон	Sean	Са́ра	Sarah
Ке́лли	Kelly	Ти́ффани	Tiffany
Джек	Jack	Джордж	George

Russian	English	Russian	English
Крис	Chris	Эдуа́рд	Edward
Стив	Steve	Пи́тер	Peter
Дайа́на	Diana	Са́ндра	Sandra
Дэ́йвид	David	Джеф	Jeff
Луи́за	Louise	Ле́сли	Lesley
До́нна	Donna	Си́нтия	Cynthia

Some Countries of the World in Russian

1. Фра́нция
2. Ита́лия
3. Вьетна́м
4. А́встрия
5. Афганиста́н
6. Аргенти́на
7. Ира́к
8. Ирла́ндия
9. Кана́да
10. Ме́ксика
11. Португа́лия
12. И́ндия
13. Брази́лия
14. Чи́ли
15. Болга́рия
16. Алжи́р
17. Япо́ния
18. Казахста́н
19. Изра́иль
20. Да́ния
21. Швейца́рия
22. Пакиста́н
23. Гре́ция
24. Австра́лия
25. Кита́й
26. Экуадо́р
27. Че́хия
28. Герма́ния
29. По́льша
30. Эфио́пия
31. Ту́рция
32. Голла́ндия
33. Ара́вия
34. Украи́на
35. Узбекиста́н
36. Коре́я

Some Countries of the World in English

1. France
2. Italy
3. Vietnam
4. Austria
5. Afghanistan
6. Argentina
7. Iraq
8. Ireland
9. Canada

10. Mexico	19. Israel	28. Germany
11. Portugal	20. Denmark	29. Poland
12. India	21. Switzerland	30. Ethiopia
13. Brazil	22. Pakistan	31. Turkey
14. Chile	23. Greece	32. Holland
15. Bulgaria	24. Australia	33. Arabia
16. Algeria	25. China	34. Ukraine
17. Japan	26. Ecuador	35. Uzbekistan
18. Kazakhstan	27. Czech Republic	36. Korea

The following are arranged alphabetically according to their position in the Russian alphabet. See how quickly you can recognize them. Some of them you will spot immediately, but some are truly opaque. Note that the correct Russian spelling does not necessarily correspond to the English pronunciation.

American States

Áйдахо	Калифо́рния	Нью-Йо́рк
Áйова	Канза́с	Нью-Ме́ксико
Алаба́ма	Кенту́кки	Нью-Хэ́мпшир
Аля́ска	Колора́до	Ога́йо
Аризо́на	Конне́ктикут	Оклахо́ма
Арканза́с	Луизиа́на	Ореѓо́н
Вайо́минг	Массачу́сетс	Пенсильва́ния
Вашингто́н	Миннесо́та	Ро́д-Айленд
Вермо́нт	Миссиси́пи	Се́верная Дако́та
Вирги́ния	Миссу́ри	Се́верная Кароли́на
Виско́нсин	Мичига́н	Теннесси́
Гава́йи	Монта́на	Теха́с
Де́лавэр	Мэн	Флори́да
Джо́рджия	Мэ́риленд	Ю́жная Дако́та
За́падная Вирги́ния	Небра́ска	Ю́жная Кароли́на
Иллино́йс	Нева́да	Ю́та
Индиа́на	Нью-Дже́рси	

The Cyrillic Alphabet

Below you will find the Russian alphabet in upper and lower case, with phonetic transcription.

Letter	Transcription	Letter	Transcription
А а	[a]	Р р	[r]
Б б	[b]	С с	[s]
В в	[v]	Т т	[t]
Г г	[g]	У у	[u]
Д д	[d]	Ф ф	[f]
Е е	[ye/e]	Х х	[kh]
Ё ё	[yo]	Ц ц	[ts]
Ж ж	[zh]	Ч ч	[ch]
З з	[z]	Ш ш	[sh]
И и	[i]	Щ щ	[sh']
Й й	[y]	— ъ	hard sign
К к	[k]	— ы	[y]
Л л	[l]	— ь	soft sign
М м	[m]	Э э	[e]
Н н	[n]	Ю ю	[yu]
О о	[o]	Я я	[ya]
П п	[p]		

2 The Noun

Имя существительное

Professions

актёр/актри́са	actor/actress
архите́ктор	architect
баскетболи́ст (ка)	basketball player
библиоте́карь	librarian
бизнесме́н	businessman
био́лог	biologist
врач	doctor
журнали́ст (ка)	journalist
касси́р (ша)	cashier
компози́тор	composer
медсестра́/медбра́т	nurse
ме́неджер	manager
меха́ник	mechanic
официа́нт (ка)	waiter/waitress
певе́ц/певи́ца	singer
писа́тель	writer
поэ́т	poet
программи́ст	programmer

продаве́ц/продавщи́ца	salesclerk
профе́ссор	profcssor
режиссёр	director
секрета́рь	secretary
спортсме́н (ка)	athlete
тенниси́ст (ка)	tennis player
учи́тель (ница)	teacher (elem.)
фе́рмер	farmer
фи́зик	physicist
фило́соф	philosopher
хи́мик	chemist
хоккеи́ст (ка)	hockey player
худо́жник	artist, painter
хулига́н	hooligan
юри́ст	lawyer

Places of Employment

библиоте́ка	library
больни́ца	hospital
Голливу́д	Hollywood
заво́д	factory
киносту́дия	movie studio
консервато́рия	conservatory
институ́т	institute
лаборато́рия	laboratory
магази́н	store
музе́й	museum
рестора́н	restaurant
ры́нок	outdoor market
суд	court
университе́т	university
фе́рма	farm
фи́рма	firm, company
шко́ла	school

Nationalities

| америка́нец/америка́нка | American |
| англича́нин/англича́нка | Englishman/woman |

италья́нец/италья́нка	Italian
кана́дец/кана́дка	Canadian
не́мец/не́мка	German
поля́к/по́лька	Pole
ру́сский/ру́сская	Russian
францу́з/францу́женка	Frenchman/woman

Verbs

де́лать	to do, make
жить	to live
рабо́тать	to work

Adjectives

америка́нский	American
англи́йский	English
голливу́дский	Hollywood
изве́стный	famous
кана́дский	Canadian
по́льский	Polish
пуэрторика́нский	Puerto Rican
ру́сский	Russian

VOCABULARY PRACTICE 1

Try to guess who the following famous people are, and then select their profession from the three choices. It might help you to recognize them if you sound out the names.

1. Мо́царт—э́то изве́стный (врач, юри́ст, компози́тор).

2. Достое́вский—э́то изве́стный ру́сский (фе́рмер, продаве́ц, писа́тель).

3. Дже́ннифер Ло́пез—э́то изве́стная америка́нская (библиоте́карь, певи́ца, писа́тель).

4. Леона́рдо да Ви́нчи—э́то изве́стный италья́нский (жудо́жник, юри́ст, меха́ник).

5. Ше́кспир—э́то изве́стный англи́йский (бизнесме́н, профе́ссор, писа́тель).

6. Николь Кидман—это известная голливудская (журналистка, актриса, спортсменка).

7. Майкл Джордан—это известный американский (химик, фермер, баскетболист).

8. Федерико Феллини—это известный итальянский (врач, режиссёр, физик).

9. Александр Пушкин—это известный русский (поэт, кассир, бизнесмен).

10. Вейн Грецкий—это известный канадский (биолог, менеждер, хоккеист).

11. Джулия Робертс—это известная американская (официантка, актриса, кассирша).

12. Мадам Кюри—это известный франко-польский (физик, секретарь, программист).

13. Рикки Мартин—это известный пуэрториканский (продавец, певец, учитель).

14. Сократ—это известный древнегреческий[1] (философ, теннисист, химик).

15. Эм-н-эм—это известный американский (юрист, медбрат, хулиган).

VOCABULARY PRACTICE 2

Fill in the blanks below with the profession that works at the place indicated.

Example: <u>Композитор</u> работает в консерватории.

1. _____ работает в библиотеке.

2. _____ работает на ферме.

3. _____ работает в суде.

4. _____ работает в школе.

5. _____ работает в киностудии.

6. _____ работает в лаборатории.

---

[1] Ancient Greek.

7. _____ рабо́тает в музе́е.

8. _____ рабо́тает в университе́те.

9. _____ рабо́тает на заво́де.

10. _____ рабо́тает в магази́не.

Vocabulary Notes

1. *Gender.* All Russian nouns can be identified as one of three genders: masculine, feminine, and neuter. An adjective will agree with the noun it modifies rather than with the subject of the sentence. In Russian you correctly say, **«Она́ хоро́ший профе́ссор»** ("*She is a good professor*"), using the masculine adjective to modify the masculine noun **профе́ссор.** See sentence 12 of Vocabulary Practice 1 for another example of this type. Gender will be discussed fully later in this chapter.

2. *Professions.* Most modern professions exist in only one form—masculine. For older professions in which women have historically appeared in significant numbers, there is often a feminine suffix, such as in **учи́тельница** or **официа́нтка.** Compare English, where a word such as *aviatrix* has nearly disappeared, or the nonexistent *professoress,* which no one would ever use. In the middle are words such as *actress, waitress, poetess, directress,* and the like, whose use is gradually disappearing or actively discouraged. This is a situation similar to the words used to describe professions in Russian, which are largely masculine. The addition of a feminine suffix such as **-ша** would, in the nineteenth century, indicate the person's wife: **генера́лша** (general's wife), **профе́ссорша, президе́нтша.** In Modern Russian, such a suffix added to a normally masculine gender profession would be considered insulting or derogatory: **«На́ши а́вторши счита́ют . . .»** ("*Our little authoresses believe . . .*").

At this point it must be stressed that gender is a *linguistic* concept and not a sexual one. A Russian word is a certain gender most of the time because of the way it ends, not because of the person, animal, or thing to which it refers.

3. *The verb* to be. This verb has no present tense in Russian. In Russian you say, "I salesclerk," "My mother—teacher," "He interesting." The long dash is used to separate the subject from the predicate only when two nouns are involved, as in the second example here. See also Vocabulary Practice 1 above.

4. *Articles.* Russian has no articles of any kind, except in substandard colloquial speech, and even then the meaning is conveyed by enclitic particles rather than articles as traditionally used in Western European languages.

VOCABULARY PRACTICE 3

Match the famous people—real or fictional—in the left column with their nationalities in the right column. You will not necessarily know all the nationalities, but you can make intelligent guesses.

1. Да́нте	_____	индиа́нка
2. Плато́н	_____	мексика́нка
3. Билл Гейтс	_____	датча́нин
4. Мо́на Ли́са	_____	по́лька
5. Покаго́нтас	_____	францу́з
6. Пи́тер Дже́ннингс	_____	италья́нец
7. Ви́нстон Чу́рчилл	_____	поля́к
8. Наполео́н	_____	америка́нец
9. Мада́м Кюри́	_____	мексика́нец
10. Шопе́н	_____	англича́нин
11. Фри́да Ка́ло	_____	италья́нка
12. Дие́го Риве́ра	_____	кана́дец
13. Га́млет	_____	не́мец
14. Ги́тлер	_____	грек

Personal Pronouns

Singular		**Plural**	
я	I	мы	we
ты	you	вы	you
он	he/it	они́	they
она́	she/it		
оно́	it		

Personal Pronoun Notes

1. The singular pronoun **ты** is used in addressing one person with whom you are familiar. This individual may be a family member, a close friend, a child, an animal, God, or anyone who invites you to address him or her familiarly. The pronoun **вы** is used to address strangers, those in a position of authority, people who are significantly older, in-laws, as well as familiar people in the plural: **«Дети! Что вы делаете?!»** (*"Children! What are you doing?!"*)

2. The third-person singular pronouns **он** and **она** may also refer to objects whose gender is, respectively, masculine or feminine. The neuter pronoun **оно** can refer to objects only.

Gender, Number, and Case of Nouns

Russian nouns are defined by gender, number, and case. They can be masculine, feminine, or neuter; singular or plural; and appear in any of six cases: nominative, accusative, genitive, prepositional, dative, and instrumental. Further, nouns are either animate (referring to living human beings and animals) or inanimate (referring to things).

The Russian language, like Latin and Greek, is based upon a system of endings to order its syntax. English, which was once far more complex than it is today, has only remnants of the case system, which are reflected mostly in its pronouns: subjective (*I*), objective (*me*), and possessive (*my*). Russian makes three further distinctions for a total of six cases: subject, direct object, indirect object, location, means, and possession. The process by which nouns, pronouns, and adjectives change their forms to alter their syntactical meaning is called declension.

The first case the student of Russian learns is the nominative case. This is how words that decline appear in a dictionary. This is one of the six cases of Russian, which will be presented systematically in the course of this book.

Gender

Those who have studied French will recall the largely arbitrary nature of gender in that language. Each word is presented together with the masculine or feminine article and must be committed to memory. The long-term implications of this system entail hours of drudgery. The gender of Russian nouns, on the other hand, is usually obvious by their endings. In cases where the gender of a Russian noun does not correlate with its ending, the reason for gender is usually clear, such as the fact that the noun relates to a human being of one or the other sex.

Masculine

Russian masculine nouns generally end in a consonant. In other words, they have a "zero" ending.

Most masculine nouns end in a hard consonant, including any of the fricatives (**ж, ч, ш, щ,** and **ц**). All of the following nouns are masculine: **компью́тер** (computer), **нож** (knife), **грузи́н** (Georgian), **каранда́ш** (pencil), **бульдо́г** (bulldog), **банк** (bank), **а́втор** (author), **стол** (table), **футболи́ст** (soccer player).

Masculine nouns may also end in a soft consonant, that is, the letter **й** or any consonant (except a fricative) plus the soft sign. The following nouns are all masculine soft nouns: **музе́й** (museum), **крите́рий** (criterion), **учи́тель**[2] (teacher), **коро́ль** (king), **слу́чай** (incident), **мураве́й** (ant), **царь** (tsar), **ого́нь** (fire), **ковбо́й** (cowboy).

Some masculine nouns may end in the vowels **-a** or **-я**. The majority of words in this category refer in some way to male human beings and express mostly relationships or nicknames: **дя́дя** (uncle), **Ва́ня** (Vanya), **мужчи́на** (man), **па́па** (dad), **Ю́ра** (Yura), **ю́ноша** (young man), **де́душка** (grandfather), **Са́ша** (Sasha), **слуга́** (servant). The Russian word for judge—**судья́**—also falls into this category.

There is a small group of nouns that end in **-a** that may be either masculine or feminine depending on the referent. Such nouns are called epicene, or nouns of common gender. An example is **сирота́** (orphan). If you are speaking of a boy, you would say, **«Он бе́дный сирота»**. If the subject is a girl, the sentence is **«Она́ бе́дная сирота́»**. Interestingly, most of these words are—or once were—pejorative in meaning: **уби́йца** (murderer), **пья́ница** (drunkard), **пла́кса** (crybaby), **растя́па** (bungler), **обжо́ра** (glutton), **неря́ха** (slob), **неве́жа** (ignoramus), **кале́ка** (cripple), **лежебо́ка** (sluggard), **левша́** (a left-handed person). **У́мница** (smart person) and **работя́га** (hard worker) are among the handful of epicene nouns with a positive connotation.

Last, there is a small number of nouns that must be memorized as masculine. Most of them refer to male human beings or animals, and all of them are from the larger group of several hundred indeclinable nouns of all genders. Among them are **ма́эстро** (maestro), **атташе́** (attaché), **я́нки** (Yankee), **шимпанзе́** (chimpanzee), **хи́нди** (Hindi), **у́рду** (Urdu), **кенгуру́** (kangaroo), **флами́нго** (flamingo), **да Ви́нчи** (da Vinci). Also part of this category are words such as **Чика́го (го́род)** and **Миссиси́пи,** which is masculine when referring to the state (**штат**). It is feminine when referring to the river (**река́**).

---

[2]All nouns ending in **-тель** are masculine. The corresponding feminine suffix is **-тельница.**

The word **кóфе** in Standard Modern Russian is considered masculine—«**Онá пьёт тóлько чёрный кóфе**»—but you will occasionally hear people mistakenly saying **чёрное кóфе,** especially in the south.

Feminine

There are only two types of feminine nouns: those that end in **-а/-я** and those that end in a soft sign.

The following nouns are all feminine nouns of the first type: **сосéдка** (neighbor), **шéя** (neck), **лúния** (line), **тётя** (aunt), **недéля** (week), **хúмия** (chemistry), **ондáтра** (muskrat), **кассúрша** (cashier), **тьма** (darkness).

Remember, there are certain nouns that end in **-а** that are masculine. These generally refer to male human beings. See the third group of nouns in the category of masculine nouns above.

Feminine nouns that end in a soft sign fall into two groups: those that must be memorized and those whose gender is predictable.

The first group is unpredictable, and you must memorize them as you learn them. They will be marked as (f.) in the vocabulary lists: **любóвь** (love), **óсень** (autumn), **дверь** (door), **треть** (one-third), **смерть** (death), **национáльность** (nationality), **мéбель** (furniture), **степь** (steppe), **плóщадь** (square), **соль** (salt), **рысь** (lynx), **óчередь** (queue).

NOTE: Abstract nouns ending in **-ость** are usually feminine.

Predictable feminine nouns in **-ь** are those in which the letter preceding the soft sign is **ж, ч, ш,** or **щ.** The following are all feminine nouns: **речь** (speech), **глушь** (backwoods), **вещь** (thing), **мышь** (mouse), **мéлочь** (trifle), **ложь** (lie), **рожь** (rye), **пóмощь** (help), **молодёжь** (youth).

The handful of feminine nouns that are exceptions to the rules above (such as **мадáм, лéди, мисс, альма мáтер**) refer to women, real or figurative. These nouns are also indeclinable.

Furthermore, some indeclinable nouns are considered feminine because they take the gender of their generic category: **Миссисúпи (рекá), Таймс (газéта), «Кáрмен» (óпера), цéце (мухá), авеню́ (у́лица).**

Neuter

The last gender, neuter, can be identified by the endings **-о** (hard), **-ё** (soft stressed), **-е** (soft unstressed), or the rare **-мя.** The following are all examples of neuter nouns: **бельё** (linens), **колéно** (knee), **питьё** (drinking), **мучéнье** (suffering), **окнó** (window), **гóре** (sorrow), **зло** (evil), **плáтье** (dress), **пéние** (singing), **сóлнце** (sun), **яйцó** (egg), **богáтство** (wealth).

There are ten neuter nouns that end in **-мя**: **вре́мя** (time), **и́мя** (first name), **пле́мя** (tribe), **бре́мя** (burden), **зна́мя** (banner), **вы́мя** (udder), **пла́мя** (flame), **се́мя** (seed), **стре́мя** (stirrup), **те́мя** (top of the head, crown).

Only **и́мя** and **вре́мя** are commonly used. Four of these nouns are not used in the plural (**вы́мя, бре́мя, пла́мя,** and **те́мя**). There are three more words ending in **-мя**—**полуи́мя** (diminutive, nickname), **по́лымя** (flame), and **бере́мя** (an armful)—which are considered colloquial, dialectal, or obsolete.

There are no feminine nouns that end in **-мя,** although there are several adverbs with this ending, such as **во́время** (on time) and **стоймя́** (upright).

Some indeclinable words that refer to things are often considered neuter: **шоссе́** (highway), **ра́дио** (radio), **пари́** (bet), **меню́** (menu), **такси́** (taxi), **интервью́** (interview), **кафе́** (café), **желе́** (jelly), **кака́о** (cocoa).

TEST FOR MASTERY 1

You may not know the meanings of all the words below, but you should nonetheless be able to identify their gender according to the rules above.

1. Миссиси́пи	10. Нью-Йо́рк Та́ймс	19. Мада́м Бовари́
2. Бу́дда	11. шоссе́	20. шимпанзе́
3. пла́кса	12. Пуччи́ни	21. бельё
4. коммюнике́	13. коли́бри	22. судья́
5. кака́о	14. госуда́рство	23. скамья́
6. ма́эстро	15. глу́пость	24. флами́нго
7. те́мя	16. раствори́тель	25. Нью-Дже́рси
8. Кеннту́ки	17. кафе́	26. ночь
9. зна́мя	18. те́ма	27. Рио-Гра́нде

Nouns in the Plural

While not the most difficult part of Russian grammar, changing nouns from the singular to the plural can be tricky. Some nouns have completely different stems (**ребёнок/де́ти**). A couple of nouns are hard in the singular and soft in the plural (**сосе́д/сосе́ди**). Masculine nouns tend to have the most exceptions, while feminine and neuter nouns behave regularly. And, as in English, there are some nouns that have only singular forms, such as **молоко́** (milk) and **серебро́** (silver), and some that have only plural forms, *pluralia tantum*—**но́жницы** (scissors) and **брю́ки** (pants).

Masculine Plural

Most masculine nouns that end in a hard consonant simply add the ending **-ы.** Of course, remember to add the ending **-и** if you have a noun ending in one of the consonants of the seven-letter spelling rule: the fricatives **ж, ч, ш, щ,** and the velars **г, к, х.**

The following masculine nouns form their plurals regularly:

Singular	Plural	English
журнали́ст	журнали́сты	journalist
блокно́т	блокно́ты	pad
кошма́р	кошма́ры	nightmare
грузови́к	грузовики́	truck
флаг	фла́ги	flag
гара́ж	гаражи́	garage
блин	блины́	pancake
каранда́ш	карандаши́	pencil
осьмино́г	осьмино́ги	octopus
метео́р	метео́ры	meteor
телеско́п	телеско́пы	telescope
врач	врачи́	doctor

Part of the above category but needing special mention are masculine nouns that have a fleeting (or unstable) vowel in the nominative form. Many nouns of more than one syllable in **-ец** and **-ок** behave in this way, dropping this vowel before adding the plural ending.

Singular	Plural	English
оте́ц	отцы́	father
америка́нец	америка́нцы	American
купе́ц	купцы́	merchant
коне́ц	концы́	end
орёл	орлы́	eagle
кусо́к	куски́	piece
городо́к	городки́	little town
рису́нок	рису́нки	drawing
значо́к	значки́	lapel pin
ого́нь	огни́	fire

Masculine nouns in a soft sign or the soft vowel **-й** will drop the soft sign or the consonant **-й** and add the vowel **-и.**

Singular	Plural	English
музе́й	музе́и	museum
ковбо́й	ковбо́и	cowboy
коро́ль	короли́	king
гусь	гу́си	goose
писа́тель	писа́тели	writer
царь	цари́	tsar
ка́мень	ка́мни[3]	stone
трамва́й	трамва́и	tram

The following groups of nouns are exceptions to the rules above. The lists below are by no means exhaustive.

1. Masculine nouns in **-анин/-янин** drop the last two letters and add the vowel **-e.**

Singular	Plural	English
англича́нин	англича́не	Englishman
славяни́н	славя́не	Slav
крестьяни́н	крестья́не	peasant
дворяни́н	дворя́не	nobleman
граждани́н	гра́ждане	citizen

NOTE: Some nouns that end in **-ин** but do not have the infix **-ан-** are slightly irregular and must be memorized:

Singular	Plural	English
тата́рин	тата́ры	Tatar
болга́рин	болга́ры	Bulgarian
ба́рин	ба́ры	lord
господи́н	господа́	lord, gentleman
боя́рин	боя́ре	boyar
грузи́н	грузи́ны	Georgian
хозя́ин	хозя́ева	host

---

[3]Note the fleeting vowel.

2. Masculine nouns in **-ёнок** drop this ending and add **-ята.** This group consists primarily of baby animals.

Singular	Plural	English
гусёнок	гусята	gosling
ягнёнок	ягнята	lamb
совёнок	совята	owlet
октябрёнок	октябрята[4]	Octobrist
котёнок	котята	kitten
жеребёнок	жеребята	colt
утёнок	утята	duckling
дьяволёнок	дьявольята	imp
ребёнок	ребята[5]	kid
кенгурёнок	кенгурята	baby kangaroo

3. A small but significant group of common masculine nouns take stressed **-á/-я** to form the plural. Some of the more widely used are:

Singular	Plural	English
дом	домá	house
нóмер	номерá	number
пóезд	поездá	train
гóлос	голосá	voice
мáстер	мастерá	craftsman
крáй	края	edge
áдрес	адресá	address
цвет	цветá	color
óстров	островá	island
пáспорт	паспортá	passport
пóвар	поварá	cook
слéсарь	слесаря	metalworker
гóрод	городá	city
глаз	глазá	eye
пáрус	парусá	sail
вéчер	вечерá	evening
свúтер	свитерá	sweater
учúтель	учителя	teacher

---

[4]An Octobrist is a member of a children's scout-type organization of the Soviet period.

[5]This is an alternate plural meaning *kids* or *guys* in the colloquial sense. The normal plural of **ребёнок** is **дéти.**

This group grows by the day, with foreign borrowings particularly apt to be given the stressed **-á** ending, especially in conversation. Thus, while most authorities will roundly dismiss such forms as **компьютера́, принтера́, констру́ктора́, сектора́,** and **трактора́** as uneducated or substandard, they are far from infrequent on the street.

4. Masculine nouns whose plural ends in **-ья** must be memorized.

Singular	Plural	English
брат	бра́тья	brother
князь	князья́	prince
лист	ли́стья	leaf
друг	друзья́	friend
муж	мужья́	husband
стул	сту́лья	chair
сук	су́чья	branch
сын	сыновья́	son

NOTE: The forms **су́чья, друзья́,** and **сыновья́** undergo changes to their stems in the plural.

5. There are a number of words that have both a stressed plural in **-á/-я́** or a plural in **-ья** (stressed or unstressed), as well as a conventional plural in **-ы/-и.** The more common the meaning of the word—or the more everyday the object—the more likely it is that the ending will be irregular. Compare the following pairs:

Concrete, everyday	Abstract, figurative
пропуска́ (permits)	про́пуски (omissions, an ellipsis)
меха́ (furs)	ме́хи (bellows)
образа́ (icons)	о́бразы (images, visions)
пояса́ (belts [for clothing])	по́ясы ([geographical] belts)
учителя́ (teachers [in school])	учи́тели (teachers [of a doctrine])
ли́стья (leaves)	листы́ (sheets of paper)
мужья́ (husbands)	мужи́ ("men" [rhetorical])
зу́бья (teeth [of a tool, machine])	зу́бы (teeth [in the mouth])
счета́ (bills)	счёты (abacus)
ко́рни (roots)	коре́нья (spices)[6]
лагеря́ ([summer] camp)	ла́гери ([philosophical] camp)

---

[6]Both **счёты** and **коре́нья** in these meanings are plural only.

6. There is a small group of masculine nouns ending in **-ей** that add a soft sign to all oblique forms (all instances where an ending must be added), both singular and plural. Some examples are:

Singular	Plural	English
муравéй	муравьи́	ant
воробéй	воробьи́	swallow
ручéй	ручьи́	stream
соловéй	соловьи́	nightingale

7. There are only a few isolated examples of masculine nouns whose plurals cannot be predicted on the basis of the above rules. They are:

Singular	Plural	English
человéк	лю́ди	person
ребёнок	дéти	child
цветóк	цветы́	flower
чёрт	чéрти	devil
сосéд	сосéди	neighbor

The last two—**чёрт** and **сосéд**—are the only nouns in Russian that are hard throughout the singular but soft in the plural forms.

Neuter Plural

Neuter nouns in the plural are decidedly easier to form than masculine nouns. The fundamental rule is to remove the **-о/-е** ending and replace it with **-а/-я.** Many disyllabic nouns ending in a consonant plus **-о/-е** add an additional step by switching the stress to the other syllable:

Singular	Plural	English
окнó	óкна	window
мéсто	местá	place
здáние	здáния	building
мучéнье	мучéнья	torment
пóле	поля́	field
острие́	острия́	cutting edge
копьё	кóпья	spear
госудáрство	госудáрства	state
слóво	словá	word

Singular	Plural	English
боло́то	боло́та	swamp
мо́ре	моря́	sea
кла́дбище	кла́дбища[7]	cemetery
ружьё	ру́жья	gun
блю́дце	блю́дца	saucer
подмасте́рье	подмасте́рья	apprentice
о́зеро	озёра	lake

There are a handful of neuter nouns whose plural is formed irregularly by dropping the **-о/-е,** adding **-ья,** and usually, but not always, changing the stress:

Singular	Plural	English
де́рево	дере́вья	tree
крыло́	кры́лья	wing
помело́	поме́лья	mop
перо́	пе́рья	feather
ши́ло	ши́лья	awl
звено́	зве́нья	chain link

The neuter nouns **пла́тье/пла́тья** and **ружьё/ру́жья** may also be grouped here. These types of neuters, as well as the masculines above that end in **-ья,** will take a **-ьев** ending in the genitive plural.

The following groups of nouns are exceptions to the rules above:

1. Neuter nouns in **-мя** expand their stems before they add the normal **-а** ending. There are only six nouns of this type:

Singular	Plural	English
вре́мя	времена́	time
се́мя	семена́	seed
и́мя	имена́	first name
стре́мя	стремена́	stirrup
пле́мя	племена́	tribe
зна́мя	знамёна[8]	banner

---

[7]This ending obeys the second part of the seven-letter spelling rule: instead of **я** or **ю,** write **а** or **у** after **к, г, х** and **ж, ч, ш, щ.**

[8]Note the stress here shifts to the stem instead of to the ending.

2. Neuter nouns that form a diminutive with **-ко** form their plural by dropping the **-о** and adding **-и**:

Singular	Plural	English
окóшко	окóшки	small window
дрéвко	дрéвки	pole
вéко	вéки	eyelid
колéчко	колéчки	little ring
зёрнышко	зёрнышки	little seed
ýшко	ýшки	little ear
я́блоко	я́блоки	apple

3. Many irregular neuter nouns are remnants from the former dual number, which represented nouns in sets of two. Many of these are nouns that, in fact, come in pairs or are thought of as twos. Examples of such nouns are:

Singular	Plural	English
пдечó	плéчи	shoulder
колéно	колéни	knee
ýхо	ýши	ear
óко	óчи	eye [poetic, obs.]

NOTE: Many irregular masculine nouns in **-á** are also relics of the dual: **рукавá** (sleeves), **глазá** (eyes), **бокá** (sides), **рогá** (horns), **берегá** (shores).

4. There are three remaining exceptions for neuter plural nouns. Two of them—**нéбо** and **чýдо**—are relics of the s-stem declension, adding the infix **-ес-** in all oblique cases. The nominative plurals of these nouns are **небесá** and **чудесá**.

Finally, the one remaining irregular neuter noun is **сýдно** (vessel), which drops the **-н-** in the plural forms: **сýдно/судá**.

Feminine Plural
With the exception of changes in stress, feminine nouns are remarkably regular in their plural formation.

General Rules:

1. If the noun ends in **-a,** replace that vowel with **-ы**.

2. If the noun ends in **-я,** replace that vowel with **-и.**

3. If the noun ends in a soft sign, drop the soft sign and add **-и.**

NOTE: Remember to apply the seven-letter spelling rule to the first general rule!

There are only three words that are exceptions in the formation of feminine plurals: The words **мать** (mother) and **дочь** (daughter) expand their stems before adding the soft plural ending: **ма́тери, до́чери.** The word **ку́рица** (chicken) forms the plural by dropping a syllable: **ку́ры.**

Many common feminine nouns of two syllables[9] change their stress to the other syllable. This stress shift will serve to distinguish the nominative plural from the genitive singular. Compare:

Nominative Singular	Genitive Singular	Nominative Plural	English
сестра́	сестры́	сёстры	sister
река́	реки́	ре́ки	river
гора́	горы́	го́ры	mountain
звезда́	звезды́	звёзды	star
голова́	головы́	го́ловы	head
сирота́	сироты́	сиро́ты	orphan

Singular vs. Plural

Some nouns exist in the singular only (or primarily). Such nouns as silver, air, wood, milk, furniture, and so forth, are singular both in English and in Russian. The student must exert care, however, in the category of fruits and vegetables: English tends to use the plural in these cases, but Russian prefers the singular. **Я люблю́ карто́фель** means *I like potatoes.* Such *singularia tantum* Russian nouns are **мали́на** (raspberries), **морко́вь** (carrots), **горо́х** (peas), **клубни́ка** (strawberries), **ви́шня** (cherries), **лук** (onions), **виногра́д** (grapes), **свёкла** (beets), **изю́м** (raisins), **минда́ль** (almonds).

These nouns take singular adjectives and singular verbs.

To denote one of these fruits or vegetables, usually a diminutive suffix is used: **морко́вка** (a carrot), **горо́шина** (a pea), **карто́шка** (a potato), **изю́мина** (a raisin), and so forth.

There are, on the other hand, numerous fruits and vegetables that form the plural in a regular manner. Some of these are **помидо́р** (tomato), **апельси́н**

---

[9]A few three-syllable nouns also show this change.

(orange), **бана́н** (banana), **огуре́ц** (cucumber), **гриб** (mushroom), **пе́рсик** (peach), **арбу́з** (watermelon), **гру́ша** (pear), and others. If you are unsure, check a dictionary.

Some nouns appear in the plural only. Many of these nouns, which are exceedingly common, have no plural counterpart in English and must be memorized. Examples in the first list below are *pluralia tantum* in English as well as Russian. The second list contains examples of nouns that are not *pluralia tantum* in English.

1. **но́жницы** (scissors), **брю́ки** (pants, trousers), **тру́сики** (underpants), **кавы́чки** (quotation marks), **кани́кулы** (vacation, holidays), **очки́** (eyeglasses), **анна́лы** (annals), **оста́нки** (remains), **плоскогу́бцы** (pliers), **во́жжи** (reins).

2. **де́ньги** (money), **по́хороны** (funeral), **ро́ды** (childbirth), **сли́вки** (cream), **су́тки** (a period of 24 hours), **черни́ла** (ink), **ша́хматы** (chess), **джу́нгли** (jungle), **духи́** (perfume), **счёты** (abacus), **щи** (cabbage soup), **су́мерки** (twilight), **са́ни** (sleigh), **обо́и** (wallpaper), **воро́та** (gate), **дрова́** (firewood), **войска́** (troops), **пре́ния** (debate—note that this is neuter plural), **ви́лы** (pitchfork), **дро́жжи** (yeast).

TEST FOR MASTERY 2

Form the plurals of the following words. If you have not seen them before, treat them as regular.

1. арбу́з	11. горо́х	21. глаз
2. пла́тье	12. черни́ла	22. па́лец
3. у́хо	13. семья́	23. око́шко
4. не́бо	14. кла́дбище	24. ку́рица
5. дом	15. перо́	25. ребёнок
6. мураве́й	16. брат	26. вре́мя
7. путь	17. поросёнок	27. музе́й
8. христиани́н	18. молоко́	28. пья́ница
9. кенгуру́	19. мать	29. существо́
10. сестра́	20. господи́н	30. дя́дя

Animate vs. Inanimate

Slavic languages categorize a noun as animate or inanimate. Animate nouns refer to living human beings or animals.

Animacy may be conferred by the mind of the speaker upon an inanimate object, such as a child's toy—a marionette, a little elephant, or a teddy bear, for instance. Thus, a little boy may view his teddy bear as a living creature when he says **«Máма! Я потеря́л моего́ люби́мого ми́шку!»** (*"Mom! I lost my favorite teddy bear!"*) The usage of the genitive case for the two adjectives of the direct object follow the rule for animate direct objects: in the masculine singular, they have the same form as the genitive case.

> **NOTE:**   Although the direct object noun, **ми́шку,** is declined like a feminine noun, it is masculine. Compare **па́па, Са́ша,** etc.

Generally speaking, collective nouns are not animate, even when they refer to people. Such nouns have an accusative identical with the nominative. Examples are **наро́д** (the people), **отря́д** (detachment), **войска́** (troops). Interestingly, however, the word **пролета́рий** (proletariat) is animate.

In the middle ground, the two words for *deceased,* **мертве́ц** and **поко́йник,** are considered animate. **Труп** (corpse), however, is inanimate.[10] When you refer to the gods Mars and Jupiter, for example, they are animate. But when these names refer to the planets, they are considered inanimate.

In the realm of the unliving, there are a few objects that are considered animate: **туз, коро́ль,** and **вале́т** (the ace, king, and jack in playing cards), **ко́зырь** (trump) **болва́н** (joker), **ферзь** (the queen, a masculine noun, as are all other pieces in chess), **куми́р** (idol), **звезда́** (movie star), **автома́т** (robot), **числи́тель** (numerator), **знамени́тель** (denominator).

One piece of linguistic trivia: In Polish, the words *banana* and *dollar* are considered animate!

One last comment: The rule that an animate noun when used as a direct object is identical with the genitive case applies in the singular to masculine nouns only. In the plural, this rule applies to all genders, even neuter. Compare the two sentences: **Он уби́л насеко́мое** (*He killed an insect*) and **Он уби́л насеко́мых** (*He killed the insects*). In the first example the direct object—the neuter noun

---

[10]D. E. Rosental notes that while the first two terms for *the deceased* refer to people only, the word **труп** can also refer to animals. And the rules for animacy in the early period of Russian were much more narrow than they are today.

насеко́мое—is like the nominative. In the second, the same word, in the plural, is now animate and is identical with the genitive case. Only neuter nouns show this peculiarity of being inanimate in the singular but animate in the plural. There are, however, some masculine nouns in certain set expressions that are animate in the singular but become inanimate in the plural.

More information on these structures will be found in chapter 3 on the accusative case.

TEST FOR MASTERY 3

The nouns in the list below are either singular or plural. Identify the number and give the opposite. Also identify which nouns are animate, that is, refer to male human beings or animals.

Example: ти́гры → тигр (animate)
             бу́ква → бу́квы

Be forewarned! Unless you know the original noun, it is much harder to change a noun from the plural to the singular.

1. каранда́ш	13. ковбо́й	25. черни́ла
2. города́	14. спортсме́н	26. лук
3. кафете́рий	15. письмо́	27. гуся́та
4. конфе́та	16. хулига́ны	28. мужья́
5. де́ло	17. медсестра́	29. де́ньги
6. муравьй	18. молодёжь	30. сирота́
7. ве́щи	19. гора́	31. небеса́
8. купе́ц	20. крокоди́л	32. до́чери
9. коле́но	21. воскресе́нье	33. коле́чко
10. ра́дио	22. ку́ры	34. зда́ния
11. тру́сики	23. мужчи́на	35. пе́рья
12. яйцо́	24. имена́	36. че́рти

ANSWER KEY

Vocabulary Practice 1

1. композитор
2. писатель
3. певица
4. художник
5. писатель

6. актриса
7. баскетболист
8. режиссёр
9. поэт
10. хоккеист

11. актриса
12. физик
13. певец
14. философ
15. хулиган

Vocabulary Practice 2

1. библиотекарь
2. фермер
3. юрист
4. учитель/учительница
5. режиссёр

6. физик/химик/биолог
7. художник
8. профессор
9. механик
10. продавец/продавщица

Vocabulary Practice 3

1. Dante/итальянец
2. Plato/грек
3. Bill Gates/американец
4. Mona Lisa/итальянка
5. Pocahontas/индианка
6. Peter Jennings/канадец
7. Winston Churchill/англичанин

8. Napoleon/француз
9. Madame Curie/полька
10. Chopin/поляк
11. Frida Kahlo/мексиканка
12. Diego Rivera/мексиканец
13. Hamlet/датчанин
14. Hitler/немец

Test for Mastery 1

1. M (the state) or F (the river)
2. M (the Buddha is a male person)

3. M or F
4. N (a communiqué)

5. N

6. M (a male person)

7. N

8. M (a state)

9. N (ending in **-мя**)

10. F (a newspaper)

11. N (indeclinable)

12. M (Puccini)

13. M (an animal)

14. N

15. F (ending in **-ость**)

16. M (ending in **-тель**)

17. N (indeclinable)

18. F (unlike **тéмя,** this ends in **-а**)

19. F (a woman, indeclinable)

20. M (an animal)

21. N

22. M

23. F (ending in **-мья,** not **-мя**)

24. M (indeclinable animal)

25. M (a state)

26. F

27. F (a river)

Test for Mastery 2

1. арбýзы

2. плáтья

3. ýши

4. небесá

5. домá

6. муравьй

7. путú

8. христиáне

9. кенгурý

10. сёстры

11. no plural

12. already plural!

13. сéмьи

14. клáдбища

15. пéрья

16. брáтья

17. порося́та

18. no plural

19. мáтери

20. господá

21. глазá

22. пáльцы

23. окóшки

24. кýры

25. дéти

26. временá

27. музéи

28. пья́ницы

29. существá

30. дя́ди

Test for Mastery 3

1. карандашѝ
2. го́род
3. кафете́рии
4. конфе́ты
5. дела́
6. муравѐй
7. вещь
8. купцы́
9. коле́ни
10. ра́дио (indeclinable)
11. plural only
12. я́йца

13. ковбо́и
14. спотрсме́ны
15. пи́сьма
16. хулига́н
17. медсёстры
18. singular only
19. го́ры
20. крокоди́лы
21. воскресе́нья
22. ку́рица
23. мужчи́ны
24. и́мя

25. plural only
26. singular only
27. гусёнок
28. муж
29. plural only
30. сиро́ты
31. не́бо
32. дочь
33. коле́чки[11]
34. зда́ние
35. перо́
36. чёрт

---

[11]This is the diminutive of **кольцо́.**

3 The Accusative Case

Винительный падеж

Useful Vocabulary

Verbs

рабо́тать	to work
отдыха́ть	to relax
идти́	to go (on foot)
е́хать	to go (by vehicle)

Family Members

семья́	family	сестра́	sister
мать	mother	брат	brother
ма́ма	mom	де́ти	children
оте́ц	father	ба́бушка	grandmother
па́па	dad	де́душка	grandfather
роди́тели	parents	соба́ка	dog
дочь	daughter	ко́шка	cat
сын	son	челове́к	person

Greetings

здра́вствуй(те)	hello
до́брое у́тро	good morning
до́брый день	good day
до́брый ве́чер	good evening
споко́йной но́чи	good night
до свида́ния	good-bye
пока́	see you, bye
всего́ хоро́шего	all the best

Phrases

дава́йте познако́мимся	let's introduce ourselves
о́чень прия́тно	nice to meet you
извини́те	excuse me
пожа́луйста	please
спаси́бо	thank you
в тако́м слу́чае	in that case
мне́ пора́	it's time for me (+ Inf.)

VOCABULARY PRACTICE

Give the antonym to the words listed below:

1. мать _____

2. здра́вствуйте _____

3. дочь _____

4. до́брое у́тро _____

5. роди́тели _____

6. де́душка _____

7. отдыха́ть _____

8. брат _____

9. пожа́луйста _____

10. па́па _____

11. соба́ка _____

12. де́ти _____

The Verb Идти́

Singular	**Plural**
я иду́	мы идём
ты идёшь	вы идёте
он/она́ идёт	они́ иду́т

The Verb Éхать

Singular	Plural
я éду	мы éдем
ты éдешь	вы éдете
он/онá éдет	они éдут

CONVERSATION PRACTICE

With a friend, take the roles of the below travelers and substitute your own materials for the underlined words.

В пóезде «Москвá–Владивостóк»

Ивáн Сергéевич:	Здрáвствуйте!
Рóберт Фи́шер:	Дóбрый день.
ИС:	Извини́те, пожáлуйста, кудá вы éдете?
РФ:	Я éду в Ирку́тск.
ИС:	А я éду во Владивостóк.

(молчáние)

ИС:	Давáйте познакóмимся! Меня́ зову́т Ивáн. А вас?
РФ:	Меня́ зову́т Рóберт.
ИС:	Óчень прия́тно!

(молчáние)

ИС:	Скажи́те, пожáлуйста, отку́да вы?
РФ:	Я америкáнец. Я живу́ и рабóтаю в Нью-Йóрке.
ИС:	А я ру́сский. Я всю жизнь живу́ в Москвé.
РФ:	Гмм.

(молчáние)

ИС:	Рóберт! Вот фотогрáфия моéй семьи́. Э́то моя́ женá, мой сын, мои́ дóчери, нáши собáки и нáши кóшки.
РФ:	Э́то óчень большáя семья́. У меня́ есть тóлько золотáя ры́бка.

ИС:	В тако́м слу́чае, вы наве́рно счастли́вый челове́к!
РФ:	Ну, мне пора́ идти́. До свида́ния.
ИС:	Всего́ хоро́шего! (по́зже) Како́й стра́нный челове́к!

On the Trans-Siberian Railroad

IVAN SERGEYEVICH:	Hello!
ROBERT FISHER:	Good afternoon.
IS:	Excuse me, please, where are you going?
RF:	I'm going to Irkutsk.
IS:	I'm going to Vladivostok.

(silence)

IS:	Let's introduce ourselves! My name is Ivan. What's yours?
RF:	My name is Robert.
IS:	Nice to meet you!

(silence)

IS:	Tell me please, where are you from?
RF:	I'm an American. I live and work in New York.
IS:	And I'm Russian. I have lived in Moscow all my life.
RF:	Hmmm.

(silence)

IS:	Robert! Here is a photograph of my family. This is my wife, my son, my daughters, our dogs, and our cats.
RF:	That's a very large family. I have only a goldfish.
IS:	In that case, you must be a happy person!
RF:	Well, it's time for me to go. Good-bye.
IS:	All the best! (later) What a strange person!

Vocabulary

1. *Greetings.* There are various ways Russians greet each other. Always correct are **До́брое у́тро!** (Good morning!), **До́брый день!** (Good afternoon!), **До́брый ве́чер!** (Good evening!).

You may also say **Здра́вствуйте!** (or **здра́вствуй,** to a person whom you address as **ты,** the informal *you*). This greeting is in the form of an imperative, and you are essentially wishing someone to be healthy. This greeting roughly corresponds to the English "*Hello! How are you?*" As such, it may be said to someone only once a day.

A more informal greeting is the expression **Приве́т** (Hi).

2. *My name is. . . .* In Russian, the construction is literally "*(They) call me . . .*" The verb is third-person plural without an expressed subject, which signifies an impersonal state (*Cf.* "*I am called . . .*"). The direct object is the pronoun **меня** (*me*), and the name is provided in the nominative case.

To a child	Как тебя́ зову́т?	What's your name?
To an (adult) stranger	Как вас зову́т?	What's your name?
About a group	Как их зову́т?	What are their names?
About a girl or woman	Как её зову́т?	What's her name?
About a boy or man	Как его́ зову́т?	What's his name?

3. *Good-bye!* The most neutral expression upon taking leave is **до свида́ния.** Ivan says, **«Всего́ хоро́шего»,** which besides its literal translation of "*All the best*" can mean "*Have a nice day.*" The word **пока́** is colloquial, meaning "*Bye!*" or "*See you later.*"

4. *Possessive Pronoun Adjectives*

	Masculine	Neuter	Feminine	Plural
my	мой	моё	моя́	мои́
your	твой	твоё	твоя́	твои́
his	его́	его́	его́	его́
her	её	её	её	её

	Masculine	Neuter	Feminine	Plural
our	наш	на́ше	на́ша	на́ши
your	ваш	ва́ше	ва́ша	ва́ши
their	их	их	их	их

Like adjectives, the possessive pronouns for the first and second person singular and plural (*my, your, our, your*) agree with the nouns they modify in gender and number. Third-person possessives do not agree.

Masculine	Neuter	Feminine	Plural
мой браслёт	моё ра́дио	моя́ газе́та	мои́ де́ньги
наш дом	на́ше ра́дио	на́ша кварти́ра	на́ши де́ти
его́ брат	его́ ра́дио	его́ сестра́	его́ очки́
её отец	её ра́дио	её мать	её роди́тели
их компью́тер	их ра́дио	их шко́ла	их друзья́

Functions of the Accusative Case

The functions of the accusative case are few and easily mastered. As for the endings, only feminine nouns have accusative endings of their own; neuter nouns and masculine inanimate nouns are like the nominative case, and masculine animate nouns are like the genitive case.

Direct Object

The primary syntactical use of the accusative case is to indicate the direct object in a sentence. The direct object is the recipient or focus of the action of the verb, or to express it in a way that is more accurate for Russian, the direct object is the object of a transitive verb. This is an important point, because what may sound like a direct object in English does not always correspond to Russian usage. To telephone someone or to help someone, for instance, is expressed in Russian by means of the dative case, not the accusative (you make a telephone call or render assistance *to* someone).[1]

Consider the following examples of the accusative case as direct object:

Па́па купи́л мне но́вую маши́ну.	Dad bought me a new car.
Почему́ ты взял мой слова́рь?	Why did you take my dictionary?
Откро́йте окно́!	Open the window!
Я про́сто не могу́ вы́терпеть Ива́на Влади́мировича.	I just can't stand Ivan Vladimirovich.
На́до уважа́ть мать и отца́.	One must respect one's mother and father.

---

[1]For a comprehensive list of verbs that take the dative case, see chapter 8.

As you can see, only two forms change endings in the singular: the feminine nouns in **-а/-я** and masculine animate nouns. Masculine inanimate nouns, all neuter nouns, and feminine nouns in a soft sign remain the same as the nominative case.

The following sentences contain plural direct objects:

Ма́ма купи́ла нам но́вые кни́ги.	Mom bought us new books.
Почему́ ты взял мои́ журна́лы?	Why did you take my magazines?
Закро́йте все о́кна!	Close all the windows!
Я не могу́ вы́терпеть э́тих ма́льчиков.	I can't stand these boys.
Мы уби́ли всех насеко́мых.	We killed all the insects.
Ты зна́ешь э́тих де́вочек?	Do you know these little girls?
Он поста́вил лошаде́й в коню́шню.	He put the horses in the stable.

As you can see, the essential difference between the accusative case in the singular and the plural lies in the fact that the distinction between *animate* and *inanimate* nouns applies to all genders in the plural but only to masculine nouns in the singular. In other words, all inanimate nouns in the accusative plural are the same as the nominative plural, whereas in the singular only masculine inanimate nouns, neuter nouns, and feminine nouns in a soft sign are the same as nominative plural. And, of course, feminine nouns in **-а/-я** have their own set of endings.

Accusative Endings, Singular and Plural, for Adjectives and Nouns

	Singular		Plural	
	Adjective	**Noun**	**Adjective**	**Noun**
Masculine				
Inanimate	но́вый	журна́л	но́вые	журна́лы
Animate	но́вого	му́жа	но́вых	муже́й
Neuter				
Inanimate	большо́е	окно́	больши́е	о́кна
Animate	большо́е	насеко́мое	больши́х	насеко́мых
Feminine				
in **-а/-я**				
Inanimate	ску́чную	кни́гу	ску́чные	кни́ги
Animate	глу́пую	сестру́	глу́пых	сестёр

	Singular		Plural	
	Adjective	**Noun**	**Adjective**	**Noun**
Feminine				
in soft sign				
Inanimate	ста́рую	тетра́дь	ста́рые	тетра́ди
Animate	бе́лую	ло́шадь	бе́лых	лошаде́й

TEST FOR MASTERY 1

«Все мои деми». If Russia were to have a Pine Valley, no doubt the inhabitants would behave in much the same way as those of the eponymous American hamlet. Therefore, whereas the people in the left-hand column are in love with those in the right-hand column, the feelings are not reciprocated. Make sentences to show the relationships, and use pronouns in the second half of the sentence according to the model.

Example: Е́рика лю́бит Джек, но он не лю́бит её.

1. Та́ня/Кри́са
2. Матве́й/Джулье́тта
3. А́лла/Бори́с
4. Тим/Ма́ша
5. А́нна/Дави́д
6. Билл/Биа́нка
7. Тётя Евдо́ксия/Граф Толсто́й
8. Людми́ла/Русла́н
9. Глеб/Я́на
10. Ака́кий/Карло́тта
11. Со́ня/Родио́н

Personal Pronouns

Singular		Plural	
Nominative	**Accusative**	**Nominative**	**Accusative**
я	меня́	мы	нас
ты	тебя́	вы	вас
он	его́	они́	их
оно́	его́		
она́	её		

Let's try the same sort of exercise, except with pronouns. For each one of the matched pairs, compose a sentence according to the example:

Он / она: Он понима́ет её, а она́ не понимает его́.

1. мы / вы	6. вы / она́
2. я / она́	7. он / ты
3. ты / он	8. она́ / вы
4. вы / мы	9. я / вы
5. они́ / я	10. мы / они́

Objects of Verbs of Motion

The accusative case is also used after verbs of motion. While English changes prepositions when location switches to motion, Russian accomplishes this change of meaning by keeping the same prepositions as used in a locative meaning but changing the case from prepositional to accusative. Compare:

Он рабо́тает <u>в ба́нке</u>.	He works <u>at</u> the bank.
Он идёт <u>в ба́нк</u>.	He is going <u>to</u> the bank.

Do not use accusative case when the object of the verb of motion is a person. This usage requires the dative case: **Он идёт к ба́бушке** *(He is going to his grand-mother's).*

The preposition **за** is also used with the accusative case when motion is involved. In this usage its meaning is *behind* or *beyond.*

За́втра мы е́дем за́ город.	Tomorrow we're going out of town.
Со́лнце то́лько что зашло́ за горизо́нт.	The sun has just set beyond the horizon.
Соба́ка побежа́ла за гара́ж.	The dog ran behind the garage.

For purposes of the exercise below, recall that Russian distinguishes between going on foot (**идти́**) and going by vehicle or riding (**е́хать**). Using the correct form of the verb, compose present tense sentences with the following subjects and destinations. Remember that **идти́** is considered the default verb—if it is not absolutely necessary to use a vehicle, use **идти́.**

TEST FOR MASTERY 3

1. Ма́ша _____ в (Перетбу́рг), а Ю́ра _____ в (Москва́).

2. Я _____ в (апте́ка). Мне ну́жен аспири́н.

3. Куда́ вы _____ на (кани́кулы)? Мы _____ в (Испа́ния).

4. Са́ша! Пора́ _____ в (шко́ла)!

5. Же́ня! Куда́ ты _____? Я _____ на (рабо́та).

6. Сего́дня ве́чером мы _____ на (конце́рт).

7. Я написа́ла все пи́сьма и сейча́с _____ на (по́чта).

8. Мы _____ в (Калифо́рния) к на́шему бра́ту.

9. Они́ собира́ются _____ в (А́нглия) на ле́то.

10. По́сле заня́тий они́ _____ в (пра́чечная [*laundry*]).

11. Сего́дня я _____ в (Ита́лия).

12. Сте́фани _____ в (библиоте́ка). Она́ бу́дет занима́ться.

After Other Prepositional Constructions

There are verb-plus-preposition phrases other than verbs of motion that require the accusative case. Many of these verbs are related to the general idea of motion. Some of them are:

превраща́ться / преврати́ться + в	to turn into
ве́рить / пове́рить + в	to believe in
стреля́ть + в	to shoot at
игра́ть + в	to play (a game)
вме́шиваться / вмеша́ться + в	to interfere in
поступа́ть / поступи́ть + в	to enter, enroll in (school, the army, etc.)
жа́ловаться / пожа́ловаться + на	to complain about
серди́ться / рассерди́ться + на	to become angry at/with
отвеча́ть / отве́тить (кому) + на	to answer someone's X
наде́яться + на	to hope for, rely on, be counting on
дели́ть / раздели́ть + на	to divide into
напада́ть / напа́сть + на	to attack

Fill in the blanks:

1. В оди́н прекра́сный день Гре́гор За́мза очну́лся и уви́дел, что он _____ в (тарака́н) (*cockroach*).

2. Вы _____ в (Бог)?

3. Он смотре́л и ме́дленно _____ на (я).

4. Ты _____ в (баскетбо́л)? Нет, но я _____ в (те́ннис).

5. Не _____ в (мои́ дела́)!

6. Когда́ она́ _____ в (консервато́рия)?

7. Он тако́й зану́да (*a bore*)! Всегда́ _____ на (всё).

8. Она́ _____ на (я) и ушла́.

9. Когда́ вы _____ (*future*) ему́ на (письмо́)?

10. Мы _____ на (твоя́ по́мощь).

11. Он _____ кусо́к хле́ба на (че́тверти).

12. Мы _____ на (враг) ле́том.

With Expressions of Time

1. The accusative is used with the preposition **в** meaning *at* and with **на** meaning *for*. A different preposition with dative case is used in the meaning of *by* (**к четвергу** [by Thursday]).

В + accusative is used for hours and minutes: **в час** (at one o'clock), **в два часа́**[2] (at two o'clock), **в пять часо́в** (at five o'clock), **в де́сять мину́т тре́тьего** (at ten minutes after two), **в че́тверть шесто́го** (at quarter after five), **в три́дцать деся́того** (at nine thirty), **в по́лдень** (at noon), **в по́лночь** (at midnight).

There is one exception. The half-hour takes the preposition **в** but is used with the prepositional case: **в полови́не седьмо́го** (at half past six).

В + accusative is used for days of the week: **в понеде́льник** (on Monday), **во вто́рник** (on Tuesday), **в сре́ду** (on Wednesday), **в четве́рг** (on Thursday), **в пя́тницу** (on Friday), **в суббо́ту** (on Saturday), **в воскресе́нье** (on Sunday).

---

[2]Note that it is the number that is in the accusative case. That number then governs the use of the genitive case for the unit that follows.

Через + accusative is used to express *in* or *after* a certain period of time is over: **Мы éдем в Лóндон через недéлю** (*We are going to London in a week*); **Через нéсколько часóв он ушёл** (*He left after a few hours*).

На + accusative is used to denote a period of time to be covered after another action: **Мы éдем в Лóндон на недéлю** (*We are going to London for a week*); **Через три дня мы éдем в Áнглию на два гóда** (*In three days we are going to England for two years*).

2. The accusative case is also used to express time when the units of time are equal to the action of the verb. Compare: **Онá читáла два часá** (*She read [for] two hours*); **Онá пошлá в библиотéку на два часá** (*She went to the library for two hours*).

In English, the word *for* can be dropped in the first example but not in the second. This is a sure-fire way of testing for use of the preposition.

3. There are further instances where the accusative case is used with time but without a preposition. The most important two are with the words **каждый** and **весь**: **кáждый день, кáждую нелéдю кáждый мéсяц, кáждый втóрник, весь день, весь год, всю недéлю, всю жизнь.**

TEST FOR MASTERY 5

Replace the words in parentheses with the correct preposition or none at all.

1. Пéтя éдет (to) Нью-Йóрк (in) час.

2. Он приéхал ко мне (for) лéто.

3. Лíза сидéла дóма (all day) и писáла пíсьма.

4. Он хóдит в музéй (every week).

5. Чтó мне дéлать?! (In) недéлю Мáма приéдет к нам (for) два мéсяца!

6. Сáша живёт в э́том гóроде (whole life).

7. (On) воскресéнье онú идýт к нам (for) вечерúнку.

8. Дéти! Не беспокóйтесь! Мáма вернётся (in) час.

9. Мáма готóвила обéд (for) два часá.

10. Мы встрéтимся (at) два часá (on) срéду.

11.   —Что передаю́т по телеви́зору?—(In) полчаса́ бу́дет «60 мину́т».

12.   Я написа́ла письмо́ и (in) не́сколько мину́т иду́ (to) по́чту.

13.   —Куда́ ты идёшь (on) суббо́ту?—Я иду́ (to) кино́.

14.   Он приезжа́ет к нам (every Friday).

15.   Па́па вернётся (in) во́семь часо́в, (at) по́лночь.

CONVERSATION PRACTICE

Examine the table below concerning Olga's schedule for the coming week, and then answer the questions that follow.

Vocabulary for this section:

ры́нок	market
гото́вить/гото́вит[2]	to cook
за́втрак	breakfast
обе́д	dinner
у́жин	supper
игра́ть/игра́ет в ка́рты	to play cards
стира́ть/стира́ет бельё	to do the laundry
убира́ть/убира́ет	to clean up
отдыха́ть/отдыха́ет	to relax
мыть/мо́ет посу́ду	to wash dishes
гуля́ть/гуля́ет (до утра́)	to go out
у роди́телей	at her parents'
у́тром	in the morning, on X morning
ве́чером	in the evening, on X evening
днём	in the afternoon, on X afternoon
занима́твся/занима́ется	to study
с колвко раз	how many times
в какие дни	on what days

	Утром	Днём	Вечером
Понеде́льник	ры́нок	рестора́н	библиоте́ка
Вто́рник	гото́вит за́втрак	библиоте́ка	
Среда́	стира́ет бельё	игра́ет в ка́рты	гото́вит у́жин
Четве́рг	библиоте́ка	гото́вит обе́д	кафе́
Пя́тница	убира́ет	отдыха́ет	дискоте́ка

[2]Verbs are presented in both the infinitive and third person singular forms.

| Суббóта | мóет посýду | игрáет в скретбббль | гуляет до утрá |
| Воскресéньс | спит до 12 часóв | музéй | у родúтслсй |

Example: Когдá Óльга идёт в музéй? (When is Olga going to the museum?)

Онá идёт в музéй в воскрéсенье днём. (She's going to the museum on Sunday afternoon.)

1. Когдá Óльга идёт на рынок?

2. Чтó дéлает Óльга в срéду вéчером?

3. Когдá Óльга занимáется в библиотéке?

4. Чтó дéлает Óльга в воскресéнье ýтром?

5. Почемý онá спит так пóздно?

6. Как вы дýмаете: почемý онá отдыхáет в пятницу днём?

7. Когдá Óльга стирáет?

8. Скóлько раз в недéлю Óльга хóдит в библиотéку?

9. Чтó дéлает Óльга во втóрник вéчером?

10. В какúе дни Óльга не готóвит дóма? Почемý?

11. Чтó дéлает Óльга в четвéрг вéчером?

12. Когдá Óльга игрáет в кáрты?

13. Как вы дýмаете: её квартúра чúстая и порядочная (neat)?

14. Как по-вáшему: Óльга хорóшая студéнтка?

Reading

Read the text below, and underline all words in the accusative case. Be sure you understand the reasons why these words are in the accusative.

Рáно ýтром. Ктó кудá идёт?

Рáно ýтром. Все кудá-то идýт.

Мáрта Антóновна идёт в шкóлу. Онá учúтельница. Онá берёт с собóй свои кнúги и ýтреннюю газéту.

Вади́м Петро́вич—инжене́р. Он идёт на заво́д, где он рабо́тает. Так-как на заво́де нет столо́вой, он верёт с собой бутербро́д с ветчино́й и ко́ка-ко́лу.

Ма́ша и Па́ша ещё ма́ленькие. Их ма́ма ведёт их в де́тский сад. Они́ беру́т с собой кни́ги, тетра́ди, и карандаши́. Они́ бу́дут обе́дать в столо́вой при шко́ле.

Ве́ра Арка́дьевна идёт на по́чту. Она́ рабо́тает там ме́неджером. А что́ де́лают её рабо́тники? Ну, почтальо́ны но́сят по́чту, коне́чно!

Наш па́па опа́здывает на рабо́ту, и поэ́тому он е́дет в свою́ фи́рму на такси́. Он архите́ктор и рабо́тает в большо́й, изве́стной фи́рме.

А ба́бушка никуда́ не идёт. Она́ на пе́нсии уже́ пять лет. Она́ сиди́т до́ма и убира́ет кварти́ру, чита́ет детекти́вы, пи́шет пи́сьма. Ка́ждое у́тро де́душка сиди́т в ку́хне, чита́ет газе́ту, и жа́луется на совреме́нную молодёжь.

Early Morning. Who's Going Where?

It's early in the morning. Everyone is going somewhere.

Marta Antonovna is going to school. She is a teacher. She is taking her books and the morning newspaper with her.

Vadim Petrovich is an engineer. He is going to the factory where he works. Since there is no cafeteria at the factory, he is taking a ham sandwich and a coca-cola with him.

Masha and Pasha are still little. Their mother is taking them to kindergarten. They are taking books, notebooks, and pencils with them. They will be having lunch at the school cafeteria.

Vera Arkadievna is going to the post office. She works there as a manager. And what do her employees do? Well, mail carriers carry mail, of course!

Our dad is late for work, so he is going to his firm by taxi. He is an architect and works in a big, famous firm.

But grandmother isn't going anywhere. She has been retired for five years already. She sits at home and cleans the apartment, reads murder mysteries, and writes letters. Every morning grandfather sits in the kitchen, reads the newspaper, and complains about the kids today.

ANSWER KEY

Vocabulary Practice

1. оте́ц

2. до свида́ния

3. сын

4. до́брый ве́чер

5. де́ти

6. ба́бушка

7. рабо́тать

8. сестра́

9. спаси́бо

10. ма́ма

11. ко́шка

12. роди́тели

Test for Mastery 1

1. Та́ня лю́бит Криса, но он не лю́бит её.

2. Матве́й лю́бит Джулье́тту, но она́ не лю́бит его́.

3. А́лла лю́бит Бори́са, но он не лю́бит её.

4. Тим лю́бит Ма́шу, но она́ не лю́бит его́.

5. А́нна лю́бит Дави́да, но он не лю́бит её.

6. Билл лю́бит Биа́нку, но она́ не лю́бит его́.

7. Тётя Евдо́ксия лю́бит Гра́фа Толсто́го, но он не лю́бит её.

8. Людми́ла лю́бит Русла́на, но он не лю́бит её.

9. Глеб лю́бит Я́ну, но она́ не лю́бит его́.

10. Ака́кий лю́бит Карло́тту, но она́ не лю́бит его́.

11. Со́ня лю́бит Родио́на, но он не лю́бит её.

Test for Mastery 2

1. Мы понима́ем вас, а вы не понима́ете нас.

2. Я понима́ю её, а она́ не понима́ет меня́.

3. Ты понима́ешь его́, а он не понима́ет тебя́.

4. Вы понима́ете нас, а мы не понима́ем вас.

5. Они́ понима́ют меня́, а я не понима́ю их.

6. Вы понима́ете её, а она́ не понима́ет вас.

7. Он понима́ет тебя́, а ты не понима́ешь его́.

8. Она́ понима́ет вас, а вы не понима́ете её.

9. Я понима́ю вас, а вы не понима́ете меня́.

10. Мы понима́ем их, а они́ не понима́ют нас.

Test for Mastery 3

1. е́дет в Петербу́рг/е́дет в Москву́

2. иду́ в апте́ку

3. е́дете на кани́кулы/е́дем в Испа́нию

4. идти́ в шко́лу

5. идёшь/иду́ на рабо́ту

6. идём на конце́рт

7. иду́ на по́чту

8. е́дем в Калифо́рнию

9. е́хать в А́нглию

10. иду́т в пра́чечную

11. е́ду в Ита́лию

12. идёт в библиоте́ку

Test for Mastery 4

1. преврати́лся в тарака́на

2. ве́рите в Бо́га

3. стреля́л на меня́

4. игра́ешь в баскетбо́л/игра́ю в те́ннис

5. вме́шивайся в мои́ дела́

6. поступи́ла в консервато́рию

7. жа́луется на всё

8. рассерди́лась на меня́

9. отве́тите ему́ на письмо́

10. наде́емся на твою́ по́мощь

11. раздели́л на че́тверти (*divided into quarters*)

12. напа́ли на врага́

Test for Mastery 5

1. в/через

2. на

3. весь день

4. ка́ждую неде́лю

5. через/на

6. всю жизнь

7. В/на

8. через

9. (*no preposition*)

10. в/в

11. Через

12. через/на

13. в/в

14. ка́ждую пя́тницу

15. через/в

Conversation Practice: Olga's Schedule

1. О́льга идёт на ры́нок в понеде́льник у́тром.

2. В сре́ду ве́чером О́льга гото́вит у́жин.

3. О́льга занима́ется в библиоте́ке в понеде́льник ве́чером, во вто́рник днём, и в четве́рг у́тром.

4. В воскресе́нье у́тром О́льга спит до 12 часо́в.

5. Потому́ что в суббо́ту ве́чером она́ гуля́ла до утра́.

6. Она́ отдыха́ет в пя́тницу днём, потому́ что ве́чером она́ идёт на дискоте́ку.

7. О́льга стира́ет в сре́ду у́тром.

8. О́льга хо́дит в библиоте́ку три ра́за в неде́лю: в понеде́льник ве́чером, во вто́рник днём, и в четве́рг у́тром.

9. Во вто́рник ве́чером она́ ничего́ не де́лает.

10. О́льга не гото́вит до́ма в понеде́льник днём, потому́ что она́ обе́дает в рестора́не.

11. В черве́рг ве́чером О́льга идёт в кафе́.

12. Она́ игра́ет в ка́рты в сре́ду днём.

13. Наве́рно (*probably*) нет. Она́ мо́ет посу́ду то́лько раз (*once*) в неде́лю.

14. Наве́рно нет. Она́ всё вре́мя гуля́ет!

Ра́но у́тром. Кто́ куда́ идёт?

Ра́но у́тром. Все куда́-то иду́т.

Ма́рта Анто́новна идёт в <u>шко́лу</u>. Она́ учи́тельница. Она́ берёт с собо́й <u>свои́ кни́ги</u> и <u>у́треннюю газе́ту</u>.

Вади́м Петро́вич—инжене́р. Он идёт на <u>заво́д</u>, где он рабо́тает. Так-как на заво́де нет столо́вой, он верёт с собо́й <u>бутербро́д</u> с ветчино́й и <u>ко́ка-ко́лу</u>.

Ма́ша и Па́ша ещё ма́ленькие. Их ма́ма ведёт <u>их</u> в <u>де́тский сад</u>. Они́ беру́т с собо́й <u>кни́ги</u>, <u>тетра́ди</u>, и <u>карандаши́</u>. Они́ бу́дут обе́дать в столо́вой при шко́ле.

Ве́ра Арка́дьевна идёт на <u>по́чту</u>. Она́ рабо́тает там ме́неджером. А что́ де́лают её рабо́тники? Ну, почтальо́ны но́сят <u>по́чту</u>, коне́чно!

Наш па́па опа́здывает на <u>рабо́ту</u>, и поэ́тому он е́дет в <u>свою́ фи́рму</u> на такси́. Он архите́ктор и рабо́тает в большо́й, изве́стной фи́рме.

А ба́бушка никуда́ не идёт. Она́ на пе́нсии уже́ <u>пять</u> лет. Она́ сиди́т до́ма и убира́ет <u>кварти́ру</u>, чита́ет <u>детекти́вы</u>, пи́шет <u>пи́сьма</u>. <u>Ка́ждое у́тро</u> де́душка сиди́т в ку́хне, чита́ет <u>газе́ту</u>, и жа́луется на <u>совреме́нную молодёжь</u>.

4 The Adjective

Имя прилагательное

Useful Vocabulary

бéдный	poor	жгýчий	burning
бéлый	white	жёлтый	yellow
блúзкий	near	здéшний	local
богáтый	rich	здорóвый	healthy
больнóй	sick	зелёный	green
большóй	big	извéстный	famous
велúкий	great	интерéсный	interesting
вкýсный	tasty, good	корóткий	short
высóкий	high, tall	красúвый	beautiful, pretty
глубóкий	deep	крáсный	red
глýпый	stupid, silly	крутóй	steep
глухóй	deaf	лёгкий	light, easy
голубóй	light blue	лúшний	extra, superfluous
грóмкий	loud	мáленький	small
грязный	dirty	мéлкий	petty
далёкий	far off	мúлый	nice, sweet
дешёвый	cheap	млáдший	younger
длúнный	long	мóдный	fashionable
дóбрый	good, kind	молодóй	young
дорогóй	dear, expensive	мýдрый	wise

некраси́вый	ugly	сла́дкий	sweet
немо́дный	unfashionable	совреме́нный	contemporary
ни́зкий	low	ста́рший	elder
но́вый	new	ста́рый	old
о́стрый	sharp	стро́гий	stern, strict, severe
плохо́й	bad	сухо́й	dry, arid
по́здний	late	счастли́вый	happy, lucky
поле́зный	useful	ти́хий	quiet
после́дний	last	то́нкий	thin
прекра́сный	fine, beautiful	тру́дный	difficult
ре́дкий	rare	тя́жкий	heavy
све́жий	fresh	у́зкий	narrow
све́тлый	light	у́мный	smart
се́верный	northern	холо́дный	cold
сего́дняшний	today's	хоро́ший	good
си́льный	strong	худо́й	bad
симпати́чный	nice	чёрный	black
си́ний	dark blue	чи́стый	clean
ску́чный	boring	широ́кий	wide
сла́бый	weak	шу́мный	noisy

VOCABULARY PRACTICE

Choose the adjective that would be *least likely* to describe the subject.

1. Моя́ ма́ма: то́нкая, краси́вая, зелёная, до́брая

2. Наш президе́нт: изве́стный, му́дрый, америка́нский, вку́сный

3. Мой го́род: шу́мный, мла́дший, зелёный, дорого́й

4. Э́тот рестора́н: дорого́й, мо́дный, дешёвый, круто́й

5. Чёрная икра́: вку́сная, дорога́я, ру́сская, шу́мная

6. Америка́нский флаг: жёлтый, кра́сный, си́ний, бе́лый

7. Моя́ де́вушка: до́брая, у́зкая, молода́я, у́мная

8. Э́тот ру́сский рома́н: совреме́нный, се́верный, плохо́й, ску́чный

9. Моя́ сестра́: мла́дшая, ста́ршая, глу́пая, зде́шняя

10. Сверхчелове́к (*Superman*): си́льный, у́мный, сла́бый, симпати́чный

11. Шокола́д: ме́лкий, сла́дкий, вку́сный, дорого́й

12. Де́ти: здоро́вые, хоро́шие, гря́зные, гро́мкие

CONVERSATION PRACTICE

Како́й прекра́сный день!

ВА́НЯ: Ма́ша! Како́й сего́дня прекра́сный де́нь!

МА́ША: Да. Не́бо голубо́е, со́лнце жёлтое, а там далёкие облака́ бе́лые.

В: Мне совсе́м не хо́чется занима́ться сего́дня. А ты как ду́маешь?

М: Дава́й пое́дем на фильм!

В: Нет, я не хочу́. Дава́й лу́чше пое́хать в дере́вню.

М: Но дере́вня—э́то са́мое ску́чное ме́сто в ми́ре!

В: Нет, Ма́ша. Там интере́сно. Мо́жно дыша́ть све́жим во́здухом, лежа́ть на со́лнце, е́здить верхо́м, купа́ться в реке́, собира́ть я́годы, лови́ть ры́бу—всё, что мы не мо́жем де́лать в го́роде.

М: Ну, ла́дно. Я не хочу́ спо́рить.

(пото́м, на вокза́ле)

В: Два биле́та в Переде́лкино. Туда́ и обра́тно.

КАССИ́Р: 2.000 рубле́й.[1]

В: Мо́жно плати́ть креди́тной ка́рточкой?

К: Пожа́луйста. Вот вам биле́ты.

(пото́м, на платфо́рме)

В: Мы опозда́ли на у́тренний по́езд на 30 мину́т.

М: Жаль. А когда́ бу́дет сле́дующий?

В: Через час. Ну, что́ де́лать? Нам на́до бу́дет ждать.

(через 2 часа́, в Переде́лкино)

В: Ну, вот мы и прие́хали! Кака́я краси́вая, ти́хая, зелёная дере́вня!

М: Но смотри́, Ва́ня—пока́ мы говори́ли и реша́ли, куда́ е́хать, э́ти далёкие, бе́лые облака́ станови́лись всё черне́е и черне́е . . .

В: Бо́же мой! Дождь!

М: Я тебе́ сказа́ла, нам лу́чше бы́ло ходи́ть в кино́.

---

[1]Where Americans use commas, Russians use periods, and vice versa in numerical designations.

What a Beautiful Day!

VANYA:	Masha! What a beautiful day it is today!
MASHA:	Yes. The sky is blue, the sun is yellow, and the far-off clouds are white.
V:	I don't feel like studying at all today. What do you think?
M:	Let's go to a movie!
V:	No, I don't want to. Let's go to the countryside instead.
M:	But the countryside is the most boring place in the world!
V:	No, Masha. It's interesting. You can breathe fresh air, lay in the sun, go horseback riding, swim in the river, gather berries, go fishing—everything that we can't do in the city.
M:	Well, okay. I don't want to argue.

(later at the train station)

V:	Two tickets to Peredelkino. Round trip.
CASHIER:	2,000 rubles.
V:	Can I pay with a credit card?
C:	Of course. Here are your tickets.

(later on the platform)

V:	We missed the morning train by 30 minutes.
M:	What a pity. When's the next one?
V:	In an hour. Well, what can we do? We'll just have to wait.

(two hours later, in Peredelkino)

V:	Well here we are! What a beautiful, quiet, green village!
M:	But look, Vanya—while we were talking and deciding on where to go, those far-off, white clouds were getting blacker and blacker.
V:	My God! Rain!
M:	I told you we should have gone to the movies.

Adjectives are the jewels of a language. Their judicious use adds much to the speaker's style, as well as defining a level of education. Russian adjectives agree completely with nouns explicit or implied. This means that they have gender, number, and case. Adjectives may be qualitative or relative, long or short, predicative or attributive, as we shall see below. They also form degrees of comparison that may be used predicatively or attributively. There are also two special types of adjectives, possessives and those formed from names of animals, that have unique formations and declensions.

Gender

Like nouns, adjectives are composed of a stem plus an ending, which may, in the case of short-form adjectives, include the zero ending. Adjectives may be masculine, neuter, or feminine in the singular. They have only one ending for all genders throughout the plural.

Masculine adjectives are characterized by the two-letter ending **-ый**. This ending may be changed for one of three reasons:

1. After **ж, ч, ш, щ,** and **к, г, х,** write **и** instead of **ы** (the seven-letter spelling rule): **хоро́ший, ру́сский, жгу́чий, све́жий.**

2. If the ending of an adjective is stressed, the masculine form is written **-о́й**: **глухо́й, молодо́й, большо́й, дорого́й.**

3. If an adjective has a stem ending in a soft consonant (primarily the soft consonant **н,** use the soft ending **-ий: после́дний сего́дняшний, зде́шний, ли́шний.**

The most commonly used soft adjectives are:

Russian	English	Russian	English
у́тренний	morning	ле́тний	summer
зи́мний	winter	осе́нний	autumn
весе́нний	spring	по́здний	late
ра́нний	early	вчера́шний	yesterday's
сего́дняшний	today's	прошлого́дний	last year's
за́втрашний	tomorrow's	тогда́шний	of that time
тепе́решний	present	дре́вний	of old, ancient
да́вний	of long ago	двухле́тний	two (etc.)-year-old
пре́жний	former	да́льний	far off, distant
зде́шний	local	ни́жний	lower
ве́рхний	upper	сре́дний	middle
пере́дний	front	вну́тренний	inner, interior
за́дний	back	сосе́дний	neighboring
вне́шний	outer, external	после́дний	last (in a series)
кра́йний	extreme	дома́шний	domestic
си́ний	(dark) blue	и́скренний	sincere
ли́шний	extra, spare	ка́рий	brown, hazel (as of eyes)[2]
посторо́нний	alien, strange		
вече́рний	evening		

---

[2]This is the only soft adjective in Russian whose stem does not end in the consonant **-н-.**

Neuter adjectives end in **-oe.** Some environments may affect this ending:

1. Do not write unstressed **o** after **ж, ч, ш, щ,** and **ц,** write **e** instead (the five-letter spelling rule): **хоро́шее, све́жее, жгу́чее.**

   NOTE: The letters **к, г,** and **x** do not belong to this spelling rule. Thus, the correct neuter form is **ру́сское.**

2. In soft adjectives, write **e** instead of **o: после́днее, вчера́шнее, весе́ннее, си́нее.**

Feminine adjectives end in **-ая.** The only exception is that soft adjectives take the ending **-яя.**

Adjective Endings

	Regular	**Soft**	**Spelling Rule**	**End Stressed**
Masculine	-ый	-ий	-ий	-о́й
Neuter	-ое	-ее	-ее	-о́е
Feminine	-ая	-яя	(-ая)	-а́я

NOTE: Remember that masculine adjectives follow the seven-letter spelling rule, but neuter adjectives follow the five-letter spelling rule.

Plural

Adjectives in the plural no longer distinguish gender. The same ending is used for all adjectives, with modifications for the seven-letter spelling rule and softness. Thus, the only possible endings for plural adjectives are **-ые** (the normal ending) and **-ие** (after soft consonants and spelling-rule consonants).

TEST FOR MASTERY 1

For the following adjective/noun combinations, add the correct endings. Be sure to pay attention to the gender of the noun and whether the noun is singular or plural.

1. ру́сск_____ зима́

2. зи́мн_____ день

3. си́н_____ пла́тье

4. Больш_____ бале́т

5. Бел_____ дом

6. послéдн_____ нóвость

7. хорóш_____ погóда

8. свéж_____ молокó

9. плох_____ рáдио

10. чёрн_____ кóфе

11. молод_____ дéвушка

12. англи́йск_____ словáрь

13. жёлт_____ такси́

14. си́н_____ небесá

15. дáльн_____ востóк

16. пятилéтн_____ дéвочка

17. совремéнн_____ áвтор

18. ми́л_____ сосéди

19. óстр_____ ножи́

20. здéшн_____ библиотéка

21. рýсск_____ речь

22. извéстн_____ музéй

23. молод_____ дерéвья

24. хорóш_____ сочинéние

25. ти́х_____ студéнт

26. плох_____ официáнтка

27. Нóв_____ рýсск_____ слóво

28. Крáсн_____ плóщадь

29. сéверн_____ вéтер

30. дли́нн_____ дорога

CONVERSATION PRACTICE

You have met Yermak, a resident of Siberia, who wants to know what it's like where you come from. Whenever he tells you something about his little village, you respond by saying that it's just the opposite in your big city.

Example: YERMAK: У нас мáленькие здáния.
              YOU: А у нас больши́е здáния.

Respond to Yermak:

1. У нас тóлько зелёные банáны.

2. У нас скýчные музéи.

3. У нас óчень немóдные магази́ны.

4. Ýлицы у нас таки́е ýзкие!

5. У меня́ тóлько рýсские кни́ги.

6. У нас в райóне бéдные лю́ди.

7. У нас больши́е озёра, краси́вые леса́.

8. У нас холо́дные, стро́гие зи́мы.

9. Авто́бусы здесь ста́рые, о́чень плохи́е.

10. У нас такси́ быва́ют чёрные.

Demonstrative Adjectives

There are two demonstrative adjectives in Russian: **э́тот** (this) and **тот** (that). The word **э́тот**, however, has a broader translation in English and can be rendered as either *this* or *that*. In English we tend to overuse the word *that* without reference to proximity or comparison with another *this* (*That's interesting. That's a good idea. I like that.*) A good rule of thumb is not to use **тот** except when you have already used **э́тот** in the same sentence.

The plurals of these words are **э́ти** and **те**.

DEMONSTRATIVE ADJECTIVE PRACTICE

Fill in the blank with the opposite adjectives.

Example: Э́ти кни́ги ста́рые, <u>а те кни́ги но́вые</u>.

1. Э́ти ребя́та шу́мные, _____.

2. Э́тот магази́н дорого́й, _____.

3. Э́ти зада́чи тру́дные, _____.

4. Э́то бельё гря́зное, _____.

5. Э́та кни́га ску́чная, _____.

6. Э́тот учени́к у́мный, _____.

7. Э́ти зда́ния ни́зкие, _____.

8. Э́тот суп вку́сный, _____.

9. Э́ти города́ бли́зкие, _____.

10. Э́та де́вушка больна́я, _____.

Comparative Adjectives

Comparative adjectives come in a compound form, which is used attributively, and a simple form, which is used predicatively. Only qualitative adjectives—adjectives of size, dimension, taste, weight, temperature, and various qualities referring to people or things—can be compared. Relative adjectives cannot be used comparatively, since they do not exist in a more or less relationship to the object. In both English and Russian, it is not possible to compare the adjectives that appear in combinations such as *wooden table, autumn day, Russian winter, fox coat, dad's office, the national budget,* and so forth. Most relative adjectives describe material, time, place, intention (*student cafeteria*), and ownership. The easiest rule of thumb to follow, however, is to test your sentence in English. If the adjective cannot be transformed by adding the suffix *-er* or by using *more,* then the comparative degree cannot be formed in Russian.

Simple (or Short-Form) Comparatives

Simple-form comparison is used predicatively. Regard the following sentences:

Ива́н умне́е, чем Лари́са.	Ivan is smarter than Larisa.
О́льга ста́рше, чем сестра́.	Olga is older than her sister.
Во́лга длине́е, чем Дон.	The Volga is longer than the Don.

The second element of all three sentences is the simple comparative adjective: *smarter, older, longer.* A comparative adjective used predicatively means that it describes the subject of a sentence that consists only of a subject, a copulative verb (*is*), and the predicate. In last position stands the object that is being compared. This comparison may be expressed either by using **чем** plus the nominative case or by placing the object in the genitive case, which is statistically more frequently encountered.

NOTE: The simple-form comparative is never declined!

Formation

1. If the stem of the adjective ends in a consonant that does not normally undergo an alternation (see section 2 below), simply add the suffix **-ee.**

Positive	Comparative	English
интере́сный	интере́снее	interesting
си́льный	сильне́е	strong

Positive	Comparative	English
сла́бый	слабе́е	weak
ску́чный	скучне́е	boring
счастли́вый	счастли́вее	happy
у́мный	умне́е	smart
о́стрый	остре́е	sharp
све́тлый	светле́е	light
му́дрый	мудре́е	wise
глу́пый	глупе́е	stupid

In adjectives whose stem consists of only one syllable, the stress is usually on the first **e** of the ending. In longer adjectives, the stress falls on the stem: **интере́снее** (more interesting), **внима́тельнее** (more attentive), **споко́йнее** (calmer), **прия́тнее** (more pleasant), **краси́вее** (prettier), **изве́стнее** (more famous), **и́скренее** (more sincere), **ра́достнее** (more joyous). Exceptions to this rule include **холодне́е** (colder), **веселе́е** (happier), **здорове́е** (healthier), and **тяжеле́е** (harder).

2. If the stem of the adjective ends in **г, к, х,** or **д, т, ст,** this stem consonant undergoes an alternation before adding a single **-е** to form the comparative. The ending of this type of comparative is never stressed.

Positive	Comparative	English
дорого́й	доро́же	expensive
стро́гий	стро́же	strict
ти́хий	ти́ше	quiet
кре́пкий	кре́пче	strong
гро́мкий	гро́мче	loud
молодо́й	моло́же	young
бога́тый	бога́че	rich
просто́й	про́ще	simple
то́лстый	то́лще	fat
твёрдый	твёрже	hard

A large number of adjectives, but not all, whose stems end in **к** or **ок** form their simple comparatives by dropping this suffix, followed by an alternation in the final stem consonant:

Positive	Comparative	English
ни́зкий	ни́же	low
высо́кий	вы́ше	high, tall

Positive	Comparative	English
у́зкий	у́же	narrow
коро́ткий	коро́че	short
гла́дкий	гла́же	smooth

3. The remainder may be considered exceptions to the above rules, even though their differences may appear slight:

Positive	Comparative	Positive	Comparative
плохо́й	ху́же	сла́дкий	сла́ще
хоро́ший	лу́чше	глубо́кий	глу́бже
большо́й	бо́льше	дешёвый	деше́вле
ма́ленький	ме́ньше	ра́нний	ра́ньше
то́нкий	то́ньше	по́здний	позднѐе *or* по́зже
далёкий	да́льше	ста́рый	старѐе (for things)
ме́лкий	ме́льче		ста́рше (for people)

4. Some adjectives do not form simple comparatives. Among them are:

- all adjectives with the suffix **-ск-,** such as **ру́сский, дру́жеский** (friendly), **мастерско́й** (masterly);

- all adjectives with the suffix **-ов-/-ев-,** such as **делово́й** (business), **ма́ссовый,** (mass, bulk), **ра́нговый** (class, rank), **ла́сковый** (affectionate);

- all deverbal adjectives (adjectives derived from verbs) ending in **-лый,** such as **уста́лый** (tired), **устаре́лый** (antiquated), **отста́лый** (backward, retarded);

- miscellaneous adjectives: **го́рький** (bitter), **де́рзкий** (impertinent), **ро́бкий** (shy), **ли́пкий** (sticky), **ско́льзкий** (slippery), **ве́тхий** (rundown), **го́рдый** (proud), **ли́шний** (extra), **пло́ский** (flat), **больно́й** (sickly), **гнило́й** (rotten), **стра́нный** (strange).

These adjectives form the comparative, if they form the comparative at all, by means of an auxiliary word. This is called the compound comparative and will be discussed in the next section.

NOTE: As it turns out, the comparative degree of adverbs is formed in exactly the same way as adjectives. Thus, **гро́мче** means not only *louder* but also *more loudly.* You will need this information in order to do several of the sentences that follow.

TEST FOR MASTERY 2

You may not have seen all of the adjectives below in the aforementioned rules, but you should be able to form the simple comparative nonetheless. Form comparative sentences from the adjective and nouns given below:

Example: большо́й: Москва́, Петербу́рг →
Москва́ бо́льше, чем Петербу́рг.

1. бли́зкий: Кана́да, Кита́й

2. интере́сный: Босто́н, Филаде́льфия

3. высо́кий: ма́ма, па́па

4. бога́тый: я, Билл Гейтс

5. лёгкий: ру́сский язы́к, испа́нский язы́к

6. сухо́й: Саха́ра, Нью-Йо́рк

7. дешёвый: ходи́ть в теа́тр, ходи́ть в кино́

8. гро́мкий: дети, взро́слые

9. круто́й: А́льпы, Аппала́чи

10. ре́дкий: серебро́, зо́лото

11. си́льный: Сверхчелове́к, локомоти́в

12. краси́вый: Мадо́нна, Бри́тни Спирс

13. большо́й: Теха́с, Аля́ска

14. холо́дный: в Сиби́ри, во Фдори́де

15. сла́дкий: арбу́з, лимо́н

16. чи́стый: у меня́ в кварти́ре, до́ма у роди́телей

17. тёмный: на се́вере ле́том, на се́вере зимо́й

18. счастли́вый: я, мои́ роди́тели

19. стро́гий: ма́ма, па́па

20. здоро́вый: А́рнольд Шва́рценнегер, Ву́дди А́ллен

COMPARATIVE ADJECTIVE PRACTICE

Complete the following sentences by saying that the subject "*keeps getting more and more*" of the description mentioned.

Example: Москва́ большо́й го́род <u>и стано́вится всё бо́льше и бо́льше</u>.
(Moscow is a large city and keeps getting bigger and bigger.)

1. В Нью-Йо́рке о́чень гро́мко _____.

2. Здесь жа́рко ле́том _____.

3. Мой па́па о́чень стро́гий _____.

4. Ва́ня высо́кий па́рень _____.

5. Жить здесь хорошо́ _____.

6. Ба́бушка о́чень сла́бая _____.

7. Весно́й в Петербу́рге но́чи све́тлые _____.

8. Он всегда́ прихо́дит по́здно, но начина́ет приходи́ть _____.

9. Фи́зика тру́дный предме́т _____.

10. Твоя́ дочь краси́вая де́вушка _____.

Expressions Used with Comparative Adjectives

1. *Much Xer:* Use **гора́здо** or **намно́го** (or the colloquial and emphatic **куда́**) with the comparative:

Филаде́льфия гора́здо скучне́е, чем Нью-Йо́рк.	Philadelphia is much more boring than New York.
Мой брат намно́го умне́е, чем моя́ сестра́.	My brother is much smarter than my sister.

2. *A little Xer:* Prefix the comparative with **по-,** which adds the meaning of *a little more, a bit more:*

Мы сейча́с покупа́ем поме́ньше ма́сла.	We are now buying a bit less butter.
Пого́да сего́дня тёплая, но она́ могла́ бы быть потепле́е.	The weather is warm today, but it could be a bit warmer.
Покупа́йте проду́кты подеше́вле.	Buy cheaper groceries.

For Additional Practice

You can redo Test for Mastery 2 above, using **гораздо** or **намно́го** (much more) or prefixing the comparative adjective with **по-**. For example: **Москва́ гора́здо бо́льше, чем Петербу́рг.**

3. *As X as possible:* Use the Russian expression **как мо́жно** plus the comparative:

Приди́те как мо́жно ра́ньше.	Come as early as possible.
Сде́дай э́то как мо́жно скоре́е.	Do this as soon as possible.
Она́ реша́ет зада́чи как мо́жно сложне́е.	She works on problems that are as hard as possible.
На́до жить как мо́жно деше́вле.	Live as cheaply as you can.
Говори́ как мо́жно ти́ше.	Speak as quietly as possible.

4. *The Xer the Xer:* Use comparatives with the correlatives **чем . . . тем.**

Чем бо́льше, тем лу́чше.	The more the better.
Чем скоре́е, тем лу́чше.	The sooner the better.
Чем ча́ще он гуля́ет, тем ме́ньше он занима́ется.	The more often he goes out, the less he studies.
Чем трудне́е зада́чи, тем бо́льше они́ мне нра́вятся.	The harder the problems, the more I like them.

NOTE: It is interesting that in the English expressions the two words *the* are not articles but remnants of adverbial forms from Old English. Knowing this, the Russian construction may not seem so strange.

Using only the second part produces an abbreviated expression:

Тем ху́же для ней!	So much the worse for her!
Тем лу́чше!	So much the better! All the better!
Тем бо́льше для нас!	The more for us!

5. Additional meaning of **скоре́е:** The word **скоре́е** also means *rather* or *sooner,* such as in the expression **скоре́е всего́** (most likely).

Compound (or Short-Form) Comparative Adjectives

The long form of the comparative degree must be used when the comparative is used attributively, that is, when it appears in front of the noun it modifies rather than in a predicative position. The sentence *My house is nicer than yours* illustrates the use of the predicative comparative, *house* being the subject and *nicer* the predicate. *I live in a nicer house than you do* is an instance where the long form comparative must be used.

The formation of the long form comparative is relatively simple, since it corresponds closely to English usage. The adjective remains unchanged—except for the necessary agreement with the noun in gender, case, and number—and the word **бо́лее** (more) or **ме́нее** (less) is used as an auxiliary. Thus, *I live in a nicer house than you do* becomes in Russian **Я живу́ в бо́лее краси́вом до́ме, чем вы.**

As you can see, the long form is necessary when you sense that the adjective must be declined. It is not possible in Russian to utter a sentence of the type **Я живу́ в краси́вее∗ до́ме, чем вы** because the mind of the Russian speaker demands that an adjective following a preposition and standing before a noun agree with that noun.[3] The force of the preposition **в** here (or any word governing case, for that matter) is not as easy to negate or ignore as it would be in English. Therefore, whatever case is required in a given instance must be acknowledged by using the correct form of the adjective, plus the word **бо́лее,** to indicate the comparison.

Note also that the long-form comparative may be used in place of the short form at your discretion. You may say either **Этот журна́л интере́снее, чем тот** (This magazine is more interesting than that one) or **Это бо́лее интере́сный журна́л, чем тот** (This is a more interesting magazine than that one).

Last, the long-form comparative may be used with any qualitative adjective, including those that were excluded above from use with the short form (see number 4, page 67 above.)

TEST FOR MASTERY 3

Change the following comparatives from short forms to long forms according to the model. Note that you will have to change the wording somewhat to accommodate the new structure.

_____
[3]The asterisk indicates a hypothetical form that does not exist in the language.

Examples: Эта книга полезнее, чем ваша. → Это более полезная книга, чем ваша.[4]

Сверхчеловек сильнее, чем Спайдермен. → Сверхчеловек более сильный сьерхгерой, чем Спайдермен.

1. Моя сестра умнее, чем ваша.

2. Этот университет старее, чем тот.

3. Филадельфия скучнее, чем мой город.

4. Романы Толстого длинее, чем романы Тургенева.

5. Мой дядя богаче, чем твой.

6. Её ребёнок счастливее, чем мой.

7. Этот язык труднее, чем китайский!

8. Лоис Лейн слабее, чем Кларк Кент.

9. Ночи у нас темнее, чем у вас.

10. Антарктика холоднее, чем Северная Америка.

Superlative Degree of Adjectives

Compound Form

As it turns out, the compound superlative is the more widely used of the two, and it is the only one that conveys the absolute idea of superlativeness. To give an example using the adjective *tall,* the compound form in Russian will mean *the tallest,* whereas the simple form conveys the idea of *a very tall* or *a most tall* person or thing, which may or may not be the tallest of the group. Thus, there may be an emotional value attached to the use of the simple superlative.

Superlative adjectives, both simple and compound, may be used both attributively and predicatively.

The formation of the compound superlative is uncomplicated: use the adjective **самый** as an auxiliary preceding the adjective, making sure that both are in the correct gender, number, and case.

---

[4]Note the change from the demonstrative adjective **эта** to the pronoun **это!**

Ива́н—са́мый высо́кий ма́льчик в на́шей гру́ппе.	Ivan is the tallest boy in our class.
Я купи́ла са́мые дороги́е ту́фли в магази́не.	I bought the most expensive shoes in the store.
Билл Гейтс—са́мый бога́тый челове́к в ми́ре.	Bill Gates is the richest man in the world.

Sometimes the words **наибо́лее** (most) or **наиме́нее** (least) can be used in place of **са́мый,** but this usage is considered bookish or official. Thus, you may see either **Э́то наибо́лее интере́сная статья́ в э́той кни́ге** or **Э́то са́мая интере́сная статья́ в э́той кни́ге,** both meaning *This is the most interesting article in this book.* As you can see by the example, in this construction the word **наибо́лее** is not declined.

Note that to express *the best,* you may use either **са́мый хоро́ший** or **са́мый лу́чший,** the latter being the more common. Similarly, *the worst* can be expressed either **са́мый плохо́й** or **са́мый ху́дший.**

TEST FOR MASTERY 4

From the following information, construct sentences containing adjectives in the superlative degree:

Example: Эверест/высо́кий/гора́/мир →
              Эвере́ст—э́то са́мая высо́кая гора́ в ми́ре.

NOTE: If you need a brush-up on the endings of the prepositional case, see chapter 6, pp. 102–103.

1. Нил/дли́нный/река́/мир

2. Росси́я/большо́й/страна́/мир

3. Кита́йский/тру́дный/язы́к/мир

4. Моя́ мла́дшая сестра́/глу́пый/де́вочка/на́ша шко́ла

5. Достое́вский/вели́кий/писа́тель/Росси́я 19-го ве́ка

6. Брази́лия/большо́й/страна́/Ю́жная Аме́рика

7. Рокфе́ллер/бога́тый/миллионе́р/Нью-Йо́рк

8. Э́ти словари́/поле́зный/кни́га/библиоте́ка

9. Ю́лия Пе́ссина/у́мный/учени́ца/наш класс

10. Арме́ния/краси́вый/страна́/(на) Кавка́з

11. На́ша библиоте́ка/ти́хий/ме́сто/наш го́род

12. Байка́л/глубо́кий/о́зеро/мир

13. Мой де́душка/до́брый/челове́к/на́ша дере́вня

14. Аля́ска/большо́й/штат/Аме́рика

15. Во́лга/дли́нный/река́/Евро́па

The syntax of sentences containing superlative comparisons permits several variants. As in the exercise above, you may use the preposition **в** and the prepositional case or one of the following:

Genitive: Эвере́ст—э́то са́мая высо́кая гора́ ми́ра.
The preposition **среди́:** Эвере́ст—э́то са́мая высо́кая среди́ гор ми́ра.
The preposition **из:** Эвере́ст—э́то са́мая высо́кая из всех гор в ми́ре.

The last example is particularly common in written Russian. Once you feel that your command of the genitive plural is strong enough, try the above exercise using the preposition **из** modeled on the third example above. Answers are provided following the previous exercise.

One additional, extremely common construction in Russian is **оди́н из** followed by the compound superlative. Thus, if you are not sure whether the Volga is the longest, or whether the Matterhorn is the highest, or whether Vasya Kropotkin is the stupidest, you can say that they are one of the longest, highest, or stupidest. Again, if you feel comfortable with the genitive plural, try the following exercise. Remember to use the correct form: **оди́н, одно́, одна́.**

TEST FOR MASTERY 5

Example: Ва́ся Кропо́ткин/глу́пый/учени́к/на́ша шко́ла →
Ва́ся Кропо́ткин—оди́н из са́мых глу́пых ученико́в в на́шей шко́ле.

1. Филаде́льфия/ску́чный/го́род/Аме́рика

2. Толсто́й/вели́кий/писа́тель/мир

3. Э́то/вку́сный/колбаса́/гастроно́м

4. Га́рвардский университе́т/ста́рый/вуз/Аме́рика

5. На́ша библиоте́ка/ти́хий/ме́сто/го́род

6. Миссиси́пи/дли́нный/река́/мир

7. Гренла́ндия/большо́й/о́стров/мир

8. И́нгмар Бе́ргман/изве́стный/кинорежиссёр/мир

9. Конне́ктикут/ма́ленький/штат/Аме́рика

10. Профе́ссор Ле́нсон/кру́пный/учёный/Аме́рика

Simple Form

The simple superlative, which is formed by means of a suffix, is used not so much to express the absolute superlative (*the tallest building*) as it is to express a value judgment on the part of the speaker and may be used when no comparison is made (*a most interesting film*). Of course, this form may be used as an absolute superlative, which will be clear from the context. Therefore, it is fair to translate the simple superlative as *a most, a very,* or *an extremely.* The emphasis on the indefinite article points to the fact that the speaker has in mind one of only many such superlative things. Note that like the compound comparative, the simple comparative is declined.

Formation

Only adjectives that have a simple comparative can form the simple superlative (see pp. 65 and 67 above). Certain other adjectives, even if they form the simple comparative, do not form the simple superlative. Among them are **ги́бкий, гро́мкий, молодо́й, родно́й, сухо́й, у́зкий.**

    1. Adjectives whose stems end in **г, к,** or **х** mutate the final consonant into **ж, ч,** or **ш** and add the ending **-айший: стро́гий/строжа́йший, ти́хий/тиша́йший, вели́кий/велича́йший, глухо́й/глуша́йший, высо́кий/высоча́йший.**

    2. Almost all other adjectives add **-ейший** to their stems: **но́вый/нове́йший, глу́пый/глупе́йший, ми́лый/миле́йший.**

3. Some adjectives form the simple superlative irregularly: **плохóй/хýдший, мáленький/мéньший, корóткий/кратчáйший, хорóший/лýчший, тя́жкий/ тягчáйший, дорогóй/дражáйший.**[5]

Two adjectives, **высóкий** and **ни́зкий**, have two simple superlatives: **высочáйший** (the highest, physically) and **вы́сший** (highest, supreme, higher, e.g., higher education), as in **в вы́сшей стéпени** (in the highest degree) and **вы́сшее óбщество** (high society); **нижáйший** (lowest, humblest) and **ни́зший** (lowest, lower, e.g., lower school), as in **ни́зшая температýра зимы́** (the lowest temperature of the winter) and **ни́зшие слýжащие** (the lowest ranking employees).

Note also **дальнéйший** (further, furthest) and **позднéйший** (subsequent).

4. The prefix **наи-** may be added to convey emphasis on the high degree of the adjective. Its usage is considered bookish or formal. Compare here the English, which does an excellent job of conveying the meaning of the prefix **наи-** in the following set expression: **с наилýчшими пожелáниями** (with [my] very best wishes).

5. The prefix **пре-** added to the simple adjective has the meaning of *very* or *extremely* and may have the connotation of *excessively, overly:* **предли́нный** (very long, too long), **непрепри́ятный** (very/extremely unpleasant).

Some Notes on Style

The simple superlative has the effect of being bookish or literary and is thus rarely heard in normal conversation, although occasionally it is encountered in the speech of educated people. However, there are certain set expressions that you will see with some frequency that use the simple superlative. Some of them are:

в ближáйшее врéмя	in the near future
милéйшие лю́ди	the nicest people
всё к лýчшему	all for the best
до мельчáйших подрóбностей	down to the smallest details
онá измени́лась к хýдшему	she changed for the worse
нет ни малéйшего сомнéния	there's not the slightest doubt
с величáйшим удовóльствием	with the greatest pleasure
с глубочáйшим уважéнием	with the deepest respect
вы́сшее образовáние	higher (college) education
чистéйший вздор	pure nonsense
егó злéйший враг	his worst (most evil) enemy
ценнéйшее кáчество	a most valuable quality

---

[5]This form is considered old-fashioned and may add an ironic tone.

Another Way to Form the Superlative

Instead of using the compound or simple superlative as described above, Russian conversation has a quick and easy way of expressing the superlative. This is to use the comparative plus the expressions **всех** (than anyone) or **всего** (than anything): **Ива́н Ива́нович был бога́че, чем други́е поме́щики** (*Ivan Ivanovich was richer than the other landowners*); **Ива́н Ива́нович был бога́че всех** (*Ivan Ivanovich was the richest of all*); **Он пи́шет лу́чше, чем он говори́т** (*He writes better than he speaks*); **Он пи́шет лу́чше всего́** (*He writes best of all*). Note that the last two examples use the comparative adverb.

TEST FOR MASTERY 6

Compose sentences describing the subject as one of the X-est of its class. The words following **из** will be in the genitive plural.

Example: Пу́шкин/вели́кий поэ́т → Пу́шкин—оди́н из
величáйших ру́сских поэ́тов.

1. Байка́л/глубо́кий/о́зеро

2. Пари́ж/краси́вый/го́род

3. «Касабла́нка»/интере́сный/фильм

4. Ру́сский язы́к/тру́дный/язы́к

5. Моско́вский университе́т/кру́пный/вуз

6. Миссиси́пи/дли́нный/река́

7. Билл Гейтс/бога́тый/челове́к

8. Это/но́вый/зда́ние

9. Радми́ла/хоро́ший/студе́нтка

10. Моя́ маши́на/плохо́й/маши́на

11. Этот го́род/ску́чный/ме́сто

12. Мадо́нна/энерги́чная/хулига́нка

13. Моя́ соба́ка/счастли́вый/живо́тное

14. Ги́тлер/злой/вождь

15. Да́ша Иво́лгина/несно́сная (*unbearable*)/спле́тница (*gossip*)

Long-Form vs. Short-Form Adjectives

Adjectives may be used in the long form or the short form. There are many instances wherein the use of either is considered the speaker's choice, and in these cases the choice of the short form is a sign of an educated speaker. Long form, however, tends to predominate in normal conversation.

Short Form

Short adjectives must be used predicatively.[6] They have masculine, feminine, neuter, and plural forms and do not decline. Long-form adjectives may be used either predicatively or attributively. Each of the following sentences conveys the same meaning: **Она́ была́ о́чень краси́вая** vs. **Она́ была́ о́чень краси́ва.** In the first example, the use of the long form may indicate that the speaker views the adjective as being intrinsic to the subject, whereas the short adjective in the companion sentence indicates that she was beautiful at that time and may no longer be. In other words, the short-form adjective is impermanent. Thus, adjectives such as **ру́сский, деревя́нный, золото́й, фиоле́товый, тре́тий,** all adjectives in **-ский,** and many others do not form short adjectives since they cannot be thought of as *more or less.*

Short-form adjectives may also convey a sense that the adjective is *excessively so,* with or without the word **сли́шком** (too): **Э́ти ту́фли мне малы́** may mean *These shoes are (too) small for me;* **Он для э́того ещё мо́лод** indicates that *He is still (too) young for that.*

The short form is used when followed by an infinitive, by the word **что́бы,** by prepositions, or when the adjective governs a word in an oblique case (see the last example below):

Я гото́в помога́ть вам во всём.	I am ready to help you with anything.
Он сли́шком бо́лен, что́бы прийти́.	He is too sick to come.
Они́ глухи́ к ва́шим про́сьбам.	They are deaf to your requests.
Вы дово́льны мое́й рабо́той?	Are you satisfied with my work?

Differences in Meaning between Long- and Short-form Adjectives

The student should become familiar with the following morphological differences between the use of long and short forms:

---

[6]There are a handful of set expressions that do not follow this rule. They will be learned as separate vocabulary entries.

Он прав.	He is right (vs. wrong).
Он пра́вый.	He is right wing.
Эта де́вочка жива́я и весёлая.	This girl is lively and happy.
Эта де́вочка едва́ жива́.	This girl is barely alive.
Он серди́тый челове́к.	He is an ill-tempered man.
Он о́чень серди́т.	He is very angry.
Она́ занята́я же́нщина.	She is a busy woman.
Сего́дня ве́чером она́ занята́.	Tonight she's busy.
Это свобо́дная страна́.	This is a free country.
За́втра я свобо́дна весь день.	Tomorrow I'm free all day.
Он уве́ренный челове́к.	He is a self-assured person.
Он в э́том уве́рен.	He is sure of that.

The adjective **рад, ра́да, ра́ды** is the only adjective commonly used in Modern Russian that exists in short form only.

The short form is used with the subjects **э́то** and **всё: Всё бы́ло я́сно** (*Everything was clear*); **Э́то о́чень тру́дно** (*That's very difficult*).

TEST FOR MASTERY 7

Replace the English word with the correct form of the adjective as appropriate:

1. Она́ была́ умна́ и (beautiful).

2. Мой брат всегда́ (ready) на всё.

3. За́втра ве́чером он заболе́л, и сего́дня ещё (sick).

4. Мой дя́дя о́чень (sick) челове́к.

5. Это ме́сто (free)?

6. В (free) вре́мя я чита́ю стихи́.

7. Он ещё не (married).

8. Мы купи́ли биле́ты на (express) по́езд.

9. Я не (agree) с ним.

10. Эта у́лица (too short) для на́шей маши́ны.

11. Он сли́шком (busy) для тебя́.

12. Са́ша! Ты сего́дна не (well)? Жаль.

13. Моя́ жена́ (happy and healthy) же́нщина.

14. Таки́е (hungry) де́ти!

15. Де́ти! Вы (hungry)?

Special Uses of Adjectives

Substantivized Adjectives

Original adjective–noun combinations, over time and with extended use, came to be used in an abbreviated fashion. The noun of the original expression was dropped, leaving only a substantivized adjective, which functions as a noun and behaves completely like a regular adjective whose gender is derived from the missing noun.

Some common adjectives used as nouns are:

Substantivized adjective	Missing noun	English
столо́вая	ко́мната	dining room
гости́ная		living room
пере́дняя		vestibule
ва́нная		bathroom
операцио́нная		operating room
бу́лочная	ла́вка	bakery
моло́чная		dairy
пивна́я		pub
больно́й	челове́к	patient
взро́слый		adult
вое́нный		soldier
рабо́чий		worker
насеко́мое	существо́	insect
живо́тное		animal

Substantivized adjective	Missing noun	English
шампа́нское	вино́	champagne
тока́йское		Tokay
бургу́ндское		Burgundy
пе́рвое	блю́до	first course
второ́е		second course
тре́тье		third course
сла́дкое		dessert

Adjectives Derived from Participles (Deverbal Adjectives)

The derivation and use of Russian participles is a difficult issue, which will be discussed in the last chapter. Yet, one mention is merited at this point, if only to stress the fact that a participle is nothing but a verb in the form of an adjective. Thus, when you encounter an unusual form of a verb, it is probably a participle. Try to think of it as an adjectival phrase modifying a noun: the person who is washing the dishes, the book that was lying on the table, the article that had been published last year, and so on.

The following substantivized adjectives are a sample of those derived from participles: **да́нные** (data, i.e., things that have been given); **начина́ющий** (a beginner, i.e., someone who is beginning); **уча́щийся** (a student, i.e., someone who is studying); **обвиня́емый** (the accused, i.e., the person who is accused); **ископа́емые** (minerals, i.e., things that are being mined); **трудя́щийся** (worker, i.e., a person who labors); **говоря́щий** (a speaker, i.e., the person who is speaking); **куря́щий** (a smoker, i.e., a person who smokes); **млекопита́ющее** (a mammal, i.e., a being that feeds milk to its young); **пресмыка́ющееся** (a reptile, i.e., a being that creeps).

The following adjectives are also participles derived from verbs, but they can be used as adjectives as well as participles. The following list should be considered only a handful out of the thousands of such words: **блестя́щий** (shining); **бы́вший** (former); **невыноси́мый** (intolerable); **рассе́янный** (distracted, scattered); **откры́тый/закры́тый** (open/closed); **выдаю́щийся** (outstanding); **небью́щийся** (unbreakable); **забы́тый** (forgotten); **оде́тый** (dressed); **приближа́ющийся** (approaching).

ANSWER KEY

Test for Mastery 1

1. ру́сская

2. зи́мний

3. си́нее

4. Большо́й

5. Бе́лый

6. после́дняя

7. хоро́шая

8. све́жее

9. плохо́е

10. чёрный[7]

11. молода́я

12. англи́йский

13. жёлтое

14. си́ние

15. да́льний

16. пятиле́тняя

17. совреме́нный

18. ми́лые

19. о́стрые

20. зде́ншяя

21. ру́сская

22. изве́стный

23. молоды́е

24. хоро́шее

25. ти́хий

26. плоха́я

27. Но́вое ру́сское сло́во[8]

28. Кра́сная

29. се́верный

30. дли́нная

Conversation Practice (some possible responses)

1. А у нас жёлтые бана́ны.

2. А у нас интере́сные музе́и.

3. А у нас то́лько мо́дные магази́ны.

4. А у́лицы у нас о́чень широ́кие.

5. А у меня́ то́лько англи́йские кни́ги.

6. А у нас бога́тые лю́ди.

7. А у нас ма́ленькие озёра, худы́е леса́.

8. А у нас тёплые, мя́гкие зи́мы.

9. А авто́бусы у нас но́вые, о́чень хоро́шие.

10. А у нас такси́ быва́ют жёлтые.

---

[7]Remember that **ко́фе** is masculine.

[8]**Но́вое ру́сское сло́во** is a well-known Russian émigré newspaper published in New York since 1905.

Demonstrative Adjective Practice

1. Э́ти ребя́та шу́мные, а те ребя́та ти́хие.

2. Э́тот магази́н дорого́й, а тот магази́н дешёвый.

3. Э́ти зада́чи тру́дные, а те зада́чи лёгкие.

4. Э́то бельё гря́зное, а то бельё чи́стое.

5. Э́та кни́га ску́чная, а та кни́га интере́сная.

6. Э́тот учени́к у́мный, а тот учени́к глу́пый.

7. Э́ти зда́ния ни́зкие, а те зда́ния высо́кие.

8. Э́тот суп вку́сный, а тот суп невку́сный.

9. Э́ти города́ бли́зкие, а те города́ далёкие.

10. Э́та де́вушка больна́я, а та де́вушка здоро́вая.

Test for Mastery 2

1. Кана́да бли́же, чем Кита́й.

2. Босто́н интере́снее, чем Филаде́льфия.

3. Па́па вы́ше, чем ма́ма.

4. Билл Гейтс бога́че, чем я.

5. Ру́сский язы́к ле́гче, чем кита́йский язы́к.

6. Саха́ра су́ше, чем Нью-Йо́рк.

7. Ходи́ть в кино́ дешёвле, чем ходи́ть в теа́тр.

8. Де́ти гро́мче, чем взро́слые.

9. А́льпы кру́че, чем Аппала́чи.

10. Зо́лото ре́же, чем серебро́.

11. Сверхчелове́к сидьне́е, чем локомоти́в.

12. Мадо́нна краси́вее, чем Бри́тни Спирс

13. Аля́ска бо́льше, чем Теха́с.

14. В Сибири холоднее, чем во Фдориде.

15. Арбуз слаще, чем лимон.

16. У меня в квартире чище, чем дома у родителей.

17. На севере зимой темнее, чем на севере летом.

18. Я спастливее, чем мои родители.

19. Мама строже, чем папа.

20. Арнольд Шварценнегер здоровее, чем Вудди Аллен.

Comparative Adjective Practice

1. и становится всё громче и громче.

2. и становится всё жарче и жарче.

3. и становится всё строже и строже.

4. и становится всё выше и выше.

5. и становится всё лучше и лучше.

6. и становится всё свабее и слабее.

7. и становитая всё светлее и светлее.

8. всё позже и позже.

9. и становится всё труднее и труднее.

10. и становится всё красивее и красивее.

Test for Mastery 3

1. У меня более умная сестра, чем у вас.

2. Я учусь в более старом университете, чем вы.

3. Филадельфия более скучный город, чем мой город.

4. Толстой писал более длинные романы, чем Тургенев.

5. У меня более богатый дядя, чем у тебя.

6. У неё бо́лее счастли́вый ребёнок, чем у меня́.

7. Э́то бо́лее тру́дный язы́к, чем кита́йский!

8. Ло́ис Лейн бо́лее сла́бый журнали́ст, чем Кларк Кент.

9. У нас бо́лее тёмные но́чи, чем у вас.

10. Анта́рктика бо́лее холо́дное ме́сто, чем Се́верная Аме́рика.

Test for Mastery 4

1. Нил—э́то са́мая дли́нная река́ в ми́ре.

2. Росси́я—э́то са́мая больша́я страна́ в ми́ре.

3. Кита́йский язы́к—э́то са́мый тру́дный язы́к в ми́ре.

4. Моя́ мла́дшая сестра́—э́то са́мая глу́пая де́вочка в на́шей шко́ле.

5. Достое́вский—э́то са́мый вели́кий писа́тель в Росси́и 19-го ве́ка.

6. Брази́лия—э́то са́мая больша́я страна́ в Ю́жной Аме́рике.

7. Рокфе́ллер—э́то са́мый бога́тый челове́к в Нью-Йо́рке.

8. Э́ти словари́—са́мые поле́зные кни́ги в библиоте́ке.

9. Ю́лия Пе́ссина—са́мая у́мная учени́ца в на́шем кла́ссе.

10. Арме́ния—э́то са́мая краси́вая страна́ на Кавка́зе.

11. На́ша библиоте́ка—са́мое ти́хое ме́сто в на́шем го́роде.

12. Байка́л—э́то са́мое глубо́кое о́зеро в ми́ре.

13. Мой де́душка—э́то са́мый до́брый челове́к в на́шей дере́вне.

14. Аля́ска—э́то са́мый большо́й штат в Аме́рике.

15. Во́лга—э́то са́мая дли́нная река́ в Евро́пе.

Test for Mastery 4, Part 2, Using the preposition "из"

1. Нил—э́то са́мая дли́нная из всех рек ми́ра.

2. Росси́я—э́то са́мая больша́я из всех стран ми́ра.

3. Китайский—э́то са́мый тру́дный из всех языко́в ми́ра.

4. Моя́ мла́дшая сестра́—са́мая глу́пая из всех де́вочек в на́шей шко́ле.

5. Достое́вский—э́то са́мый вели́кий из всех писа́телей Росси́и 19-го ве́ка.

6. Брази́лия—э́то са́мая больша́я из всех стран Ю́жной Аме́рики.

7. Рокфе́ллер—э́то са́мый бога́тый из всех миллионе́ров Нью-Йо́рка.

8. Э́ти словари́—э́то са́мые поле́зные из всех книг в библиоте́ке.

9. Ю́лия Пе́ссина—э́то са́мая у́мная из учени́ц в нашем кла́ссе.

10. Арме́ния—э́то са́мая краси́вая из всех стран на Кавка́зе.

11. На́ша библиоте́ка—э́то са́мое ти́хое из всех мест в на́шем го́роде.

12. Байка́л—э́то са́мое глубо́кое из всех озёр в ми́ре.

13. Мой де́душка—э́то са́мый до́брый из всех люде́й в на́шей дере́вне.

14. Аля́ска—э́то са́мый большо́й из всех штатов в Аме́рике.

15. Во́лга—э́то са́мая дли́нная из всех рек в Евро́пе.

Test for Mastery 5

1. Филаде́льфия—оди́н из са́мых ску́чных городо́в Аме́рики.

2. Толсто́й—оди́н из са́мых вели́ких писа́телей ми́ра.

3. Э́то одна́ из са́мых вку́сных колба́с в гастроно́ме.

4. Га́рвардский университе́т—оди́н из са́мых ста́рших ву́зов Аме́рики.

5. На́ша библиоте́ка—одно́ из са́мых ти́хих мест в го́роде.

6. Миссиси́пи—одна́ из са́мых дли́нных рек ми́ра.

7. Гренла́ндия—оди́н из са́мых больши́х острово́в ми́ра.

8. И́нгмар Бе́ргман—оди́н из са́мых изве́стных кинорежиссёров ми́ра.

9. Коннекти́кут—оди́н из са́мых ма́леньких шта́тов в Аме́рике.

10. Профе́ссор Ле́нсон—оди́н из са́мых кру́пных учёных в Аме́рике.

Test for Mastery 6

1. Байка́л—одно́ из гдубоча́йших озёр ми́ра.

2. Пари́ж—оди́н из красиве́йших городо́в в Евро́пе.

3. «Касабла́нка»—оди́н из интересне́йших америка́нских фи́льмов

4. Ру́сский язы́к—оди́н из трудне́йших языко́в в ми́ре.

5. Моско́вский университе́т—оди́н из крупне́йших ву́зов в ми́ре.

6. Миссиси́пи—одна́ из длинне́йших рек ми́ра.

7. Билл Гейтс—оди́н из богате́йших люде́й в ми́ре.

8. Э́то одно́ из нове́йших зда́ний в на́шем го́роде.

9. Радми́ла—одна́ из на́ших лу́чших студе́нток.

10. Моя́ маши́на—одна́ из ху́дших маши́н в ми́ре.

11. Э́тот го́род—одно́ из скучне́йших мест на э́той плане́те.

12. Мадо́нна—одна́ из энергичне́йших хулига́нок в Аме́рике.

13. Моя́ соба́ка—одно́ из счастливе́йших живо́тных в ми́ре.

14. Ги́тлер—оди́н из зле́йших вожде́й в исто́рии.

15. Да́ша Иво́лгина—одна́ из несносне́йших спле́тниц в на́шем городке́.

Test for Mastery 7

1. краси́ва (Note: You cannot mix long and short forms in the same sentence. Because the adjective **умна́** is used first, the short form **краси́ва** must follow.)

2. гото́в

3. бо́лен

4. больно́й

5. свобо́дно

6. свобо́дное

7. жена́т

8. ско́рый

9. согла́сен/согла́сна

10. узка́

11. за́нят

12. здоро́в

13. счастли́вая и здоро́вая

14. голо́дные

15. го́лодны

5 The Verb

Глагол

Useful Vocabulary

бежа́ть	to run	мёрзнуть	to freeze
везти́	to transport	написа́ть	to write, compose
вести́	to lead, conduct	нарисова́ть	to paint
взять	to take	нести́	to carry
грести́	to row, rake	освободи́ть	to free, liberate
грызть	to chew, gnaw	печь	to bake
дава́ть	to give	пла́кать	to cry
дать	to give	поги́бнуть	to perish
дости́гнуть	to achieve	поня́ть	to understand
е́здить	to go	посеща́ть	to visit
есть	to eat	преподава́ть	to teach
ждать	to wait	привы́кнуть	to become used to
жить	to live	приня́ть	to receive
зада́ть	to pose	прода́ть	to sell
зайти́	to drop in	проч́есть	to read
заня́ть	to occupy	расти́	to grow
идти́	to go	рисова́ть	to draw
исче́знуть	to disappear	роди́ться	to be born
красть	to steal	сотвори́ть	to create

стричь	to cut	учи́ться	to study
умере́ть	to die	ходи́ть	to go
хоте́ть	to want		

VOCABULARY PRACTICE

Cross out the verb in each group that does not belong. Look for meaning first of all, then check verb forms.

1. преподава́ть/учи́ться/прочёсть/печь

2. роди́ться/е́здить/ходи́ть/идти́

3. роди́ться/дости́гнуть/умере́ть/жить

4. дать/есть/красть/хоте́ть

5. мёрзнуть/нарисова́ть/написа́ть/сотвори́ть

6. жить/зайти́/расти́/есть

7. пла́кать/дости́гнуть/привы́кнуть/мёрзнуть

8. стричь/вести́/нести́/вести́

Russian Verbs

On the surface, the Russian verb is much easier than the verb in English. There are, for instance, only five tenses: one present, two past, and two future. The formation of the past tense is accomplished with an ease unknown in most European verb systems. One of the future tenses is very similar to the English construction. Yet the deeper one probes into the intricacies of the Russian verb system, the clearer it becomes that Russian can hold its own when it comes to any of the world's complex systems of verbs.

The Infinitive

The majority of Russian infinitives are characterized by their endings. The overwhelming majority of infinitives end in **-ть.** Two less frequent though still common endings for infinitives are **-ти** and **-чь.** There are no other infinitive endings possible in Russian.

Past Tense

Formation

The formation of the past tense is very uncomplicated:

First, remove the infinitive ending (**-ть**) and replace it with the ending **-л.** Then, adjust for gender. Russian verbs agree in gender and number with their subjects. Therefore, the full endings will be **-л** (masculine), **-ла** (feminine), **-ло** (neuter), **-ли** (plural).

For the plural forms **мы, вы,** and **они,** plural verbs are used, even when **вы** refers to only one person: **Юлия Яковлевна, где вы родились?** (*Yuliya Yakovlevna, where were you born?*).

For verbs in **-ся,** disregard this particle while you form the past tense, and then return it to the verb in the correct form: **-ся** after consonants and **-сь** after vowels (**он родился, она родилась**).

Even the so-called irregular verbs in Russian are formed regularly according to this rule: **дал, хотел,** and **бежал.** One exception is the verb **есть,** which has the past tense **ел, ела, ело, ели.**

Special Cases

1. There are a few verbs that end in a consonant plus **-ть,** such as **грызть, красть,** and **прочесть,** whose past tense is unpredictable and will therefore be provided. The past tense of the above verbs is **грыз/ла, крал/а, прочёл/прочла.**

2. Some infinitives in **-нуть** and **-ереть** drop this ending completely in the past tense: **достигнуть, достиг/ла;** and **умереть, умер/умерла.** Other common verbs of this type are **исчезнуть, мёрзнуть, погибнуть,** and **привыкнуть.**

3. And what if an infinitive does not end in **-ть?** In that case, the past tense will be provided for you in the glossary. Some examples of verbs of this type:

идти	шёл, шла, шло, шли
нести	нёс, несла, несло, несли
везти	вёз, везла, везло, везли
вести	вёл, вела, вело, вели
зайти	зашёл, зашла, зашло, зашли

расти́	рос, росла́, росло́, росли́[1]
грести́	грёб, гребла́, гребло́, гребли́

Since many of these verbs are verbs of motion and/or are used with numerous prefixes, they are not a problem for native speakers. You, however, will have to memorize these forms.

A not insignificant group of verbs has an infinitive ending in **-чь.** Throughout their conjugation, these verbs show an underlining **к** or **г** that alternates with **ч** or **ж** when appearing before the vowel **-e-.** The past tense, coincidentally, turns out to be the stem of the present tense:

Infinitive	печь	стричь
First-person singular	пеку́	стригу́
Second-person singular	печёшь	стрижёшь
Third-person plural	пеку́т	стригу́т
Past masculine	пёк	стриг
Past feminine	пекла́	стригла́

All verbs of the above types are end stressed both in the conjugation and in the past-tense forms.

Stress Patterns

Verbs have three stress patterns in the past tense: always stem, always ending, and shifting stress. In this last pattern, the stress falls on the stem, except for the feminine form, which takes the stress on the ending:

жить	жил, жила́, жи́ло, жи́ли
взять	взял, взяла́, взя́ло, взя́ли

Most verbs in **-нять** and **-дать** also have a shifting stress pattern, but in the masculine, neuter, and plural the stress falls on the prefix. Here are a few examples:

поня́ть	по́нял, поняла́, по́няло, по́няли
заня́ть	за́нял, заняла́, за́няло, за́няли
приня́ть	при́нял, приняла́, при́няло, при́няли
прода́ть	про́дал, продала́, про́дало, про́дали
зада́ть	за́дал, задала́, за́дало, за́дали

---

[1] Note the vowel change from **-a-** in the present-tense stem to **-o-** in the past tense.

All other irregularities in stress will be given in the glossary.

It is essential to remember that in order to form the past tense you must work with the infinitive and not the conjugated form or present-tense stem. In order to emphasize the importance of this process, you are presented with a challenging exercise below.

TEST FOR MASTERY 1

Change the following sentences from the present tense to the past tense. Be sure that your verb agrees in gender and number with the subject.

1. Мы ждём автобус.

2. Офелия живёт в Грузии.

3. Профессор Павлов, где вы преподаёте?

4. Памела говорит по телефону весь день.

5. Дети сидят у себя в комнате и пишут сочинения.

6. Рада хорошо учится.

7. Этерея прекрасно читает по-китайски.

8. Этот хулиган всегда крадёт мои вещи.

9. Мама печёт пирожки.

10. Цветы растут медленно.

11. Что ты рисуешь?

12. Она всегда даёт деньги бедным.

13. Почему Андрюша плачет?

14. В этом магазине продают книги.

15. Бернард посещает музеи в Москве.

TEST FOR MASTERY 2

Culture Quiz. Place the names of the world-famous figures into the blanks, and change the verbs to the past tense. **Чайковский, Толстой, Пикассо, Горбачёв, Чехов, Марк Твейн, Линкольн, Сервантес, Вашингтон, да Винчи, Ломоносов, Шекспир**

1. _____ (сотворить) политику «Гласность».

2. _____ (написать) «Войну́ и мир».

3. _____ (быть) пе́рвый америка́нский президе́нт.

4. _____ (основа́ть) Моско́вский университе́т.

5. _____ (написать) рома́н «Дон Кихо́т».

6. _____ (написа́ть) пье́су «Три сестры́».

7. _____ (написа́ть) пье́су «Га́млет».

8. _____ (нарисова́ть) карти́ну «Гуе́рника».

9. _____ (освободи́ть) америка́нских рабо́в.

10. _____ (написа́ть) бале́т «Лебеди́ное о́зеро».

11. _____ (быть) америка́нский писа́тель.

12. _____ (нарисова́ть) карти́ну «Мо́на Ли́са».

Introduction to Verbs of Motion

Verbs of motion will be covered more fully in a later chapter, but their formation and use in the past tense will serve as an appropriate introduction.

Nonprefixed, indeterminate verbs of motion—that is, verbs whose basic meaning is the activity itself, with no destination or time frame specified—are synonymous in the past tense with the past tense of *to be*. Compare: **Вчера́ я был в библиоте́ке** (*Yesterday I was at the library*) with **Вчера́ я ходи́л в библиоте́ку** (*Yesterday I went to the library*). The first sentence specifies location, the second, motion. Both sentences convey the same information. The verb of motion implies that there was a round trip, that although yesterday you went to the library, you are no longer there and have returned.

TEST FOR MASTERY 3

Change the following past-tense sentences from location to motion sentences. Be sure to change the object of motion to the accusative case. Remember to use **ходи́л** for most places but **е́здил** for places that cannot logically be reached without using a vehicle, such as cities and countries.

Some adverbs of time you may wish to review before doing this exercise are вчера́ (yesterday), **когда́-нибудь** (ever), **вчера днём** (yesterday afternoon), **вчера́ ве́чером** (last night), **ле́том** (in the summer), **на про́шлой неде́ле** (last week), **сего́дня у́тром** (this morning), **в про́шлом году́** (last year).

1. Вчера́ мы бы́ли в музе́е.

2. Ле́том она́ была́ в А́нглии.

3. Где ты был вчера́ ве́чером?

4. Вы когда́-нибудь бы́ли в Афри́ке?

5. На про́шлой неде́ле Бо́ря был в Кремле́.

6. В декабре́ Гали́на была́ в Вашингто́не.

7. Сего́дня у́тром мы бы́ли в це́ркви.

8. Вчера́ днём она́ была́ в бу́лочной.

9. Где вы бы́ли в про́шлом году́?

10. На день рожде́ния я была́ в Пари́же.

CONVERSATION PRACTICE

The teacher is asking the students where they went yesterday and how it was. Answer the teacher with the information provided. Here are some adjectives you will need: **ве́село** (fun), **ску́чно** (boring), **интере́сно** (interesting), **ти́хо** (quiet), **жа́рко** (hot), **хо́лодно** (cold), **шу́мно** (noisy), **вла́жно** (humid).

Example: Учи́тель: Джон, где ты был вчера́?
Джон: (музе́й) Я ходи́л в музе́й. Там бы́ло ску́чно.

1. Мэ́ри: Мавзоле́й Ле́нина

2. Магда: По́льша

3. А́нна: А́фрика

4. Дже́ссика: мо́ре

5. Ва́ня и Та́ня: Третьяко́вка[2]

6. И́горь: «Де́тский мир»[3]

7. Ка́тя: Аля́ска

8. Ю́лия: рабо́та

9. Гри́ша: библиоте́ка

10. Па́мела: като́к (*ice skating rink*)

---

[2] The Tretyakov Gallery in Moscow is famous for its Russian art.

[3] Children's World, the largest store for children's clothing and toys in Moscow.

ANSWER KEY

Vocabulary Practice

1. печь (not having to do with school)

2. роди́ться (not a verb of motion)

3. дости́гнуть (not having to do with life)

4. красть (not irregular)

5. мёрзнуть (not transitive)

6. зайти́ (not having to do with growing)

7. пла́кать (not a **-нуть** infinitive)

8. стричь (not a **-ти** infinitive)

Test for Mastery 1

1. Мы жда́ли авто́бус.

2. Офе́лия жила́ в Гру́зии.

3. Профе́ссор Па́влов, где вы преподава́ли?

4. Па́мела говори́ла по телефо́ну весь день.

5. Де́ти сиде́ли у себя́ в ко́мнате и писа́ли сочине́ния.

6. Ра́да хорошо́ учи́лась.

7. Этере́я прекра́сно чита́ла по-кита́йски.

8. Э́тот хулига́н всегда́ крал мой ве́щи.

9. Ма́ма пекла́ пирожки́.

10. Цветы́ расли́ ме́дленно.

11. Что ты рисова́л(а)?

12. Она́ всегда́ дава́ла де́ньги бе́дным.

13. Почему́ Андрю́ша пла́кал?

14. В э́том магази́не продава́ли кни́ги.

15. Берна́рд посеща́л музе́и в Москве́.

Test for Mastery 2

1. Горбачёв сотворил политику «Гласность».

2. Толстой написал «Войну и мир».

3. Вашингтон был первый американский президент.

4. Ломоносов основал Московский университет.

5. Сервантес написал роман «Дон Кихот».

6. Чехов написал пьесу «Три сестры».

7. Шекспир написал пьесу «Гамлет».

8. Пикассо нарисовал картину «Гуерника».

9. Линкольн освободил американских рабов.

10. Чайковский написал балет «Лебединое озеро».

11. Марк Твейн был американский писатель.

12. Да Винчи нарисовал картину «Мона Лиса».

Test for Mastery 3

Did you remember to make sure that your verbs agreed in gender and number with the subject of the sentence?

1. Вчера мы ходили в музей.

2. Летом она ездила в Англию.

3. Куда ты ходил вчера вечером?

4. Вы когда-нибудь ездили в Африку?

5. На прошлой неделе Боря ходил в Кремль.

6. В декабре Галина ездила в Вашингтон.

7. Сегодня утром мы ходили в церковь.

8. Вчера днём она ходила в булочную.

9. Куда вы ездили в прошлом году?

10. На день рождения я ездила в Париж.

Conversation Practice

Your answers may differ from those below.

1. Я ходи́ла в Музе́й Ле́нина. Там бы́ло ти́хо.

2. Я е́здила в По́льшу. Там бы́ло ве́село.

3. Я е́здила в А́фрику. Там бы́ло жа́рко.

4. Я е́здила на мо́ре. Там бы́ло вла́жно.

5. Мы ходи́ли в Третьяко́вку. Там бы́ло интере́сно.

6. Я ходи́л в «Де́тский мир». Там бы́ло шу́мно.

7. Я е́здила в Аля́ску. Там бы́ло хо́лодно.

8. Я ходи́ла на рабо́ту. Там бы́ло, как всегда́, ску́чно.

9. Я ходи́л в библиоте́ку. Там бы́ло ти́хо.

10. Я ходи́ла на като́к. Там бы́ло ве́село.

6 The Prepositional Case

Предложный падеж

Useful Vocabulary

Transportation

автóбус	bus	платфóрма	platform
аэропóрт	airport	пóезд	train
велосипéд	bicycle	самолёт	plane
вокзáл	train station	стáнция	metro station
метрó	metro, subway	стоя́нка	taxi stand
остановка	bus stop	таксú	taxi

Points of the Compass

юг	south	юго-зáпад	southwest
céвер	north	юго-востóк	southeast
востóк	east	céверо-зáпад	northwest
зáпад	west	céверо-востóк	northeast

Events

вы́ставка	exhibit	собрáние	meeting
заня́тия	class(es), school	вечерúнка	party
лéкция	lecture	пóхороны	funeral
свáдьба	wedding		

Places

Вселе́нная	the Universe	полуша́рие	hemisphere
Мле́чный путь	the Milky Way	по́чта	post office
на́бережная	embankment, coast	предприя́тие	enterprise, business
о́зеро	lake	рай	paradise
пляж	beach	ры́нок	market
полуо́стров	peninsula		

Verbs

жени́ться (на)	to marry (for men)
игра́ть (на)	to play (an instrument)
наста́ивать (на)	to insist on
находи́ться	to be located
нужда́ться (в)	to need
обвиня́ться (в)	to be accused of
ошиба́ться (в)	to be mistaken in
подозрева́ть (в)	to suspect of
признава́ться (в)	to admit to
сомнева́ться (в)	to doubt
убежда́ть (в)	to convince of
уверя́ть (в)	to assure of
уча́ствовать (в)	to take part in

VOCABULARY PRACTICE

Choose the correct prepositional phrase:

1. Нам бы́ло ве́село (на по́хоронах/на сва́дьбе).

2. Он прие́хал в Петербу́рг (на по́езде/на велосипе́де).

3. Мы обы́чно покупа́ем о́вощи и фру́кты (на ры́нке/на по́чте).

4. Анта́рктика нахо́дится (на се́вере/на ю́ге).

5. Босто́н нахо́дится (на ю́го-за́паде/на се́веро-восто́ке).

6. Спортсме́ны (уча́ствуют в/признаю́тся в) соревнова́нии.

7. Гости́ница «Укра́ина» располо́жена (на полуо́строве/на на́бережной) Москвы́-реки́.

8. Мы сиде́ли (на пля́же/на предприя́тии) и загора́ли.

9. Ви́ка хорошо́ (игра́ет на/нужда́ется в) балала́йке.

10. Мле́чный путь нахо́дится (во Вселе́нной/в аэропорту́).

CONVERSATION PRACTICE

Уро́к геогра́фии

Говоря́т:	Ничего́ не зна́ющий Са́ша
	Всезна́ющая ма́ма
Са́ша:	Ма́ма, где мы живём?
Ма́ма:	Мы живём в ма́ленькой кварти́ре.
С:	Где нахо́дится на́ша кварти́ра?
М:	Она́ нахо́дится на широ́ком проспе́кте.
С:	А где нахо́дится э́тот проспе́кт?
М:	В о́чень большо́м го́роде.
С:	В како́м большо́м го́роде?
М:	В го́роде Нью-Йо́рк.
С:	А где нахо́дится наш го́род?
М:	Он нахо́дится в шта́те Нью-Йо́рк.
С:	А мам, где нахо́дится э́тот штат?
М:	Нью-Йо́рк нахо́дится на восто́чной на́бережной на́шей страны́.
С:	А в како́й стране́ мы живём?
М:	В Соединённых Шта́тах Аме́рики, коне́чно.
С:	Но я не зна́ю, где нахо́дится э́та страна́.
М:	Она́ нахо́дится в Се́верной Аме́рике.
С:	Гмм. А где нахо́дится Се́верная Аме́рика?
М:	На За́падном полуша́рии.
С:	Пра́вда? А где оно́ нахо́дится?
М:	За́падное полуша́рие нахо́дится на на́шей Земле́.
С:	Ах, да! А где нахо́дится Земля́?
М:	Она́ нахо́дится в Со́лнечной систе́ме.
С:	В Со́лнечной систе́ме? А где э́то?
М:	Со́лнечная систе́ма нахо́дится в Мле́чном пути́.
С:	Ха-ха! И скажи́, мам, где нахо́дится э́тот Мле́чный путь?
М:	Он нахо́дится вон там, во Вселе́нной.
С:	Вот как!

The Geography Lesson

SPEAKERS: Know-Nothing Sasha
                 Know-Everything Mom

SASHA: Mom, where do we live?
MOM: We live in a small apartment.
S: Where is our apartment?
M: It's on a wide street.
S: Where is this street?
M: In a very big city.
S: In what big city?
M: In New York City.
S: Where is our city (located)?
M: It is (located) in the state of New York.
S: Where is this state, Ma?
M: New York is on the east coast of our country.
S: In what country do we live?
M: In the United States of America, of course.
S: But I don't know where that country is.
M: It is in North America.
S: Hmm. And where is North America?
M: In the Western Hemisphere.
S: Really? And where is that?
M: The Western Hemisphere is on our Earth.
S: Oh, right! And where is Earth?
M: It's in the solar system.
S: In the solar system? Where's that?
M: The solar system is in the Milky Way.
S: Ha, ha. And tell me, Mom, where is this Milky Way?
M: It's way over there, in the Universe.
S: You don't say!

The Prepositional Case

The prepositional case is so named because it never occurs without a preposition. You may find that in older Russian grammars this case is called the locative. This is a falsely inclusive title, since the true locative—pertaining to location only and masculine nouns only—is a subcase of the prepositional and will be discussed later in this chapter. The five prepositions that govern this case will be dealt with separately in the sections that follow.

Endings

Nouns

In the singular, all masculine,[1] feminine, and neuter[2] nouns take the ending **-е,** except for the following: masculines in **-ий,** neuters in **-ие,** feminines in **-ия,** and feminines in **-ь.** These nouns remove the last letter and replace it with **-и: сцена́рий** becomes **в сцена́рии, зда́ние** becomes **в зда́нии, Фра́ция** becomes **во Фра́ции,** and **дверь** becomes **на две́ри.**

In the plural all nouns, without exception, take the ending **-ах/-ях: в шко́лах, на ле́кциях, на дверя́х, в музе́ях, на о́кнах, на авто́бусах, в теа́трах, на стола́х, в круга́х, в ряда́х, в институ́тах, на у́лицах, на заво́дах, на моста́х, в тетра́дях, в сцена́риях, на да́чах, в ба́нках.**

Nouns: Prepositional Case Formation

	Singular	Plural
Masculine nouns in **-ий**	-и в санато́рии	-ях в санато́риях
All remaining masculine nouns	-е на столе́ в музе́е о писа́теле	-ах/-ях на стола́х в музе́ях о писа́телях
Feminine nouns in **-ия**	-и на ле́кции в аудито́рии	-ях на ле́кциях в аудито́риях
Feminine nouns in **-ь**	-и в тетра́ди	-ях в тетра́дях
All remaining feminine nouns	-е в кни́ге на ку́хне	-ах/-ях в кни́гах на ку́хнях

---

[1] Except for the locative case in stressed **-у́,** which will be discussed below on p. 110.

[2] Neuter nouns ending in **-мя** take the ending **-и: вре́мя** becomes **вре́мени.**

Neuter nouns	-и	-ях
in **-ие**	в зда́нии	в зда́ниях
All remaining	-е	-ах/-ях
neuter nouns	в мо́ре	в моря́х
	на окне́	на о́кнах

Adjectives

Adjective endings are equally uncomplicated, as long as you keep in mind the spelling rules:

Five-letter spelling rule:
After **ж, ч, ш, щ,** and **ц,** do not write an unstressed **о.** Write **е** instead.

Seven-letter spelling rule:
After **ж, ч, ш, щ,** and **к, г, х,** do not write **ы.** Write **и** instead.

Masculine and neuter adjectives take the ending **-ом,** feminine adjectives take the ending **-ой,** and plural adjectives take the ending **-ых,** all endings subject to application of the spelling rules.

Adjectives: Prepositional Case Formation

	Singular	Plural
Masculine		
но́вый	но́вом	но́вых
большо́й	большо́м	больши́х
хоро́ший	хоро́шем	хоро́ших
после́дний	после́днем	после́дних
Neuter		
но́вое		
большо́е	Same as masculine	
хоро́шее		
после́днее		
Feminine		
но́вая	но́вой	но́вых
больша́я	большо́й	больши́х
после́дняя	после́дней	после́дних

Adjective Ending Notes

1. The adjective **большо́й** illustrates the application of the seven-letter spelling rule in the plural.

2. The adjective **хоро́ший** is governed by both the five-letter spelling rule (in the singular) and the seven-letter spelling rule (in the plural forms).

3. The adjective **после́дний** is a soft adjective and shows soft endings.

The Prepositions в and на

These two prepositions are used to indicate location. **B** usually shows location in or within an enclosed space (the library, Moscow, the United States, the cafeteria, July, the magazine, a good mood, the store, a black dress, ecstasy); **на** is used in the meaning *on* (the table, the floor, your nose, the wall, the door, the street, a bench, the Moon, Mars).

NOTE: **B** will become **во** in front of consonant clusters, especially those beginning with the sounds [f/v]: **во Флори́де** (in Florida), **во Фра́нции** (in France), **во дворе́** (in the yard), **во всём** (in everything), **во вся́ком слу́чае** (in any case), **во-вторы́х** (in the second place).

Both **в** and **на** may be used to translate *at*. **Ha** is used to express *at* a certain function, event, or occasion where people gather to do something: **на собра́нии, на вечери́нке, на по́хоронах, на ле́кции, на конце́рте, на сва́дьбе, на рабо́те, на заня́тиях, на уро́ке, на о́пере, на экза́мене, на конфере́нции;** or with certain public buildings where **на** may be translated as *at* or *in:* **на по́чте, на ста́нции, на вы́ставке, на вокза́ле, на телегра́фе, на предприя́тии, на заво́де, на фа́брике.**

B is used to translate *at* where English may also allow *in*. Russian perceives the location as within an enclosed or circumscribed building or place rather than at a broader location, as does English. The following phrases will all use **в** to translate *at: at the university, at school, at the library, at Princeton, at the movies, at the drugstore, at the bank*, and *at the store*.

NOTE: To translate "at" a person's house, use the preposition **у** plus genitive case:

Вчера он был у Ивана (*He was at Ivan's yesterday*).

Idiomatic Uses of в

1. This preposition is used with certain time expressions: **в апре́ле** (in April), **в э́том году́** (this year), **в кото́ром часу́** (at what time), **в полови́не пе́рвого** (at 12:30).

2. Use **в** when talking about wearing clothes: **Она́ была́ в черном пла́тье** (*She was wearing a black dress*).

3. This preposition expresses certain moods: **в восто́рге** (in ecstasy), **в го́ре** (in grief), **в волне́нии** (in agitation/agitatedly), and so forth.

4. Certain verbs require the use of the preposition **в** plus the prepositional case. Among them are:

нужда́ться в	to be in need of something
обвиня́ть в	to accuse (someone) of something
ошиба́ться в	to err in something
подозрева́ть в	to suspect (someone) of something
признава́ться в	to confess, admit to something
сомнева́ться в	to doubt something
убежда́ть в	to convince (someone) of something
уверя́ть в	to assure (someone) of something
уча́ствовать в	to take part in something

Similarly, nouns derived from such verbs will also take **в** plus prepositional case: **нужда́ в по́мощи** (need for help), **оши́бка в оце́нке** (a mistake in judgment).

Idiomatic Uses of На

You must make a special effort to learn which nouns are used with **на**. In addition to the rules on p. 104 above, the following might help you sort the various categories of nouns.

1. Use **на** with certain geographical places or areas that do not have well-defined borders, such as mountain ranges, peninsulas, islands, or points of the compass. The translation is usually *in,* although you will see both *on* and *at* used in the following expressions:

на Кавка́зе	in the Caucasus
на фро́нте	at the front

на Камчáтке	on Kamchatka
на Украине[3]	in Ukraine
на Гавайях	in Hawaii
на Крáсной плóщади	on Red Square
на Урáле	in the Urals
на Кубе	on/in Cuba
на Аляске	in Alaska
на Корéйском полуóстрове	on the Korean Peninsula
на рынке	at the market
на востоке	in the East
на юго-зáпаде	in the Southeast
на пляже	at the beach

2. Use **на** to express the means of transportation and transportation centers: **на пóезде, на велосипéде, на автóбусе, на метрó, на самолёте, на такси, на вокзáле, на платфóрме, на стáнции, на стоянке, на остановке.**

3. Use **на** after certain verbs: **игрáть на** (to play a musical instrument), **говори́ть/писáть на** (to speak a language), **жени́ться на** (to marry), **настáивать на** (to insist on).

4. **На** is used with certain miscellaneous expressions:

на свéжем вóздухе	in the fresh air
на сóлнце	in the sun
на рассвéте	at dawn
на сквознякé	in a draft
на рóдине	in one's native land
на дáче	at one's summer house
на бýдущей/этой недéле	next/this week
на морóзе	in the cold weather
на закáте	at sunset
на пéнсии	retired
на свобóде	at large
на клáдбище	at the cemetery

---

[3] You will also hear **в Украине** these days due to the influence of the political situation after the breakup of the Soviet Union.

TEST FOR MASTERY 1

In the following sentences, choose the correct preposition, **в** or **на**:

1. Моя́ сестра́ говори́т _____ трёх языка́х.

2. Дава́й встре́тимся _____ Не́вском проспе́кте.

3. Сего́дня у́тром я была́ _____ по́чте и _____ магази́не.

4. Рим нахо́дится _____ Ита́лии.

5. Я рабо́таю _____ э́том ста́ром заво́де.

6. Они́ у́чатся _____ университе́те.

7. Ко́шка лежи́т _____ со́лнце.

8. Она́ прие́хала _____ апре́ле э́того го́да.

9. Я сомнева́юсь _____ э́том!

10. Ты прие́хал _____ по́езде, и́ли _____ самолёте?

TEST FOR MASTERY 2

Remember your geography? See if you can identify the location of the following geographical place names, using the verb **находи́ться** with the correct preposition, followed by the prepositional phrase. In alphabetical order, the places you will need for your answers are **Австра́лия, А́нглия, Аргенти́на, Афганиста́н, Африка, Брази́лия, Гре́ция, Кавка́з, Калифо́рния, Кана́да, Кита́й, Перу́, По́льша, Сиби́рь, Тибе́т, Ти́хий океа́н, Фра́нция, Швейца́рия, Южная Аме́рика, Япо́ния.**

Example: Рим? → Рим нахо́дится в Ита́лии.

1. Пари́ж?

2. Ло́ндон?

3. Варша́ва?

4. Река́ Нил?

5. Буэ́нос-А́йрес?

6. Ме́лбурн?

7. Торо́нто?

8. А́льпы?

9. Бейджи́нг?

10. О́зеро Байка́л?

11. Арме́ния?

12. Кабу́л?

13. Лос-А́нджелес?   17. Эве́рест?

14. То́кио?   18. Боли́вия?

15. Ли́ма?   19. Гава́йи?

16. Амазо́нка?   20. Афи́ны?

More Prepositions That Require the Prepositional Case

1. The meaning of the preposition **о** is *of, about,* or *concerning:*[4] **Что́ ты зна́ешь о Фра́нции?** (*What do you know about France?*); **Я ча́сто ду́маю о бра́те, кото́рый живёт на Камча́тке** (*I often think about my brother who lives in Kamchatka*).

The preposition **о,** when followed by a non-iotated vowel (a vowel that does not begin with the sound [y] changes for the sake of euphony to **об: Он всегда́ ду́мает об А́нне** (*He is always thinking about Anna*); **Что ты зна́ешь об э́том?** (*What do you know about this?*); **Ва́ня ничего́ не зна́ет об Оде́ссе** (*Vanya doesn't know anything about Odessa*).

Last, three phrases show a further mutation of **о** to **обо: обо мне** (about me), **обо всём** (about everything), **обо всех** (about everyone).

2. The preposition **при** is sometimes difficult to translate.

In its physical sense, it means *in the area of, attached to,* or may disappear in translation: **столо́вая при заво́де** (the factory['s] cafeteria), **При до́ме был огоро́д** (The house had a vegetable garden).

It means *under* or *at the time of* in the temporal sense of *during:* **при Петре́ пе́рвом** (during the reign of Peter I), **при феодали́зме** (under feudalism).

Last, **при** may be used in expressions of condition: **при нали́чии** (in the presence of), **при отсу́тствии** (in the absence of), **при жела́нии** (with the desire, desirous of), **при по́мощи** (with the help of), **Я э́то сде́лаю при трёх усло́виях** (*I'll do this on three conditions*).

It may also be used idiomatically: **Нельзя́ так говори́ть при де́тях** (*You shouldn't talk like that in front of the children*); **Э́то произошло́ при свиде́телях** (*That happened before witnesses*).

---

[4] Another preposition, **про** plus the accusative case, is more widely used in conversation than **о** plus the prepositional. The latter form is more common in written Russian.

And it can be used in the meaning *on,* indicating possession: **У меня́ нет при себе́ де́нег** (*I have no money on me*); **У тебя́ е́сть при ссбе́ конфе́ты?** (*Do you have any candy with you?*).

3. Use **по** for *upon* or *after.* You will come to know these expressions gradually through memorization and use. This form is considered somewhat formal: **по оконча́нии университе́та** (upon finishing the university, after graduating), **по прие́зде в Москву́** (upon arriving in Moscow), **по возвраще́нии в Вашингто́н** (upon returning to Washington), **по прие́зде домо́й** (upon arriving home).

This preposition is also used with expressions of grieving, e.g., **пла́кать по му́же** (to mourn one's husband), **тоскова́ть по ро́дине**[5] (to yearn for/miss one's native land).

TEST FOR MASTERY 3

Fill in the blanks with the appropriate preposition:

1. Мы всегда́ обе́даем _____ столо́вой _____ университе́те.

2. _____ оконча́нии институ́та Ната́ша поступи́ла на рабо́ту.

3. Мы бы́ли _____ Кавка́зе _____ про́шлом году́.

4. _____ кото́ром часу́ ты придёшь домо́й?

5. Что ты зна́ешь _____ рабо́те Эйнште́йна?

6. Соба́ка сиди́т _____ со́лнце и спит.

7. Де́душка уже́ _____ пе́нсии, а ба́бушка ещё рабо́тает _____ заво́де.

8. Поли́тика «перестро́йка» начала́сь _____ Горбачёве.

9. _____ по́хоронах жена́ пла́кала _____ поко́йном му́же.

10. Я уверя́ю вас _____ моём по́лном соде́йствии.

11. Автомоби́ли нужда́ются _____ бензи́не.

12. Ва́ня хорошо́ игра́ет _____ балала́йке.

---

[5] Some sources note that the preposition **по** in the second example may govern dative case as well.

The "Locative" Case

Properly speaking, the locative case is a subcase of the prepositional. In fact, some sources consider the locative—along with the partitive genitive, which also has endings separate from the standard genitive—as one of the eight cases of Russian, making life even harder for students. Like the prepositional, the locative is used only with prepositions—in this case **в** and **на**—and only to express location. There are a limited number of masculine nouns in this category, and they must be memorized. This is easier done than said, since most of them occur with great frequency throughout conversational Russian, and by the time students arrive at an explanation of these forms, they have already learned them.

The ending for the locative case is a stressed **-ý/-ю́.**

The following masculine nouns constitute an inclusive list of this category:

в аду́	in hell	на меху́	fur-lined
в аэропорту́	at the airport	в мозгу́	in the brain
на балу́	at the ball	на мосту́	on the bridge
на берегу́	on the shore	на носу́	on one's nose
на боку́	on one's side	в полку́	in the regiment
на борту́	on board	на полу́	on the floor
в бою́	in battle	в порту́	in the port
в бреду́	in delirium	на посту́	at one's post
в виду́	in view (of), in mind	в поту́	in a sweat
в глазу́	in one's eye	в пруду́	in the pond
в году́	in a year	в раю́	in paradise
на Дону́	on the Don	во рту (рот)	in one's mouth
в жару́	in the heat	в ряду́	in a row
на краю́	on the edge	в саду́	in the garden
в кругу́	in a circle	в снегу́	in the snow
в Крыму́	in the Crimea	в строю́	in formation
на лбу (лоб)	on one's forehead	в/на углу́	in/on the corner
в лесу́	in the woods	в цвету́	in bloom
на лугу́	in the meadow	в часу́	at the hour
на льду (лёд)	on the ice	на шелку́	silk-lined
в меду́	in the honey	в шкафу́	in the cupboard

Locative Notes

In some instances, both the locative and the prepositional forms are used, with different meanings: **в/на кругу́** indicates within a circular area, while **в/на кру́ге** refers to the circumference of a circle; **в углу́** means *in the corner,* while **в угле́** means *in the angle* (geometry).

The nouns above are used in a literal locative meaning only with the prepositions **в** and **на.** With the three other prepositions, **о, при,** and **по,** normal prepositional endings in **-e** or **-и** are required:

Мы сиде́ли в вишнёвом саду́.	We sat in the cherry orchard.
Гали́на испо́лнила роль в «Вишнёвом са́де».	Galina played a part in *The Cherry Orchard.*
А́йше родила́сь в Крыму́.	Ayshe was born in the Crimea.
Она́ мно́го зна́ет о Кры́ме.	She knows a lot about the Crimea.
Они́ сидя́т в кругу́.	They are sitting in a circle.
Солжени́цын написа́л рома́н «В Кру́ге пе́рвом».	Solzhenitsyn wrote the novel *The First Circle.*

TEST FOR MASTERY 4

Supply the prepositions and nouns with the correct case endings for the following sentences:

1. Ада́м и Е́ва жи́ли _____ _____.
    Eden/paradise   (рай)

2. Что́ ты зна́ешь _____ _____ _____?
    about   life/(жизнь)   (Камча́тка)

3. Что́ он име́ет ____ _____, говоря́ э́то?
    in   mind/(вид)

4. _____ _____ росси́йские войска́ охвати́ли (*seized*) Каза́нь.
    Under   Ivan the Terrible/
    (Ива́н Гро́зный)

5. _____ _____ словаря́ вы суме́ете перевести́ э́ту статью́.
    With   the help/(по́мощь)

6. _____ _____ на ро́дину, он сра́зу же на́чал иска́ть кварти́ру.
    Upon   returning/
        (возвраще́ние)

7. Он очну́лся (*awoke*) весь _____ _____.
                         sweat (пот)

8. Он рабо́тает _____ _____ __ _____.
                bookstore (кни́жный магази́н) at the university

9. Я е́хал в Босто́н _____. _____ я встре́тил ста́рого знако́мого.
                  by train   In the train

10. Вита́лий ду́мает, что он всё зна́ет _____ и _____.
                              about everything   about everyone

11. Смотри́, что у Са́ши _____ _____?
                    mouth (рот)

12. Нельзя́ говори́ть ____ _____ _____ _____ _____.
                the neighbors (соседи) in front of Uncle Dmitri

13. Че́хов жил не́сколько лет _____.
                       Sakhalin Island

14. Влади́мир Ката́ев мно́го зна́ет _____.
                      Anton Chekhov

15. ____ _____ мы бы́ли ____ _____ и _____.
      Russia   in big cities small villages

ANSWER KEY

Vocabulary Practice

1. на сва́дьбе

2. на по́езде.

3. на ры́нке.

4. на ю́ге.

5. на се́веро-восто́ке

6. уча́вствуют в

7. на на́бережной

8. на пля́же

9. игра́ет на

10. во Вселе́нной

Test for Mastery 1

1. на трёх языка́х
2. на Не́вском проспе́кте
3. на по́чте, в магази́не
4. в Ита́лии
5. на заво́де
6. в университе́те
7. на со́лнце
8. в апре́ле
9. в э́том
10. на по́езде, на самолёте

Test for Mastery 2

1. Пари́ж нахо́дится во Фра́нции.
2. Ло́ндон нахо́дится в А́нглии.
3. Варша́ва нахо́дится в По́льше.
4. Река́ Нил нахо́дится в А́фрике.
5. Буэ́нос-А́йрес нахо́дится в Аргенти́не.
6. Ме́лбурн нахо́дится в Австра́лии.
7. Торо́нто нахо́дится в Кана́де.
8. А́льпы нахо́дятся в Швейца́рии.
9. Бейджи́нг нахо́дится в Кита́е.
10. О́зеро Байка́л нахо́дится в Сиби́ри.
11. Арме́ния нахо́дится на Кавка́зе.
12. Кабу́л нахо́дится в Афганиста́не.
13. Лос-А́нджелес нахо́дится в Калифо́рнии.
14. То́кио нахо́дится в Япо́нии.
15. Ли́ма нахо́дится в Перу́.
16. Амазо́нка нахо́дится в Брази́лии.
17. Э́верест нахо́дится в Тибе́те.
18. Боли́вия нахо́дится в Ю́жной Аме́рике.

19. Гавáи нахóдятся на Тúхом океáне.

20. Афúны нахóдятся в Грéции.

Test for Mastery 3

1. в столóвой, при университéте
2. По окончáнии
3. на Кавкáзе, в прóшлом годý
4. В котором часу
5. о рабóте
6. на сóлнце
7. на пéнсии, на завóде
8. при Горбачёве
9. На пóхоронах, по мýже
10. в моём содéйствии
11. в бензúне
12. на балалáйке

Test for Mastery 4

1. в раю́
2. о жúзни на Камчáтке
3. в видý
4. При Ивáне Грóзном
5. При пóмощи
6. При возвращéнии
7. в потý
8. в кнúжном магазúне при университéте
9. на пóезде. В пóезде
10. обо всём и обо всех
11. во ртý
12. о сосéдях при дя́де Дмúтрии
13. на Сахалúне
14. об Антóне Чéхове
15. В России, в больши́х городáх и мáленьких дерéвнях

7 Present Tense Verbs

Глаголы настоящего времени

Useful Vocabulary

Everyday Activities

бри́ться	to shave
встава́ть	to get up
гла́дить	to iron
гото́вить	to cook, prepare
гуля́ть	to go out (for a walk)
за́втракать	to eat breakfast
занима́ться	to study
идти́ за поку́пками	to go shopping
идти́ на рабо́ту	to go to work
ложи́ться спать	to go to bed
мыть посу́ду	to wash the dishes
обе́дать	to have dinner
одева́ться	to get dressed
принима́ть душ	to take a shower
рабо́тать	to work
раздева́ться	to get undressed
стира́ть бельё	to do the laundry
убира́ть	to clean/tidy up
у́жинать	to have supper
чи́стить зу́бы	to brush your teeth

Sports Verbs

бе́гать	to run, jog
гуля́ть	to walk, stroll
де́лать у́треннюю заря́дку	to do your morning exercises
е́здить верхо́м	to go horseback riding
занима́ться (+ instr.)[1]	to do, engage in
игра́ть в (+ acc.)	to play (a sport)
ката́ться на (во́дных) лы́жах	to (water) ski
ката́ться на велосипе́де	to go biking
ката́ться на конька́х	to go ice skating
ката́ться на ло́дке	to go boating
ката́ться на ро́ликах	to go roller-skating
лови́ть ры́бу	to go fishing
пла́вать	to swim
кара́тэ	karate
бейсбо́л	baseball
баскетбо́л	basketball
волейбо́л	volleyball
гольф	golf
бокс	boxing
гимна́стика	gymnastics
бег	jogging, running
стрельба́	archery
лакро́сс	lacrosse
спортсме́н(ка)	athlete (m./f.)

Sports

те́ннис	tennis
футбо́л	soccer
борьба́	wrestling
хокке́й	hockey
фигу́рное ката́ние	figure skating
аэро́бика	aerobics

---

[1] For activities that you do not play, such as gymnastics, wrestling, figure skating, aerobics, etc.

VOCABULARY PRACTICE

Say whether the following statements are true (**пра́вда**) or false (**непра́вда**).

1. Уэ́йн Гре́цкий занима́ется то́лько борьбо́й.

2. Ру́сские о́чень лю́бят фигу́рное ката́ние.

3. Америка́нцы лю́бят пла́вать на дворе́ (*outdoors*) зимо́й.

4. Нельзя́ ката́ться на ро́ликах в до́ме.

5. Та́йгер Вудс пло́хо игра́ет в гольф.

6. Я ложу́сь спать у́тром и встаю́ ве́чером.

7. На́до чи́стить зу́бы два и́ли три ра́за в день.

8. Гимна́стика—о́чень некраси́вый вид спо́рта.

9. Мо́жно лови́ть ры́бу и ле́том и зимо́й.

10. Гуля́ть—вре́дно для здоро́вья.

11. Майкл Джо́рдан плохо́й баскетболи́ст.

12. Ковбо́и (*cowboys*) хорошо́ е́здят верхо́м.

Расписа́ние на неде́лю

	воскресе́нье	понеде́льник	вторник	среда	четверг	пя́тница	суббота
9–10	бе́гать в па́рке		у́тренняя заря́дка	бе́гать на стадио́не		у́тренняя заря́дка	
10–11		стира́ть бельё			химчи́стка		убира́ть кварти́ру
11–12			гла́дить	занима́ться в библиоте́ке		писа́ть пи́сьма	то́ же
12–13		бассе́йн	то́ же		поликли́ника	гастроно́м	
13–14	гото́вить обе́д		те́ннис	мыть пол		то́ же	звони́ть ма́ме
14–15		звони́ть па́пе	занима́ться в библиоте́ке		занима́ться в библиоте́ке		занима́ться в библиоте́ке

(Continued)

	воскресе́нье	понедельник	вторник	среда	четверг	пятница	суббота
15–16	Парк культу́ры	спать	то́ же	слу́шать му́зыку	то́ же	бассе́йн	
16–17	то́ же			то́ же		занима́ться в библиоте́ке	ката́ться на ро́ликах
17–18		печь пече́нья	Профе́ссор Ивано́в		звони́ть ма́ме		то́ же
18–19							
19–20		занима́ться в библиоте́ке	мыть посу́ду	занима́ться в библиоте́ке	ветерина́р	о́пера	
20–21	звони́ть ма́ме	то́ же	занима́ться в библиоте́ке	кинотеа́тр: но́вый фильм			волейбо́л
21–22			то́ же	то́ же		то́ же	дискоте́ка
22–23						то́ же	то́ же
23–24		но́вости			но́вости		то́ же

Примечания[2]

1. Ка́ждый день Ка́тя встаёт и принима́ет душ, за́втракает в во́семь часо́в, и обе́дает в два часа́, но у́жинает когда́ уго́дно.

2. Ка́тя занима́ется в библиоте́ке четы́ре ра́за в неде́лю, три часа́ подря́д. Библиоте́ка откры́та ка́ждый день с 10 утра́ до 10 но́чи.

3. Иногда́ по вечера́м Ка́тя смо́трит телеви́зор.

4. Ка́ждый ве́чер в 10 ч. Ка́тя гуляет со свое́й соба́кой.

5. Она́ ложи́тся спать не по́зже, чем час но́чи.

CONVERSATION PRACTICE

Answer the questions based on Katya's weekly schedule above and the information added in the remarks that follow. Some of your answers will be based on your personal opinion.

---
[2] See the answer key for translating help with the **Примечания.**

1. Что́ де́лает Ка́тя по среда́м в час дня?

2. Когда́ Ка́тя хо́дит в бассе́йн? Что́ она́ там де́лает?

3. Ско́лько раз в неде́лю она́ звони́т ма́ме? А па́пе? Когда́?

4. По каки́м дням Ка́тя занима́ется в библиоте́ке?

5. Что́ де́лает Ка́тя у́тром по суббо́там?

6. Почему́ она́ хо́дит к ветерина́ру по четверга́м?

7. К кому́ она́ идёт по вто́рникам в пять часо́в?

8. Кто́ тако́й Профе́ссор Ивано́в?

9. Когда́ Ка́тя хо́дит в кино́? На о́перу?

10. Ка́тя ча́сто смо́трит телеви́зор?

11. Когда́ Ка́те не́когда (*has no time*) гуля́ть со свое́й соба́кой? Почему́?

12. Когда́ Ка́тя чи́стит зу́бы? А вы?

13. Ка́тя игра́ет в спорт? В како́й вид спо́рта? Когда́?

14. Как вы ду́маете—Ка́тя хоро́шая спортсме́нка? А вы?

15. Что́ де́лает Ка́тя по суббо́там у́тром?

16. Когда́ Ка́тя хо́дит в поликли́нику? Почему́?

17. Когда́ Ка́тя пи́шет пи́сьма?

18. Ка́тя принима́ет душ или ва́нну (*bath*)?

19. Когда́ обе́дают ру́сские? А америка́нцы?

20. Как по-ва́шему: Ка́тя лю́бит му́зыку?

21. В како́й час Ка́тя свобо́дна ка́ждый день? Как вы ду́маете: что она́ де́лает в э́тот час?

22. Ка́тя мно́го чита́ет? Когда́?

23. Что́ де́лает Ка́тя в Па́рке культу́ры? Когда́?

24. Ка́тя ча́сто хо́дит в кино́?

25. Что́ де́лает Ка́тя в ку́хне? Когда́?

Conversation Notes

1. On a Russian calendar, the week begins with Monday. The seven days of the week, which are not capitalized, are **понеде́льник, вто́рник, среда́, четве́рг, пя́тница, суббо́та, воскресе́нье.**

To say *on a given day* of the week, use **в** plus the accusative case: **в понеде́льник, во вторник, в среду, в четверг, в пятнипу, в субботу, в воскресенье.** To say that something occurs regularly on a certain day, use **по** plus the dative plural: **по понеде́льникам, по вто́рникам, по среда́м, по четверга́м, по пя́тницам, по суббо́там, по воскресе́ньям.** Compare *on Monday* with the first construction and *on Mondays* with the second. Similarly, this latter construction is used to express something regularly occurring during a specific time of day: **по утра́м** (in the mornings), **по дня́м** (in the afternoons), **по вечера́м** (in the evenings), **по нача́м** (during the night[s]).

2. To express A.M. and P.M., Russians use genitive expressions that pertain to parts of the day: **утра́** (in the morning), **дня** (in the afternoon), **ве́чера** (in the evening), and **но́чи** (at night). These are used with specific clock times. If you wish to focus on an extended part of a single day, use the instrumental expressions **у́тром, днём, ве́чером,** and **но́чью:**

Она́ игра́ет в те́ннис по утра́м.	She plays tennis in the mornings
Она́ игра́ет в те́ннис за́втра у́тром.	She is playing tennis tomorrow morning.
Мы встре́тимся в 9 часо́в утра́.	We will meet at 9:00 A.M.

3. Note that the schedule above lists clock times according to a 24-hour clock. Whereas English uses this mainly in military and scientific contexts, it is widespread in Russia, turning up in any kind of schedule (TV, movies, transportation, etc.).

When read aloud, do not use the numbers higher than twelve. For 22:00, say **де́сять часо́в ве́чера** (10:00 P.M.).

4. To express *from* a certain time *to* another time, you must change the numbers to the genitive case. The numeral *one* is not used; just place the noun **час** into the genitive case.

Nominative	Genitive
два	двух
три	трёх
четы́ре	четырёх
пять	пяти́
шесть	шести́
семь	семи́
во́семь	восьми́
де́вять	девяти́
де́сять	десяти́

5. The nouns for people who engage in certain sports are usually formed by adding the suffix **-ист(ка)** to the sport: **те́ннис/тенниси́ст(ка), баскетбо́л/баскетболи́ст(ка), хокке́й/хоккеи́ст(ка), фигу́рное ката́ние/фигури́ст(ка).** There are, of course, exceptions: **бокс/боксёр, гимна́стика/гимна́ст, бег/бегу́н, стрельба́/стреле́ц.**

First-Conjugation Verbs

There is a type of first-conjugation verb—the **рабо́тать, де́лать, чита́ть** type—that lulls beginning students of Russian into a false sense of security that all Russian verbs are easy and that everything conjugates the same way as the above verbs do. Nothing could be further from the truth. First-conjugation verbs are a royal mess. They are so difficult to classify that most systems appear forced and wind up being more difficult to learn than the verbs themselves. For the faint of heart, the best advice is to learn the infinitive, the first-person singular, and the second-person singular. These three forms will tell you all you need to know about how a verb behaves: its stress pattern, its present-tense stem, and its past-tense stem. All remaining parts of the verb are predictable from these three forms.

For the more courageous, this chapter will take them into the morass of first-conjugation verbs to see if some sense can be made of them.

But first, to prove this point, examine the list below and try to discern what these verbs have in common: **жить, пить, верну́ться, тоскова́ть, дрема́ть, ждать, боро́ться, привы́кнуть, красне́ть, мыть, вести́, красть, стричь, грызть, умере́ть, поня́ть, жела́ть.** The answer, not so surprisingly, is that they have nothing in common—except the fact that they are all first-conjugation verbs. Each one of them represents its own type of first-conjugation verb. Each one of these verbs is conjugated in its own way.

It is obvious from this list that there seems to be no single way of identifying the conjugation pattern of a verb. The verb **жить** ends in **-ить,** just like the second-conjugation verb **купи́ть.** The verb **жела́ть** ends in **-ать,** the same as **крича́ть,** but the former is first conjugation and the latter is second conjugation. From their infinitives alone, **мыть** and **грызть** appear to be conundrums. The only way to make any sense out of them, it seems, is to memorize the three parts as suggested above. Once you have several hundred verbs under your belt, a pattern will begin to emerge, and you will begin to make intelligent guesses as to how a verb should be conjugated. This is what a native speaker—particularly a child—does, after all.

So without further ado, let us tackle each one of the verbs in the famous list above to discuss its peculiarities as a first-conjugation verb.

Monosyllabic Verbs in -ить

Except for the verb **жить,** all verbs of this type (and all prefixed forms derived from such verbs) belong to this conjugation and have the following pattern:

Пить (to drink)	Бить (to beat)	Лить (to pour)	Шить (to sew)
пью	бью	лью	шью
пьёшь	бьёшь	льёшь	шьёшь
пьёт	бьёт	льёт	шьёт
пьём	бьём	льём	шьём
пьёте	бьёте	льёте	шьёте
пьют	бьют	льют	шьют

As you can see, the present-tense stem is a consonant + a soft sign, followed by stressed first-conjugation endings. This conjugation pattern will also apply to prefixed infinitives based on these verbs, such as **напи́ть, вы́пить, перепи́ть, допи́ть, недопи́ть, попи́ть,** and **отпи́ть**—to give a handful of examples for the verb **пить** alone.

As for the verb **жить** and its prefixed forms, it appears to be a unique verb of this type, expanding the stem to **жив-** and adding stressed first-conjugation endings: **живу́, живёшь, живёт, живём, живёте, живу́т.**

Infinitives in -чь

These verbs are one of two types: underlying **-к-** stems or underlying **-г-** stems. Two examples are:

Стричь	**Печь**
(to cut)	**(to bake)**
стригу́	пеку́
стрижёшь	печёшь
стрижёт	печёт
стрижём	печём
стрижёте	печёте
стригу́т	пеку́т

Because of a phonetic phenomenon that traces its origins to Old Russian, it is not possible to have the velars **г** or **к** before the vowels **е/ё**.[3] In these positions, the consonants will mutate to **ж** and **ч**, respectively.

Note that from the infinitive alone it is not possible to predict which consonant is part of the underlying stem.

Other verbs that belong to this type are **мочь (мог-)** (can, to be able), **сечь (сек-)** (to cut to pieces), **жечь (жг-)** (to burn), **влечь (влек-)** (to draw, drag), **лечь (ляг-)** (to lie down), **течь (тек-)** (to flow), **воло́чь (волок-)** (to drag), **толо́чь (толок-)** (to pound, crush), **помо́чь (помог-)** (to help), **запря́чь (запряг-)** (to harness).

All verbs of this type are end stressed throughout the conjugation, except in the case of a perfective verb prefixed in **вы-**, such as **вы́сечь: вы́секу, вы́сечешь, вы́сечет, вы́сечем, вы́сечете, вы́секут.** Verbs of this type are always stressed on the prefix.

Infinitives in -овать

This is an enormous group of verbs that continues to grow by the day. The suffix roughly corresponds to the popularity of the English suffix *-ize* (*prioritize, standardize*) in that it is used to form new Russian verbs, most of them based on foreign words. In some cases they are replacing native Russian locutions. In current colloquial Russian, it is now more common to say **паркова́ть маши́ну** (*to park the car*) than it is to use the older expression **ста́вить маши́ну (на стоя́нку)**.

Before verbs of this type are conjugated, a change must be made to the suffix: the **-ова-** is replaced with the vowel **-у-** before regular unstressed first-conjugation endings are added. The student must make every effort to distinguish these verbs from those in a consonant + **ать** or risk sounding childish (*I knowed that*).

---

[3] The one exception is the verb **ткать** (to weave), which is conjugated: **тку, ткёшь, ткёт, ткём, ткёте, ткут.**

The conjugation of verbs of this type is as follows:

Голосовáть (to vote)	Демонстри́ровать (to demonstrate)	Стартовáть (to start [sports])	Совéтовать (to advise)
голосу́ю	демонстри́рую	старту́ю	совéтую
голосу́ешь	демонстри́руешь	старту́ешь	совéтуешь
голосу́ет	демонстри́рует	старту́ет	совéтует
голосу́ем	демонстри́руем	старту́ем	совéтуем
голосу́ете	демонстри́руете	старту́ете	совéтуете
голосу́ют	демонтсри́руют	старту́ют	совéтуют

There are also several verbs that have the soft variation of the suffix, **-евать**. In these verbs, the **-ева-** is replaced with the vowel **-ю** before regular endings. Stress varies. For example:

Плевáть (to spit)	Воевáть (to wage war)
плюю́	вою́ю
плюёшь	вою́ешь
плюёт	вою́ет
плюём	вою́ем
плюёте	вою́ете
плюю́т	вою́ют

Some interesting examples of new verbs formed with this suffix from the current Russian press are **парковáть** (to park), **прессинговáть** (to put pressure on), **приорити́ровать** (to prioritize), **лобби́ровать** (to lobby), **информи́ровать** (to brief), and **тести́ровать** (to test).

Infinitives in -авать

Verbs of this type drop the **-ва-** altogether before adding regular stressed first-conjugation endings. The most common verbs of this type are prefixed forms of **давáть**, **-знавáть**, and **-ставáть**.

Давáть (to give)	Узнавáть (to recognize)	Вставáть (to get up)
даю́	узнаю́	встаю́
даёшь	узнаёшь	встаёшь

даёт	узнаёт	встаёт
даём	узнаём	встаём
даёте	узнаёте	встаёте
даю́т	узнаю́т	встаю́т

Some other verbs of this type are **продава́ть** (to sell), **преводава́ть** (to teach), **передава́ть** (to transmit, broadcast), **раздава́ть** (to distribute), **задава́ть** (to ask), **признава́ть** (to admit), **сознава́ть** (to realize), **переста́ва́ть** (to stop), **достава́ть** (to get, obtain), and **уставать** (to get tired).

Infinitives in -ывать[4]

All verbs of this type are imperfective and all conjugate regularly, according to the paradigm of **де́лать** or **рабо́тать**.

Note that because of the seven-letter spelling rule, this ending may occasionally appear as **-ивать,** as in **спра́шивать.**

Infinitives in a Consonant + ать

This is perhaps the most exasperating class of verbs in Russian. In addition to categories three through five above, there are hundreds upon hundreds of other verbs that end in a consonant + **ать** whose conjugations are unpredictable and must be memorized. There are, however, only two major types of these verbs.

Conjugated Like **Рабо́тать**

Because verbs of this type are commonly learned early in one's study of Russian, students come to rely on the paradigm. They are conjugated as follows:

---

[4] Many of these verbs are secondary imperfectives, formed from originally imperfective verbs that became perfective with the addition of a suffix that changed their meaning. Consider, for example, the following verbs:

Imperfective	**Perfective**	**Perfective**	**Secondary Imperfective**
чита́ть	прочита́ть	перечита́ть (to re-read)	перечи́тывать
писа́ть	написа́ть	подписа́ть (to sign)	подпи́сывать

This phenomenon is widespread in Russian.

Рабо́тать (to work)	Де́лать (to do)	Отдыха́ть (to rest, relax)	Занима́ться (to study)
рабо́таю	де́лаю	отдыха́ю	занима́юсь
рабо́таешь	де́лаешь	отдыха́ешь	занима́ешься
рабо́тает	де́лает	отдыха́ет	занима́ется
рабо́таем	де́лаем	отдыха́ем	занима́емся
рабо́таете	де́лаете	отдыха́ете	занима́етесь
рабо́тают	де́лают	отдыха́ют	занима́ются

Conjugated Like Писать

Verbs of this type change the final consonant of the stem before adding the endings. Unlike second-conjugation verbs, these changes are permanent throughout the conjugation (i.e., present or future perfective tense).

Писа́ть (to write)	Пла́кать (to cry)	Маха́ть (to wave)	Сказа́ть (to say)	Иска́ть (to look for)
пишу́	пла́чу	машу́	скажу́	ищу́
пи́шешь	пла́чешь	ма́шешь	ска́жешь	и́щешь
пи́шет	пла́чет	ма́шет	ска́жет	и́щет
пи́шем	пла́чем	ма́шем	ска́жем	и́щем
пи́шете	пла́чете	ма́шете	ска́жете	и́щете
пи́шут	пла́чут	ма́шут	ска́жут	и́щут

Conjugated Like Ждать

Yet one last category of verbs that end in a consonant + -ать are largely monosyllabic and add the same endings as the писать group above. Occasionally these verbs show a fleeting vowel.

Ждать (to wait for)	Брать (to take)	Звать (to call)	Ора́ть (to yell)	Врать (to tell lies)
жду	беру́	зову́	ору́	вру
ждёшь	берёшь	зовёшь	орёшь	врёшь
ждёт	берёт	зовёт	орёт	врёт
ждём	берём	зовём	орём	врём
ждёте	берёте	зовёте	орёте	врёте
ждут	беру́т	зову́т	ору́т	врут

Verbs That End in -ять

Some verbs that end in **-ять** keep the **-я-** throughout the conjugation. This is a productive category of verbs, that is, new verbs continue to be formed according to this pattern.

Гуля́ть (to walk)	Теря́ть (to lose)	Добавля́ть (to add)	Явля́ться (to be)
Гуля́ю	теря́ю	добавля́ю	явля́юсь
гуля́ешь	теря́ешь	добавля́ешь	явля́ешься
гуля́ет	теря́ет	добавля́ет	явля́ется
гуля́ем	теря́ем	добавля́ем	явля́емся
гуля́ете	теря́ете	добавля́ете	явля́етесь
гуля́ют	теря́ют	добавля́ют	явля́ются

Others in this group drop the **-я-.**

Ла́ять (to bark)	Та́ять (to melt)	Наде́яться (to hope [for])	Смея́ться (to laugh [at])
ла́ю	та́ю	наде́юсь	смею́сь
ла́ешь	та́ешь	наде́ешься	смеёшься
ла́ет	та́ет	наде́ется	смеётся
ла́ем	та́ем	наде́емся	смеёмся
ла́ете	та́ете	наде́етесь	смеётесь
ла́ют	та́ют	наде́ются	смею́тся

Note, however, that there are some second-conjugation verbs that end in **-ять,** such as **стоя́ть** and **боя́ться.** These will be appropriately marked.

Verbs in -нять

Though small as a group, these verbs are widely used and must be learned thoroughly. Generally speaking, the infinitive forms of these verbs change stems as illustrated below.

For comparison the imperfective will be listed first, so that the relationship with the conjugated perfective form will be visible.

Imperfective Infinitive	Perfective Infinitive	Present Stem	Stress	English
понима́ть	поня́ть	пойм-	end	to understand
занима́ть	заня́ть	займ-	end	to occupy
нанима́ть	наня́ть	найм-	end	to rent
принима́ть	приня́ть	приму-[5]	shifting	to accept
поднима́ть	подня́ть	подним-	shifting	to lift
отнима́ть	отня́ть	отним-	shifting	to take away
обнима́ть	обня́ть	обним-	shifting	to embrace
снима́ть	снять	сним-	shifting	to take off

Verbs in -еть

Russians readily form verbs from adjectives and nouns by means of this productive suffix.

Красне́ть (to turn red, to blush)	Старе́ть (to grow old)	Худе́ть (to become thin)	Толсте́ть (to become fat)	Камене́ть (to turn to stone)
красне́ю	старе́ю	худе́ю	толсте́ю	камене́ю
красне́ешь	старе́ешь	худе́ешь	толсте́ешь	камене́ешь
красне́ет	старе́ет	худе́ет	толсте́ет	камене́ет
красне́ем	старе́ем	худе́ем	толсте́ем	камене́ем
красне́ете	старе́ете	худе́ете	толсте́ете	камене́ете
красне́ют	старе́ют	худе́ют	толсте́ют	камене́ют

Verbs in -оть

There are very few verbs of this type. Here are two common ones:

Моло́ть (to grind)	Боро́ться (to struggle, fight [for])
мелю́	борю́сь
ме́лешь	бо́решься
ме́лет	бо́рется
ме́лем	бо́ремся
ме́лете	бо́ретесь
ме́лют	бо́рются

---

[5] Like the verb **прийти́,** this verb drops the **-й-** in the conjugation.

Monosyllabic Verbs in -ыть

These verbs and their prefixed forms are all stem stressed.

Мыть (to wash)	Крыть (to cover)	Выть (to howl)	Открыть (to open, uncover)
мо́ю	кро́ю	во́ю	откро́ю
мо́ешь	кро́ешь	во́ешь	откро́ешь
мо́ет	кро́ет	во́ет	откро́ет
мо́ем	кро́ем	во́ем	откро́ем
мо́ете	кро́ете	во́ете	откро́ете
мо́ют	кро́ют	во́ют	откро́ют

There are a few exceptions: **плыть, плыву́, плывёшь** (to swim) is the most common.

Infinitives Ending in Stressed -ти or a Consonant + ть

These verbs are invariably end stressed.

Идти́ (to go)	Нести́ (to carry)	Красть (to steal)	Цвести́ (to blossom)	Грызть (to gnaw)
иду́	несу́	краду́	цвету́	грызу́
идёшь	несёшь	крадёшь	цветёшь	грызёшь
идёт	несёт	крадёт	цветёт	грызёт
идём	несём	крадём	цветём	грызём
идёте	несёте	крадёте	цветёте	грызёте
иду́т	несу́т	краду́т	цвету́т	грызу́т

Exceptional First-Conjugation Forms

Infinitive	Present Tense	English
нача́ть	начну́, начнёшь	to begin
стать (встать)	ста́ну, ста́нешь	to become (to get up)
взять	возьму́, возьмёшь	to take
одеть	оде́ну, оде́нешь	to dress
петь	пою́, поёшь	to sing
умере́ть	умру́, умрёшь	to die
гнить	гнию́, гниёшь	to rot
брить	бре́ю, бре́ешь	to shave
ошиби́ться	ошибу́сь, ошибёшься	to be mistaken

Irregular Verbs

There are only a handful of truly irregular verbs in Russian. These verbs have characteristics of both first and second conjugation.

Дать (to give)	Хотеть (to want)	Есть (to eat)	Бежать (to run)
дам	хочу́	ем	бегу́
дашь	хо́чешь	ешь	бежи́шь
даст	хо́чет	ест	бежи́т
дади́м	хоти́м	еди́м	бежи́м
дади́те	хоти́те	еди́те	бежи́те
даду́т	хотя́т	едя́т	бегу́т

Second-Conjugation Verbs

On the surface, Russian verbs of the second conjugation appear to the beginning student to be much harder than first-conjugation verbs. Fortunately, this is not the case, and these verbs unlock their simplicity of form and ease of conjugation with the memorization of a few key principles.

There are only three types of infinitives: verbs in **-ить**, verbs in **-еть**, and many verbs that end in **ж, ч, ш,** or **щ** plus **-ать**. Here are three typical examples:

Говори́ть (to talk)	Ви́деть (to see)	Молча́ть (to be silent)
говорю́	ви́жу	молчу́
говори́шь	ви́дишь	молчи́шь
говори́т	ви́дит	молчи́т
говори́м	ви́дим	молчи́м
говори́те	ви́дите	молчи́те
говоря́т	ви́дят	молча́т

> **NOTE:** The five-letter spelling rule applies with second-conjugation verbs in the first-person singular and third-person plural forms. Since you may write neither **ю** nor **я** after **ж, ч, ш, щ,** and **ц,** the endings for these forms become **-у** and **-ат.**

There are no other types of second-conjugation verbs.

Stress

Second-conjugation verbs come in any of the three stress patterns of Russian verbs: stem stress, end stress, or shifting stress.

Stem stress means that the stress always falls on the same syllable as in the infinitive, and this syllable is stressed throughout the conjugation.

End stress means that the stress always falls on the last syllable.

Shifting stress, which is the most difficult pattern to master, stresses the last syllable in the infinitive and the first-person singular and moves one syllable toward the beginning of the word in all other forms of the conjugation.

Examples

	Stem Stress	**End Stress**	**Shifting Stress**
Infinitive	по́мнить	положи́ть	плати́ть
First-person singular	по́мню	положу́	плачу́
Second-person singular	по́мнишь	положи́шь	пла́тишь

NOTE: There is no relationship between stress pattern and type of conjugation.

Consonant Alternation

Second-conjugation verbs may have a consonant alternation (mutation) in the first-person singular. This phenomenon is what makes these verbs seem so difficult for beginning students. By the intermediate level, however, with several dozen of these verbs mastered, the notion of consonant alternation is not so strange.

What is important to remember is that consonant alternation with second-conjugation verbs occurs in the first person singular only, unlike first-conjugation verbs, where the alternation is permanent throughout the conjugated forms.

The consonants that can mutate (**н** and **р** do not) are as follows:

Original Consonant	**Mutates to**	**Original Consonant**	**Mutates to**
д, з, г	ж	б	бл
т, к	ч	п	пл
с, х	ш	в	вл
ст, ск	щ	ф	фл
		м	мл

Notice that the labial consonants (those that are formed using the lips) all mutate by the addition of the letter **л.**

Examples of labial stems are **люби́ть** (to love), **купи́ть** (to buy), **лови́ть** (to catch), **графи́ть** (to make lines [on paper]), **офо́рмить** (to formalize).

Examples of other stems are **ви́деть** (to see), **плати́ть** (to pay), **вози́ть** (to convey, drive), **пригласи́ть** (to invite).

Thus, if you learn the first-person singular of a verb without any of the other forms, there is no sure way to predict the infinitive.

Examples of other verbs conjugated like **говори́ть** are **кури́ть** (to smoke), **дели́ть** (to divide), **смотре́ть** (to look), **сто́ить** (to cost), **извини́ть** (to excuse), **звони́ть** (to call on the phone), and **по́мнить** (to remember).

Some verbs conjugated like **молчать** are **лежа́ть** (to be lying down), **крича́ть** (to yell), **реши́ть** (to decide), **треща́ть** (to creak), **учи́ться** (to study), **ложи́ться** (to lie down), **слы́шать** (to hear), and **положи́ть** (to put down).

Verbs that end in a fricative (**ж, ч, ш, щ**) plus **-ать** are very often second-conjugation verbs, so be careful not to assume that they are like the first-conjugation verbs **приглаша́ть** (to invite) or **получа́ть** (to receive). There are a few verbs ending in **-ять** that are second conjugation, **стоя́ть** (to stand) being the most common. All other infinitive endings will indicate verbs of the first conjugation. It is also important to note that there are no second-conjugation verbs of one syllable, so all nonprefixed verbs of one syllable must be first-conjugation verbs.

This is the entire story of second-conjugation verbs. There are no further rules, spelling or otherwise, and there are no exceptional forms. You need remember only two things: the five-letter spelling rule and the consonant mutations or alternations that occur in the first-person singular only.

Students spend hours agonizing over what turns out to be a simple and elegant matter. If you spend the time here and try to understand what is happening, you will save countless hours in the long run on memorizing first- and second-person singular forms. To help you get started with the process, jump into the exercise that follows.

TEST FOR MASTERY 1

For each of the following infinitives below, form the first-person singular:

1. смотре́ть (to look)

2. ве́сить (to weigh)

3. висе́ть (to hang)

4. держа́ть (to hold)

5. по́мнить (to remember)

6. крути́ть (to twist)

7. ста́вить (to place, stand)

8. вари́ть (to boil)

9. хвали́ть (to praise)

10. проси́ть (to request)

11. оскорби́ть (to offend)

12. кле́ить (to glue)

13. положи́ть (to put, place)

14. роди́ть (to give birth)

15. копи́ть (to dig)

16. молча́ть (to be silent)

17. стреми́ть (to strive)

18. научи́ть (to teach)

19. тра́тить (to spend, waste)

20. слы́шать (to hear)

TEST FOR MASTERY 2

Using the same infinitives as in the exercise above, produce both the first- and the second-person singular.

Example: грузи́ть (to load) → гружу́, гру́зишь

TEST FOR MASTERY 3

Identify the following verbs as first (I) or second (II) conjugation. Remember to disregard the prefix, if any, before you consider your answer. In some cases it may not be possible to decide with certainty. In these instances, the correct conjugation will appear in parentheses in the Answer Key. See the Answer Key also for a translation of these verbs.

1. крича́ть

2. помы́ть

3. паркова́ть

4. перепи́сывать

5. принести́

6. смотре́ть

7. зако́нчить

8. нали́ть

9. уходи́ть

10. спра́шивать[6]

---

[6] Remember the seven-letter spelling rule!

11. задава́ть
12. помести́ться
13. му́чить
14. га́снуть
15. подожда́ть

16. хохота́ть
17. продли́ть
18. прогоре́ть
19. прожи́ть
20. укра́сть

ANSWER KEY

Vocabulary Practice

1. непра́вда
2. пра́вда
3. непра́вда
4. пра́вда
5. непра́вда
6. непра́вда

7. пра́вда
8. непра́вда
9. пра́вда
10. непра́вда
11. непра́вда
12. пра́вда

Translation of Comments to "Schedule for the Week"

1. Every day Katya gets up and takes a shower, has breakfast at eight o'clock, and has lunch at two, but has supper when it's convenient.

2. Katya studies in the library four times a week, three hours in a row. The library is open every day from 10:00 A.M. to 10:00 P.M.

3. Sometimes Katya watches television in the evenings.

4. Every night at 10:00 o'clock, Katya goes for a walk with her dog.

5. She goes to sleep no later than 1:00 A.M.

Conversation Practice

Your answers may vary.

1. По среда́м в час дня Ка́тя мо́ет пол.

2. Ка́тя хо́дит в бассе́йн по понеде́льникам и по пя́тницам. Наве́рно, она́ там пла́вает.

3. Ка́тя звони́т ма́ме три ра́за в неде́лю: по воскресе́ньям в во́семь часо́в, по четверга́м в пять часо́в, и по суббо́там в час дня. Па́пе Ка́тя звони́т по понеде́льникам в два часа́ дня.

4. В библиоте́ке Ка́тя занима́ется в понеде́льник ве́чером, во вто́рник днём и ве́чером, в сре́ду у́тром и ве́чером, в четве́рг днём, и да́же в пя́тницу днём и в суббо́ту днём.

5. У́тром по суббо́там Ка́тя убира́ет кварти́ру.

6. Она́ туда́ хо́дит, потому́ что она́ там рабо́тает. (Или потому́ что её соба́ка боле́ет.)

7. По вто́рникам в пять часо́в она́ хо́дит к Профе́ссору Ивано́ву.

8. Мо́жет быть, Профе́ссор Ива́нов—её руководи́тель.

9. Ка́тя хо́дит в кино́ по среда́м ве́чером, а на о́перу по пя́тницам.

10. Нет, Ка́те не́когда (*Katya has no time*) смотре́ть телеви́зор!

11. Ка́те не́когда гуля́ть со свое́й соба́кой по утра́м. Почти́ (*almost*) ка́ждый день она́ занима́ется спо́ртом.

12. Ка́тя чи́стит зу́бы у́тром и ве́чером.

13. Да, Ка́тя игра́ет в волейбо́л и те́ннис, бе́гает, пла́вает, ката́ется на ро́ликах, и танцу́ет на дискоте́ке. Она́ занима́ется спо́ртом почти́ ка́ждый день.

14. Да, по-мо́ему, Ка́тя хоро́шая спортсме́нка.

15. По суббо́там у́тром Ка́тя убира́ет кварти́ру.

16. Ка́тя хо́дит в поликли́нику по четверга́м. Мо́жет бы́ть, у неё плохо́е здоро́вье.

17. Ка́тя пи́шет пи́сьма у́тром, по пя́тницам.

18. Ка́тя принима́ет душ.

19. Ру́сские обе́дают днём. Америка́нцы обе́дают ве́чером.

20. Да, по-мо́ему, Ка́тя о́чень лю́бит му́зыку. Она́ слу́шает му́зыку, хо́дит на о́перу, и хо́дит на дискоте́ку.

21. Ка́ждый день Ка́тя свобо́дна в шесть часо́в. Наве́рно, она́ и́ли занима́ется и́ли смо́трит телеви́зор и́ли слу́шает му́зыку и́ли чита́ет.

22. По-мо́ему, да. Она́ чита́ет, когда́ она́ занима́ется в библиоте́ке.

23. В Па́рке культу́ры Ка́тя гуля́ет по воскресе́ньям в три часа́.

24. Нет, Ка́тя хо́дит в кино́ то́лько раз в неде́лю, по среда́м.

25. В ку́хне Ка́тя гото́вит за́втрак ка́ждое у́тро и обе́д по воскресе́ньям.

Test for Mastery 1

1. смотрю́
2. ве́шу
3. вишу́
4. держу́
5. по́мню
6. кручу́
7. ста́влю
8. варю́
9. хвалю́
10. прошу́
11. оскорблю́
12. кле́ю
13. положу́
14. рожу́
15. коплю́
16. молчу́
17. стремлю́
18. научу́
19. тра́чу
20. слы́шу

Test for Mastery 2

1. смотрю́, смо́тришь
2. ве́шу, ве́сишь
3. вишу́, виси́шь
4. держу́, де́ржишь
5. по́мню, по́мнишь
6. кручу́, кру́тишь
7. ста́влю, ста́вишь
8. варю́, ва́ришь
9. хвалю́, хва́лишь
10. прошу́, про́сишь
11. оскорблю́, оскорби́шь
12. кле́ю, кле́ишь
13. положу́, поло́жишь
14. рожу́, роди́шь
15. коплю́, ко́пишь
16. молчу́, молчи́шь
17. стремлю́, стреми́шь
18. научу́, нау́чишь
19. тра́чу, тра́тишь
20. слы́шу, слы́шишь

Test for Mastery 3

1. II (to shout)
2. I (to wash)
3. I (to park)
4. I (to correspond)
5. I (to bring)
6. II (to watch)
7. II (to finish)
8. I (to pour)
9. II (to leave)
10. I (to ask)

11. I (to pose, ask)
12. II (to fit)
13. II (to torment)
14. I (to extinguish)
15. I (to wait)
16. I (to guffaw, giggle)
17. II (to prolong)
18. II (to burn through)
19. I (to survive)
20. I (to steal)

8 The Dative Case

Дательный падеж

Useful Vocabulary

Verbs

(на)писа́ть	to write
(по)дари́ть	to give as a present
(по)звони́ть	to call, telephone
(по)каза́ться	to seem
(по)меша́ть	to bother, hinder, disturb
(по)нра́виться	to like, to appeal to
(по)сове́товать	to advise
аплоди́ровать	to applaud
ве́рить	to believe
дава́ть/дать	to give
надоеда́ть/надое́сть	to be sick of
покупа́ть/купи́ть	to buy
помога́ть/помочь	to help
посыла́ть/послать	to send
пра́здноваться	to be celebrated
улыба́ться/улыбну́ться	to smile

Prepositions

по	(various meanings)
к	to, toward
благодаря́	thanks to
согла́сно	according to
навстре́чу	in the opposite direction

Impersonal Expressions

на́до/ну́жно	must, have to
интере́сно	interesting
хо́лодно	cold
жа́рко	hot
тепло́	warm
ску́чно	boring
ве́село	fun
гру́стно	sad

Nouns

арти́сты	performers
ба́нка икры́	container of caviar
велосипе́д	bicycle
Восьмо́е ма́рта	International Women's Day, March 8
День побе́ды	Victory Day
день рожде́ния	birthday
детекти́в	murder mystery
духи́	perfume
золота́я цепо́чка	gold chain, necklace
зри́тели	audience, viewers
кольцо́	ring
коро́бка шокола́да	box of chocolate
ку́кла	doll
Междунаро́дный же́нский день	International Women's Day
ми́шка	teddy bear
Но́вый год	New Year's
Первома́й	May Day
пода́рок	present

пра́здник	holiday
приглаше́ние	invitation
Рождество́	Christmas
сере́бряные се́рьги	silver earrings
цветы́	flowers
шкату́лка из Па́леха	enamel Palekh box
ювели́рные изде́лия	jewelry

Other Expressions

по-мо́ему, по-тво́ему, по-на́шему, по-ва́шему	I think/in my opinion, you think/ in your opinion, etc.

The verb **дать** is one of only a handful of verbs in Russian that are truly irregular, and as such its conjugation must be memorized. Note also that **дать** is a perfective verb, so conjugating it produces the future tense.

я дам	мы дади́м
ты дашь	вы дади́те
он/она́ даст	они́ даду́т

VOCABULARY PRACTICE

Circle the most appropriate word.

1. Моя́ сестра́ о́чень лю́бит францу́зские (детекти́вы, духи́, цветы́) «Дио́р».

2. (Но́вый год, Первома́й, Междунаро́дный же́нский день) пра́зднуется 8-го ма́рта.

3. Плохи́е де́ти ча́сто (меша́ют, сове́туют, аплоди́руют) роди́телям.

4. Что́ ты (позвони́шь, напи́шешь, пода́ришь) Та́не на день рожде́ния?

5. Моя́ подру́га о́чень лю́бит ювели́рные изде́лия, осо́бенно (духи́, икру́, цепо́чки).

6. Он е́дет в Ита́лию (на конька́х, на велосипе́де, на самолёте).

7. Толсто́й (писа́л, посла́л, аплоди́ровал) рома́ны.

8. Ма́леньким де́тям нра́вятся (детекти́вы, францу́зские духи́, ми́шки и ку́клы).

9. Ива́ну (на́до, согла́сно, благодаря́) занима́ться сего́дня ве́чером.

10. Бриллиа́нты, ко́льца и брасле́ты—это (кита́йская еда́, ювели́рные изде́лия, италья́нская оде́жда).

CONVERSATION PRACTICE

Что́ подари́ть на день рожде́ния?

Анна:	Зна́ешь что́, Ва́ня? Ско́ро бу́дет день рожде́ния Наста́сьи Фили́пповны. Как по-тво́ему—что́ ей подари́ть?
Иван:	Э́то ве́чная пробле́ма! У неё всё есть. Ей ничего́ не ну́жно.
А:	Да, ты прав. Не на́до покупа́ть ей брасле́ты и́ли цепо́чки. Она́ уж не хо́чет игру́шки и́ли шкату́лки. Она́ не лю́бит ни шокола́да, ни икры́. Что́ ей подари́ть?
И:	Слу́шай, А́нечка! У меня́ о́чень хоро́шая иде́йка! Я пойду́ к Семёну Ива́новичу в кни́жный магази́н и куплю́ ей детекти́в!
А:	Како́й детекти́в? Америка́нский?
И:	Нет, по-мо́ему ей бо́льше нра́вятся ру́сские рома́ны. Что́ ты мне посове́туешь?
А:	Купи́ На́сте «Преступле́ние и наказа́ние» Достое́вского. Ей бу́дет стра́шно интере́сно.
И:	Договори́лись. Кста́ти, когда́ бу́дет её день рожде́ния? Ско́лько ей бу́дет лет?
А:	Тебе́ бы не спра́шивать о же́нском во́зрасте! Она́ пригласи́ла нас к себе́ в четве́рг. Ты свобо́ден?
И:	Го́споди, нет! У неё всегда́ таки́е стра́нные вечера́. Нам лу́чше бы сиде́ть до́ма. Я куплю́ ей э́тот рома́н за́втра и пошлю́ его́ по по́чте.

What Should We Give Her for Her Birthday?

Anna:	You know what, Vanya? Nastasya Filippovna's birthday is coming up. What do you think? What should we give her?
Ivan:	It's the eternal problem! She has everything. She doesn't need anything.
A:	Yes, you're right. We shouldn't buy her bracelets or necklaces. She doesn't want toys or enameled boxes. She doesn't like either chocolate or caviar. What to give her?

I:	Listen, Annie! I have a great idea! I'll go to Semyon Ivanovich's bookstore and buy her a murder mystery!
A:	What kind of mystery? An American one?
I:	No, I think she likes Russian novels better. What do you advise?
A:	Buy Nastya *Crime and Punishment* by Dostoevsky. She'll find it awfully interesting.
I:	OK. By the way, when is her birthday? How old is she going to be?
A:	You shouldn't ask a woman's age! She invited us to her place for Thursday. Are you free?
I:	Lord, no! She always has such strange parties. It would be better for us to stay home. I'll buy her the novel tomorrow and send it by mail.

The Dative Case

Of all the inflected forms in contemporary spoken Russian, the dative case is the most widely used, at a frequency of nearly 60 percent of declinable words in any given conversation. This case has syntactical, modal, idiomatic, and other usage—such as the expression of subjective states of being—and, as with other cases, is also governed by certain prepositions and certain verbs.

Forms and Endings

Singular

Happily, the dative case is unusually regular. Masculine and neuter singular nouns take the ending **-у/-ю.**[1] Feminine nouns ending in a consonant plus **a** or **я** take **-e,** and nouns that end in **-ия** or the soft sign take the ending **-и.**

Masculine		Neuter		Feminine	
Nominative	**Dative**	**Nominative**	**Dative**	**Nominative**	**Dative**
Ива́н	Ива́ну	окно́	окну́	газе́та	газе́те
Андре́й	Андре́ю	мо́ре	мо́рю	ку́хня	ку́хне
ру́бль	рублю́	зда́ние	зда́нию	ле́кция	ле́кции
				дверь	две́ри

---

[1] The **-у** ending is used for hard masculine and neuter nouns; the **-ю** ending for soft nouns, i.e., those masculine nouns that end in a soft sign or **-й** and those neuter nouns that end in **-е.**

The endings for adjectives are similarly uncomplicated. Masculine and neuter nouns take the endings **-ому/-ему** and feminine nouns take the ends **-ой/-ей.**[2] The possessive pronoun adjectives **мой/моё/моя, твой/твоё/твоя, наш/наше/наша,** and **ваш/ваше/ваша** behave the same way.

Masculine and Neuter	Feminine
моему́	мое́й
на́шему	на́шей
но́вому	но́вой
ру́сскому	ру́сской
хоро́шему	хоро́шей
после́днему	после́дней

Plural

All nouns, regardless of gender, take the endings **-ам/-ям.**[3]
All adjectives, regardless of gender, take the endings **-ым/-им.**[4]

> **NOTE:**   *There are <u>no</u> exceptions!*

> Examples:
> Мы купи́ли пода́рки всем на́шим ро́дственникам и друзья́м.

We bought gifts for all our relatives and friends.

> Она́ ча́сто пи́шет свои́м ста́рым знако́мым и прия́телям.

She often writes to her old acquaintances and friends.

Pronouns

The table below represents the dative case of interrogative, personal, and indefinite pronouns.

	Singular		Plural	
	Nominative	**Dative**	**Nominative**	**Dative**
Interrogative	кто?	кому́?	что?	чему́?

---

[2] Hard adjectives of all genders take the endings **-ому** or **-ой.** Soft adjectives or those that involve the five-letter spelling rule take the endings **-ему** or **-ей.**

[3] Hard nouns of all genders take **-ам.** Soft nouns of all genders take **-ям.**

[4] Most hard adjectives take the ending **-ым.** All soft adjectives and those hard adjectives to which the seven-letter spelling rule applies take the ending **-им.**

| | Singular | | Plural | |
	Nominative	Dative	Nominative	Dative
Personal	я	мне	мы	нам
	ты	тебе́	вы	вам
	он/оно́	ему́	они	им
Indefinite	всё	всему́[5]	все	всем[5]

Examples:

Я пишу́ тебе́, ты пи́шешь ему́,   I write to you, you write to him,
   он пи́шет ей, она́ пи́шет нам,   he writes to her, she writes to us,
   мы пи́шем вам, вы пишете   we write to you, you write to them,
   им, но никто́ не пи́шет мне!   but no one writes to me!

If you memorize the above Russian sentence, you will know all the dative personal pronouns, as well as the conjugation of the verb *to write!*

Uses

Indirect Object

The primary syntactical use of the dative case is to express the indirect object in a sentence. (The indirect object is usually the person or thing that receives the direct object.)

Examples

Иди́ понеси́ э́тот кило́ са́хара на́шему   Go take this kilo of sugar to our
   но́вому сосе́ду.   new neighbor's house.

Он подари́л свое́й ста́ршей сестре́   He gave his older sister Marina
   Мари́не цветы́ на день рожде́ния.   flowers for her birthday.

Она́ посла́ла приглаше́ния всем свои́м   She sent invitations to all her
   друзья́м и ро́дственникам.   friends and relatives

По суббо́там он звони́т всем чле́нам   On Saturdays he calls all the
   комите́та по улучше́нию   members of the Committee for
   студе́нческого бы́та.   the Improvement of Student Life.

---

[5] **Всё/всему́** means *everything.* **Все/всем** means *everyone, everybody,* which is plural in Russian.

Sometimes the recipient of the direct object may be expressed in Russian by using the preposition **для** plus the genitive case. Thus, **Он купи́л соба́чку свое́й де́вушке** and **Он купи́л соба́чку для свое́й де́вушки** are both acceptable sentences in Russian, corresponding closely to the English *He bought his girlfriend a dog* in the first example and *He bought a dog for his girlfriend* in the second.

Object of Verbs

The dative case is used with certain verbs, the most important of which are **помога́ть, звони́ть, аплоди́ровать, подари́ть, меша́ть, каза́ться, сове́товать, ве́рить, надое́сть, сни́ться** (to dream), **улыба́ться, хоте́ться,** and **нра́виться.**[6]

Не верь ему́—он говори́т то́лько непра́вду.	Don't believe him—he tells only lies.
Мне надое́ло твоё поведе́ние!	I'm fed up with your behavior!
Нам ка́жется, что ты права́.	It seems to us that you are right.
Ему́ не спи́тся.	He can't sleep.
Но́чью мне сни́лся стра́нный сон.	Last night I had a strange dream.
Мне о́чень хо́чется пить.	I'm really thirsty.

The case a verb governs should always be learned together with the verb. A good Russian dictionary will indicate case government by the appropriate forms of **кто́** and **что́,** for example: **зави́довать кому́; ве́рить кому́, чему́; боя́ться кого́, чего́; стать кем, чем.**

Impersonal Expressions

The dative case is used to express the logical subject in impersonal expressions. These are situations in which there is usually a subjective relationship to the situation. Thus, when one says *I am cold,* the meaning conveyed by the grammar in Russian is that *It is cold for me,* while perhaps someone else may feel fine. In fact, if the phrase *I am cold* is translated literally into Russian, the resulting sentence expresses something quite different from what is intended: *I am a cold person.* So be careful not to confuse *I am so disgusted* and *I am so disgusting,* as my grandmother always did.

---

[6] When a noun is formed from a verb, it will often govern the same case as the verb: **дари́ть де́тям** (to give children presents); **пода́рки де́тям** (presents for the children).

The most common impersonal expressions of this type are **хóлодно, теплó, жáрко, интерéсно, скýчно, грýстно, вéсело, жаль,** and others.

Тебé бýдет хóлодно! Возьми с собóй пальтó.	You'll be cold. Take a coat with you.
Нам бы́ло так скýчно на лéкции!	We were so bored at the lecture!
Мне жаль вáшу сестрý.	I'm sorry for your sister
Нам бы́ло óчень вéсело на вечери́нке.	We had a lot of fun at the party.
Почемý тебé так грýстно?	Why are you so sad?
Мне бóльно глотáть.	It hurts (me) to swallow.
Тебé легкó.	It's easy for you.
Мне бы́ло стрáшно.	I was scared.

Permission and Necessity

Expressions involving permission and necessity also require the dative case. **Мóжно** expresses permission; **нельзя́** is used to indicate that permission is being refused or that something is not permitted.

Мáма, мне мóжно пойти́ в кинó сегóдня вéчером?	Mom, may I go to the movies tonight?
Нет, тебé нельзя́. Тебé лýчше сидéть дóма, занимáться.	No. It would be better if you stayed home and studied.
Больнóму нельзя́ кури́ть.	The patient is not allowed to smoke.

Expressions of necessity use the words **надо** and **нужно** interchangeably:

Отцý нáдо поéхать в Рим на командирóвке.	My father has to go to Rome on a business trip.
Брáту нýжно ходи́ть за покýпками.	My brother has to go shopping.

If the expression of necessity involves one action at one time, then use a perfective infinitive: *Vanya has to wash* (**помы́ть**) *the dishes before he goes out tonight.* If you wish to convey a general idea of necessity, use an imperfective verb: *Vanya has to wash* (**мыть**) *the dishes every evening.*

Object of a Preposition

The dative case is used with certain prepositions. By far the most widely used are **к** and **по; благодаря́, согла́сно, вопреки́,** and **навстре́чу** are most frequently encountered in reading.

Я о́чень люблю́ е́здить к ба́бушке в дере́вню.	I really like going to Grandmother's in the countryside.
Де́ти бегу́т к реке́.	The children are running to the river.
Он подошёл к две́ри и вдру́г останови́лся.	He walked up to (as far as) the door and suddenly stopped.
Он равноду́шен к му́зыке.	He is indifferent to music.
Мы шли по у́лице и пе́ли пе́сни.	We walked down the street singing songs.
Тури́сты ходи́ли по магази́нам.	The tourists went from store to store.
А́ся рабо́тает по вечера́м.	Asya works evenings.
Ка́ждый учени́к получи́л по карандашу́.	Every pupil received one pencil.
Благодаря́ дождю́, был прекра́сный урожа́й.	Thanks to the rain, the harvest was wonderful.
Согла́сно реше́нию суда́ . . .	According to the decision of the court . . .
Вопреки́ всем тру́дностям, он око́нчил университе́т во́время.	In spite of all the difficulties, he graduated from college on schedule.

Expressions of Opinion

There are several ways to express opinion in Russian. Since Russian is not an *I/me/my*-centered language, the preferred expressions involve a passive construction using the dative case. Instead of saying **Я ду́маю, что,** a Russian is more likely to say either **по-мо́ему** or **мне ду́мается.**

По-мо́ему, Ва́ня ма́ло занима́ется.	In my opinion (I think that) Vanya studies too little.
Мне ду́мается, что она́ права́.	I think she's right.

NOTE: Pay attention to the stress in the idioms **по-мо́ему** and **по-тво́ему.** They differ from the normal declension of the possessive pronoun only by stress. The latter forms are pronounced **по твоему́ мне́нию** (in your opinion), **по моему́ распоряже́нию** (according to my instruction).

Age

The dative case is used to express age.

Де́вочка! Ско́лько тебе́ лет?	How old are you, little girl?
Мне бу́дет 4 го́да в апре́ле.	I'll be four in April.

Idiomatic Expressions

Переда́й приве́т жене́!	Give my regards to your wife!
Ве́чная па́мять геро́ям.	Eternal memory to the heroes
Чему́ вы ра́ды?	What makes you happy?
Э́то па́мятник Ю́рию Долгору́кому.	This is a monument to Yuri Dolgoruky.
Нам пора́ уйти́.	It's time for us to leave.
Вот вам приме́р.	Here's an example for you.
Ему́ по дела́м.	He got what he deserved.
Я жела́ю вам сча́стья.	I wish you happiness.
Ему́ повезло́!	He got lucky!

TEST FOR MASTERY 1

Complete the sentences below with the correct form of the dative case.

1. Андре́й всегда́ помога́ет (свой глу́пый брат и своя́ мла́дшая сестра́) и они́ помога́ют (him).

2. Зри́тели бу́рно аплоди́ровали (ру́сские балери́ны и орке́стр).

3. Что́ ты подари́л (роди́тели) на Но́вый год? Я подари́л (them) цветы́.

4. И́горь звони́т (своя́ де́вушка) ка́ждый ве́чер, но она́ никогда́ (him) не звони́т.

5. Почему́ ты так кричи́шь? Ты меша́ешь (студе́нты) занима́ться.

6. Де́ти меша́ли (ма́ма) рабо́тать. «Ся́дьте!» она́ (to them) сказа́ла.

7. Сего́дня у́тром мы звони́ли (the doctor), но его́ не́ было.

8. Всё у́тро они́ е́здили (around the city).

9. Я (to them) не нра́влюсь, а они́ (to me) не нра́вятся.

10. Ско́лько лет (your mother)? (She is) со́рок три го́да.

11. Зáвтра (I have to) сидéть дóма. У меня́ урóки по (music).

12. Я жела́ю (you all) сча́стья и здоро́вья.

13. У нас ско́ро бу́дет экза́мен по (physics) и (we will have to) мно́го занима́ться.

14. (Thanks to her help), мы сда́ли все выпускны́е экза́мены.

TEST FOR MASTERY 2

Form sentences describing what you are giving to your family members for the New Year holiday. Use the gifts suggested on the left and the family members listed on the right. Use the verb **подари́ть** or **купи́ть** in the future tense. Remember to place the direct object (what you are giving) into the accusative case and the indirect object (the recipient of your present) into the dative case.

Example: На Но́вый год я подарю́ бы́вшему му́жу коро́бочку у́гля.
(For New Year's I'm giving my former husband a box of coal.)

коро́бка шокола́да	ма́ма
золота́я цепо́чка	па́па
больша́я ба́нка икры́	брат Глеб
но́вый америка́нский детекти́в	сестра́ На́стя
шкату́лка из Па́леха	ба́бушка
дорога́я стереосисте́ма	де́душка
но́вые зу́бы	твой друг/твоя́ де́вушка
креди́тная ка́рточка	тётя Фёкла
косме́тика	дя́дя Ака́кий
япо́нский мотоци́кл	двою́родный брат Са́шка
ма́ленькая мышь	двою́родная сестра́ Ната́ша
уро́дливый га́лстук	моя́ ко́шка Клеопа́тра

TEST FOR MASTERY 3

Перепи́ска. From the following list of Russian authors, compose sentences stating who used to write to whom.

Example: Карамзи́н писа́л Держа́вину. Держа́вин писа́л Пу́шкину.

Авторы: Алекса́ндр Пу́шкин, Михаи́л Ле́рмонтов, Никола́й Го́голь, Фёдор Достое́вский, Лев Толсто́й, Ива́н Турге́нев, Михаи́л

Салтыко́в-Щедри́н, Анто́н Че́хов, Макси́м Го́рький, Евге́ний Замя́тин, Ива́н Бу́нин, Алекса́ндр Солжени́цын, Андре́й Би́тов, Васи́лий Шукши́н

Women's last names do not obey normal declension patterns for feminine nouns. They behave, rather, like the pronominal **эта.** Therefore, feminine last names endings in **-ова, -ева, -ина,** and **-ская** all take the dative ending **-ой.**

Example: Со́ня Толста́я писа́ла Мари́не Цвета́евой.
Áнна Па́влова писа́ла Ма́йе Плисе́цкой.

Moreover, some feminine surnames do not end in a typical feminine suffix. These names tend to be of foreign origin and, like most foreign words in Russian, do not decline.

Example: Áнна Ахма́това писа́ла Наде́жде Мандельшта́м.

TEST FOR MASTERY 4

Given the following information on date of birth, answer the questions: **ма́ма**—1968, **па́па**—1960, **тётя Да́ша**—1963, **соба́ка Зо́я**—2001, **Óля**—1988, **Ви́тя**—1990, **дя́дя Фома́**—1962, **ко́шка Му́рка**—2000, **ба́бушка**—1945, **де́душка**—1940.

1. Ско́лько лет ма́ме?

2. Ско́лько лет па́пе?

3. Кому́ бы́ло 40 лет в 2000-м году́?

4. Кто́ ста́рше: соба́ка и́ли ко́шка? На ско́лько лет?

5. Кто́ са́мый ста́рый челове́к? Ско́лько ему́ лет?

6. Ско́лько лет бы́ло ба́бушке в 2000-м году́?

7. Кто́ ста́рше: тётя Да́ша и́ли дя́дя Фома́?

8. Ско́лько лет бу́дет соба́чке Зо́е в 2005-м году́?

9. Ско́лько лет бы́ло ма́ме и па́пе, когда́ роди́лся Ви́тя?

10. Ско́лько лет бы́ло де́душке и ба́бушке, когда́ родила́сь Óля?

TEST FOR MASTERY 5

Given the information on the birth and death of the following luminaries of Russian literature, answer the questions that follow. Remember the agreement of numbers: if a number ends in 1, use **год;** if it ends in 2, 3, or 4, use **гóда.** For five and above, including the teens and zero, use **лет.** Also, assume that these authors reached their birthday that year.

Гóголь (1809–52)   Солженѝцын (1918–)
Пу́шкин (1799–1837)   Маякóвский (1893–1930)
Достоéвский (1821–81)   Пастернáк (1890–1960)
Тургéнев (1818–83)   Брóдский (1940–1996)
Чéхов (1860–1904)   Ахмáтова (1889–1966)
Толстóй (1826–1910)   Мандельштáм (1891–1938)

1. Скóлько лет бы́ло Гóголю, когдá он у́мер?

2. Скóлько лет бы́ло Пу́шкину, когдá он у́мер?

3. Скóлько лет бы́ло Достоéвскому, когдá он у́мер?

4. Скóлько лет бы́ло Тургéневу, когдá он у́мер?

5. Скóлько лет бы́ло Чéхову, когдá он у́мер?

6. Скóлько лет бы́ло Толстóму, когдá он у́мер?

7. Скóлько лет бы́ло Солженѝцыну, когдá он у́мер?

8. Скóлько лет бы́ло Маякóвскому, когдá он у́мер?

9. Скóлько лет бы́ло Пастернáку, когдá он у́мер?

10. Скóлько лет бы́ло Брóдскому, когдá он у́мер?

11. Скóлько лет бы́ло Ахмáтовой, когдá онá умерлá?

12. Скóлько лет бы́ло Мандельштáму, когдá он у́мер?

Constructions for Advanced Students

Два плюс два равнó четырём.   Two plus two is four.
Три умнóженное на шестнáдцать   Three multiplied by sixteen equals
    равня́ется сорокá восьми́.   forty-eight.

Почему́ на тебе́ три цепо́чки?	Why are you wearing three chains?
Э́то тебе́ не Калифо́рния!	What do you think this is—California?
Он пожа́л мне ру́ку.	He shook my hand.
По суббо́там мы обы́чно хо́дим в кино́, но в э́ту суббо́ту мы пое́дем за город.	On Saturdays we usually go to the movies, but this Saturday we are going out of town.
—Хо́чешь идти́ в музе́й?	Want to go to the museum?
—Нет. Сего́дна мне не до музе́ев.	No. I'm not up to museums today.
Нам говори́ть, а тебе́ слу́шать.	It's for us to speak and you to listen.
Вам бы похуде́ть.	You ought to lose some weight.
Ему́ бы гуля́ть побо́льше.	He should walk more.
Нам не́где сиде́ть.	We have nowhere to sit.
Мне не́ с кем говори́ть.	I have no one to talk to.
Ей не́чего сказа́ть ему́.	She has nothing to say to him.
Мне не́когда его ви́деть	I have no time to see him.

ANSWER KEY

Vocabulary Practice

1. духи́
2. Междунаро́дный же́нский день
3. меша́ют
4. пода́ришь
5. цепо́чки

6. на самолёте
7. писа́л
8. ми́шки и ку́клы
9. на́до
10. ювели́рные изде́лия

Test for Mastery 1

1. своему́ глу́пому бра́ту и свое́й мла́дшей сестре́ / ему́
2. ру́сским балери́нам и орке́стру
3. роди́телям / им
4. свое́й де́вушке / ему́
5. студе́нтам
6. ма́ме / им

7. врачу́

8. по го́роду

9. им / мне

10. ва́шей ма́тери / ей

11. мне на́до (*or* нужно) бу́дет / му́зыке

12. вам всем

13. фи́зике / нам на́до (*or* ну́жно) бу́дет

14. Благодаря́ её по́мощи

Test for Mastery 2

Your answers may vary from those given here.

1. Я подарю́ ма́ме но́вый америка́нский детекти́в.

2. Я куплю́ па́пе уро́дливый га́лстук.

3. Мы пода́рим бра́ту Гле́бу дорогу́ю стереосисте́му.

4. Глеб ку́пит сестре́ На́сте косме́тику.

5. Ма́ма пода́рит ба́бушке но́вые зу́бы.

6. Ба́бушка ку́пит де́душке коро́бку шокола́да.

7. Я куплю́ де́вушке/дру́гу но́вые часы́.

8. Ма́ма пода́рит тёте Фёкле япо́нский мотоци́кл.

9. Сестра́ На́стя пода́рит дя́де Ака́кию креди́тную ка́рточку.

10. Я куплю́ двою́родному бра́ту Са́шке большу́ю ба́нку икры́.

11. Брат Глеб пода́рит двою́родной сестре́ Ната́ше шкату́лку из Па́леха.

12. Па́па ку́пит мое́й ко́шке Клеопа́тре золоту́ю цепо́чку.

Test for Mastery 3

1. Пу́шкин писа́л Ле́рмонтову.

2. Ле́рмонтов писа́л Го́голю.

3. Го́голь писа́л Достое́вскому.

4. Достое́вский писа́л Толсто́му.

5. Толсто́й писа́л Турге́неву.

6. Турге́нев писа́л Салтыко́ву-Щедрину́.

7. Салтыко́в-Щедри́н писа́л Че́хову.

8. Че́хов писа́л Го́рькому.

9. Го́рький писа́л Замя́тину.

10. Замя́тин писа́л Бу́нину.

11. Бу́нин писа́л Солжени́цыну.

12. Солжени́цын писа́л Би́тову.

13. Би́тов писа́л Шукшину́.

Test for Mastery 4

The answers will depend on the current year. The answers that follow are based on the year 2002.

1. Ма́ме 34 го́да.

2. Па́пе 42 го́да.

3. В 2000-м году́ па́пе бы́ло 40 лет.

4. Ко́шка Му́рка ста́рше на (оди́н) год.

5. Са́мый ста́рый челове́к—э́то де́душка. Ему́ 62 го́да.

6. В 2000-м году́ ба́бушке бы́ло 55 лет.

7. Дя́дя Фома́ ста́рше на год.

8. В 2005-м году́ соба́чке Зо́е бу́дет 4 го́да.

9. Когда́ роди́лся Ви́тя, ма́ме бы́ло 22 го́да и па́пе бы́ло 30 лет.

10. Когда́ родила́сь Оля, де́душке бы́ло 48 лет и ба́бушке бы́ло 43 го́да.

Test for Mastery 5

1. Ему́ бы́ло 43 го́да.

2. Ему́ бы́ло 38 лет.

3. Ему́ бы́ло 60 лет.

4. Ему́ бы́ло 65 лет.

5. Ему́ бы́ло 44 го́да.

6. Ему́ бы́ло 84 го́да.

7. Он пока́ не у́мер!

8. Ему́ бы́ло 37 лет.

9. Ему́ бы́ло 70 лет.

10. Ему́ бы́ло 56 лет.

11. Ей бы́ло 77 лет.

12. Ему́ бы́ло 47 лет.

Aspect of Verbs

Вид глагола

Useful Vocabulary

Verbs (Imperfective Verb Listed First)

чита́ть	прочита́ть	to read
повторя́ть	повтори́ть	to review, repeat
учи́ть	вы́учить	to study
забыва́ть	забы́ть	to forget
де́лать	сде́лать	to do
покупа́ть	купи́ть	to buy
рисова́ть	нарисова́ть	to draw
стро́ить	постро́ить	to build
отвеча́ть	отве́тить	to answer
боле́ть	заболе́ть	to be sick / to get sick
убира́ть	убра́ть	to clean up
слу́шать	послу́шать	to listen to
отдыха́ть	отдохну́ть	to relax
изуча́ть	изучи́ть	to study

CONVERSATION PRACTICE

Пе́рвого Сентября́

Учи́тель:	Здра́вствуйте, друзья́! Дава́йте познако́мимся. Меня́ зову́т Анто́н Па́влович.
Ученики́:	Здра́втсвуйте, Анто́н Па́влович.
Учи́тель:	А как вас зову́т?
Учени́к:	Меня́ зову́т Ма́рк.
Учени́ца 1:	Меня́ зову́т Па́мела.
Учени́ца 2:	Меня́ зову́т Ребе́кка.
Учи́тель:	Добро́ пожа́ловать! Дава́йте начнём занима́ться. Вы уже́ прочита́ли пе́рвый уро́к?
Ребе́кка:	Да, прочита́ли.
Учи́тель:	Вы чита́ли со словарём, и́ли без словаря́?
Марк:	Я чита́л без словаря́.
Учи́тель:	А ты, Па́мела?
Па́мела:	И я без словаря́.
Ребе́кка:	Я то́же чита́ла без словаря́.
Учи́тель:	Зна́чит, вы повтори́ли слова́, кото́рые вы учи́ли в про́шлом году́?
Марк:	Да, я повтори́л все слова́.
Па́мела:	Я повторя́ла слова́, но повтори́ла ещё не все.
Учи́тель:	А ты, Ребе́кка, повторя́ла слова́?
Ребе́кка:	Я не повторя́ла. Я, наве́рное, хорошо́ вы́учила их в про́шлом году́ и сейча́с все по́мню.
Марк:	Я то́же в про́шлом году́ хорошо́ учи́л слова́, но ле́том не́которые забы́л.
Ребе́кка:	А я ле́том мно́го чита́ла по-ру́сски.
Марк:	Ну, тогда́, коне́чно, ты не забы́ла слова́.
Учи́тель:	Ребе́кка, а что ты чита́ла ле́том?
Ребе́кка:	Я чита́ла кни́ги о Росси́и. Мне интере́сно чита́ть по-ру́сски об э́той стране́. Но ещё тру́дно.
Учи́тель:	Мы бу́дем мно́го чита́ть о Росси́и. И начнём уже́ сего́дня.
Марк:	О чём мы бу́дем чита́ть сего́дня?
Учи́тель:	Сего́дня мы бу́дем чита́ть о Да́льнем Восто́ке.
Па́мела:	Прекра́сно! Мы ещё ма́ло зна́ем о Да́льнем Восто́ке.

The First of September

TEACHER:	Hello, friends! Let's introduce ourselves. My name is Anton Pavlovich.
STUDENTS:	Hello, Anton Pavlovich!
TEACHER:	And what are your names?
MALE STUDENT:	My name is Mark.
FEMALE STUDENT 1:	My name is Pamela.
FEMALE STUDENT 2:	My name is Rebecca.
TEACHER:	Welcome! Let's start working. Have you already read the first lesson?
REBECCA:	Yes, we have.
TEACHER:	Did you read with or without a dictionary?
MARK:	I read without a dictionary.
TEACHER:	And you, Pamela?
PAMELA:	I read without a dictionary, too.
REBECCA:	I also read without a dictionary.
TEACHER:	So have you (all) reviewed the vocabulary that you studied last year?
MARK:	Yes, I reviewed all the words.
PAMELA:	I reviewed (some) words, but haven't done them all.
TEACHER:	And you, Rebecca? Have you reviewed the vocabulary?
REBECCA:	No, I didn't. I guess I learned them pretty well last year, and so I remember all of them now.
MARK:	I also studied the vocabulary well last year, but over the summer I forgot some of them.
REBECCA:	I read a lot in Russian this summer.
MARK:	Well then, of course you didn't forget the vocabulary.
TEACHER:	Rebecca, what did you read this summer?
REBECCA:	I read books about Russia. It's interesting for me to read about this country in Russian. But it's still difficult.
TEACHER:	We will be reading about Russia a lot. Let's begin today.
MARK:	What are we going to read about today?
TEACHER:	Today we're going to read about the Far East.
PAMELA:	Great! We still know very little about the Far East.

Conversation Notes

1. Russian schoolchildren traditionally return to school every year on September 1, except if that date falls on a weekend. In the younger grades they bring

flowers for their teachers on the first day of school. Russian children wear uniforms. Almost every little girl wears a large bow in her hair called a **бантик.**

2. The teacher introduces himself as Anton Pavlovich, using his first name and patronymic. This is a very formal type of address. It is comparable to Western usage of an honorific such as Mr. plus last name, which is rarely encountered in Russia. To give you an idea of the formality of first name and patronymic, the Russian leader is addressed this way in almost all situations: **«Михаи́л Серге́евич, мы хоте́ли бы . . .»** would roughly correspond to "*Mr. Gorbachev, we would like to. . . .*"

3. The situation in this dialogue is a Russian language class for advanced foreigners. They are still young, so the teacher addresses them individually as **ты** but as a group as **вы** (*you all*).

Aspect

For each verb in English there exist two forms in Russian, called the imperfective and the perfective aspect. These forms serve to convey different ideas about the nature of the verb, whether the focus is on completion or result (perfective), or whether the emphasis is on the action itself (imperfective). This dual nature of the Russian verb produces an extremely simple verb system of only five tenses: the imperfective past and future, the perfective past and future, and the present tense, which is imperfective only. The concepts upon which this system depends, however, are as opaque and impenetrable as the use of articles is in English for foreign speakers. You will make progress in understanding the difference between the forms and in choosing the correct aspect, but you will never achieve complete proficiency in this area. But there is hope: first, your chances of making the right choice are 50–50, and second, if you make a mistake you will still be understood—you will just sound odd.

Perfective verbs in Russian convey the idea of completeness, and they may often point to the result or product of the action of the verb or emphasize the moment of completion. This is the bottom line. You must have a specific, compelling reason for using the perfective aspect. If you do not, then the imperfective is used. The imperfective, therefore, is the default verb.

Some words in a sentence may lead you to choose perfective. Among them are **уже́** and **наконе́ц,** which point to a result that has been awaited or expected: **«Вы уже́ прочита́ли пе́рвый уро́к?»** By using the perfective aspect, the teacher is asking whether the students have completed reading the first chapter and, by implication, whether they know the material.

If the teacher had merely asked, **«Что вы де́лали вчера́?»** (*"What did you do yesterday?"*), the reply would be **«Я чита́л уро́к»** (*"I read the lesson"*). This reply does not exclude the possibility that the student read the lesson completely! But the student is answering the question posed, which asks for a list of the activities that took place. *I read the lesson* means that *I spent some time reading the lesson.* It expresses nothing more. The lesson may have been finished or may not yet be finished. These considerations are irrelevant in the given exchange.

One last thing: Remember that all verbs in the past tense are completed. It is not sufficient to say that the action of the verb is completed and therefore the perfective is the proper choice. To use the perfective for this reason, the speaker must be focusing on the moment of completion: **Я вста́л в семь часо́в** (*I got up at seven o'clock*) or **Он пришёл домо́й о́чень по́здно** (*He came home very late*).

Comment 1

A good way to illustrate the added meanings of verbal aspect is to analyze the use of verbs in the text that begins this lesson. The teacher first says, **«Добро́ пожа́ловать! Начнём занима́ться. Вы уже́ прочита́ли пе́рвый уро́к?»** The first clue that the perfective is appropriate is the use of the word **уже́.** The teacher wants to know not only whether the students completed the first lesson but whether he may then proceed with the material, assuming that the students have learned it.

Sometimes the difference between the two aspects of the same verb is happily conveyed into English by differing translations:

Я сдава́ла контро́льную.	I took the exam.
Я сдала́ контро́льную.	I passed the exam.
Он учи́л но́вые слова́.	He studied the new words.
Он вы́учил но́вые слова́.	He learned the new words.
Вчера́ она́ реша́ла зада́чи.	Yesterday she worked on (tried to solve) the problems.
Вчера́ она́ реши́ла все зада́чи.	Yesterday she solved all the problems.
Я звони́ла ему́, но его́ не́ было до́ма.	I called him (tried calling him) but he wasn't home.
Я позвони́ла ему́ и мы реши́ли встре́титься в семь часо́в.	I called him (and spoke with him), and we decided to meet at seven.

In other words, use of the imperfective aspect implies that the subject made an attempt to perform the action of the verb; the perfective aspect conveys the added information that the action was successfully performed.

Comment 2

The question **«Вы чита́ли со словарём, и́ли без словаря́?»** can be translated as *"Did you read with a dictionary or without one?"* or as *"Did you use a dictionary while you were reading?"* There are two reasons that the imperfective verb is used here. First, the focus of the question is not on whether the assignment was finished but on whether a dictionary was or was not used. Second, the actual phrase that contains the verb accurately translates as *while you were reading*. Whenever you use an *-ing* verb form in English, you can bet that you will use an imperfective verb in Russian.

Consider the aspects of the verbs in the following dialogue:

—Вы <u>чита́ли</u> рома́н «Идио́т» Достое́вского?

—Нет, я не чита́л э́ту кни́гу.

—А «А́нну Каре́нину» Толсто́го <u>чита́ли</u>?

—Да, <u>чита́л</u>.

—Вы <u>чита́ли</u> э́тот рома́н по-ру́сски?

—Да, я <u>чита́л</u> его́ по-ру́сски со словарём.

—Вы <u>прочита́ли</u> всю кни́гу?

—Да, всю.

The first person wants to know whether the second person has read (or has ever attempted to read) *The Idiot*. The second replies that no, the action was never performed. If an action was never performed, never even begun, there can be no completion point or result. Next, the first person asks about *Anna Karenina*. The second replies, *"Yes, I did."* Now, even though one might be tempted to assume that the second person read the entire novel, there is no reason for that person to use a perfective verb, because the speaker simply states that the action took place and nothing more. Perhaps there is more; perhaps the speaker picked it up but didn't finish it.

The next question, *"Did you read this novel in Russian?"* focuses not on the completion of the novel but rather on the opposite, the process of reading itself, and that process was done in Russian. This question focuses on how the action was performed. All questions of this type use imperfective verbs. The answer, logically, states how the novel was read: in Russian and with a dictionary.

The last question finally asks something very specific: *"Did you finish reading the entire book?"* Because the word **всю** (entire, whole) points to the totality of the novel, the speaker is obliged to use the perfective verb.

Comment 3

Учи́тель:	Зна́чит, вы <u>повтори́ли</u> слова́, кото́рые вы <u>учи́ли</u> в про́шлом году́?
Марк:	Да, я <u>повтори́л</u> все слова́.
Па́мела:	Я <u>повторя́ла</u> слова́, но <u>повтори́ла</u> ещё не все.

Now the teacher wants to know about results, so he asks in the first clause whether the student reviewed the words. Does the student now know the material? The second clause, however, focuses on an action that took place some time in the past (last year), whose results, if in effect at one time, may have faded completely or have lost their force. Thus, the teacher asks about words that the student tried to learn and uses an imperfective verb. Mark answers the perfective question positively with another perfective verb. Pamela's response is more detailed, so she specifies that she tried to learn or spent some time learning the new words but didn't manage to finish reviewing them.

Comment 4

Учи́тель:	А ты, Ребе́кка, повторя́ла слова́?
Ребе́кка:	Я не повторя́ла. Я, наве́рное, хорошо́ вы́учила их в про́шлом году́ и сейча́с все по́мню.

The teacher asks here whether Rebecca spent any time reviewing—not whether she succeeded in relearning the verbs but whether any time was devoted to the task. To the imperfective answer, she answers imperfectively. The implication of her answer is *"I didn't (have to) review"* because she goes on to say that she (perfectively) learned the words so well last year that she now (successfully) remembers them all. One of the markers that will lead you to choose a perfective verb is if the verb is modified by an adverb that qualifies the results; **хорошо́** is one such adverb.

Comment 5

Марк: Я тóже в прóшлом годý хорошó учи́л словá, но лéтом нéкоторые забы́л.

Mark now adds to the conversation that he, too, spent time studying the words, but since he forgot some of them over the summer, he used the imperfective verb for *studied*.

Comment 6

Учи́тель: Ребéкка, а чтó ты чита́ла лéтом?
Ребéкка: Я чита́ла кни́ги о Росси́и. Мне интерéсно чита́ть по-рýсски об э́той странé.

The teacher now turns to Rebecca and asks what she read during the summer. He uses an imperfective verb simply to focus on the activity of reading. He is not asking her whether she finished reading the things she read; he only wants to know what it was that she read. Here the focus is on the identity of the object, rather than on the completion or result. Her answer, similarly, is a very general statement: books about Russia—not anything specific.

Verbs Associated with Learning

The imperfective and perfective verbs associated with studying and learning show some interesting characteristics between the aspects that should help you remember them. Compare the two aspects of the following verbs:

учи́ть	to try to learn or memorize, to study
вы́учить	to have learned or memorized
изуча́ть	to study (take) a subject in school
изучи́ть	to have mastered a subject, to know everything about it
сдава́ть экза́мен	to take an exam
сдать экза́мен	to pass an exam

поступа́ть в университе́т	to apply to a university
поступи́ть в университе́т	to get into a university
реша́ть зада́чу	to work on a problem
реши́ть зада́чу	to have solved a problem

The imperfective verbs of these pairs always have the connotation of trying to do something, perhaps unsuccessfully. The perfective verbs, on the other hand, state emphatically that the things have been accomplished, that a successful result has been achieved.

Summary

Infinitive

You must memorize a pair of verbs for every one English verb. Generally speaking, aspectual pairs will resemble each other, differing only by prefix or suffix. On rare occasion they will have entirely separate roots.

Past Tense

Both perfective and imperfective verbs are formed regularly from the infinitive.

Perfective verbs are ordinarily used with the words **уже́** and **наконе́ц,** the verbs **удало́сь** and **успе́ть,** and others that point to successful completion.

Perfective verbs can be used only to describe one-time actions.

Imperfective verbs are used whenever any type of frequency is involved, such as **ча́сто, ка́ждый день, раз в неде́лю, всегда́, никогда́, по суббо́там,** and so forth.

Imperfective verbs are used when the result of an action has been negated. (**Я учи́ла слова́, но забы́ла не́сколько.**)

Present Tense

Only conjugated imperfective verbs are used. Perfective verbs cannot be used because they forcefully point to a completion, which can have occurred only in the past or will have occurred in the future but, since they are not a process, cannot take place in the present tense. Therefore, the idea of verbal aspect is not relevant for the present tense.

Future Tense

Imperfective future is formed with the appropriate form of the verb **буд-** plus an imperfective infinitive.

Perfective future is formed by conjugating the perfective infinitive.

Imperative

Perfective verbs are usually used to convey one command at one time: **Съешь óвощи!** (*Eat your vegetables!*).

Imperfective verbs are used to convey general commands or suggestions: **Ешь óвощи кáждый день!** (*Eat vegetables every day!*).

TEST FOR MASTERY

Choose the correct aspect in the past tense.

1. Вчерá я (читáла/прочитáла) «Áнну Карéнину» и сегóдня ýтром (возвращáла/вернýла) эту кнúгу в библиотéку.

2. Вчерá я сидéл дóма весь день. Я (смотрéл/посмотрéл) телевúзор, (слýшал/послýшал) рáдио, (убирáл/убрáл) квартúру, и вéчером (отдыхáл/отдохнýл).

3. Лéтом рабóчие (стрóили/пострóили) дом.

4. В октябрé рабóчие наконéц (стрóили/пострóили) наш дом.

5. В мóлодости я чáсто (рисовáл/нарисовáл).

6. Вáня! Какýю красúвую картúну ты (рисовáл/нарисовáл).

7. Мне нáдо бýдет (убирáть/убрáть) квартúру, потомý что к нам приезжáют гóсти сегóдня вéчером.

8. Мáша всегдá (отвечáла/отвéтила) прáвильно.

9. Ты былá на рынке сегóдня ýтром? Чтó ты (покупáла/купúла)?

10. Сегóдня ýтром на урóке Сáша (болéл/заболéл) и пошёл домóй.

11. На прóшлой недéле я (болéл/заболéл), а тепéрь я совсéм здорóв.

12. В áвгусте мы были в Крымý и прекрáсно (отдыхáли/отдохнýли).

13. Я уже́ (учи́ла/вы́учила) грамма́тику, и я гото́ва к зачёту (*quiz*).

14. В шко́ле он (изуча́л/изучи́л) а́лгебру, но не (изуча́л/изучи́л).

15. Па́ша (чита́л/прочита́л) гро́мко.

ANSWER KEY

Test for Mastery

1. прочита́ла, верну́ла

2. смотре́л, слу́шал, убира́л, отдыха́л

3. стро́или

4. постро́или

5. рисова́л

6. нарисова́л

7. убра́ть

8. отвеча́ла

9. купи́ла

10. заболе́л

11. боле́л

12. отдохну́ли

13. вы́учила

14. изуча́л, изучи́л

15. чита́л

10 Future Tense and Imperative Mode

Будущее время и повелительное наклонение

Useful Vocabulary

Verbs

встава́ть/вста́ть	to get up
встреча́ть/встре́тить	to meet
выключа́ть/вы́ключить	to turn off
выноси́ть/вы́нести	to take out
гото́вить/пригото́вить	to prepare
де́лать/сде́лать	to do, make
есть/съесть	to eat
жа́ловаться/пожа́ловаться на (+ acc.)	to complain
занима́ться	to study
изуча́ть/изучи́ть	to study
ложи́ться/лечь	to lie down
мыть/помы́ть	to wash
обе́дать/пообе́дать	to have dinner
отдыха́ть/отдохну́ть	to rest, relax
писа́ть/написа́ть	to write
пить/вы́пить	to drink
покупа́ть/купи́ть	to buy
преподава́ть	to teach
принима́ть/приня́ть	to take (various senses)

путешéствовать	to travel
садúться/сесть	to sit down
слýшать	to listen (to)
сплéтничать	to gossip
танцевáть	to dance
трóгать/трóнуть	to touch
учить/вы́учить	to memorize
чинúть/починúть	to repair

NOTE: If no perfective is listed, it is because Russian does not normally use one.

Future Tense

As mentioned in the discussion of verbal aspect (chapter 9), there are two future tenses in Russian: imperfective future and perfective future. The imperfective future is the easier of the two, so we shall begin there.

Imperfective

The imperfective future is similar to English in that it is formed with an auxiliary verb. The Russian uses the conjugated form of the infinitive **быть** as the auxiliary, plus the imperfective infinitive.

The imperfective future implies only that an action will take place over some period of time in the future. It says nothing about the end of the action or any results, expected or otherwise. Here are some paradigms:

Читáть	Занимáться	Слýшать мýзыку
я бýду читáть	я бýду занимáться	я бýду слýшать мýзыку
ты бýдешь читáть	ты бýдешь занимáться	ты бýдешь слýшать мýзыку
он бýдет читáть	он бýдет занимáться	он бýдет слýшать мýзыку
онá бýдет читáть	она бýдет занимáться	она бýдет слýшать мýзыку
мы бýдем читáть	мы бýдем занимáться	мы бýдем слýшать мýзыку
вы бýдете читáть	вы бýдете занимáться	вы бýдете слýшать мýзыку
онú бýдут читáть	они бýдут занимáться	они бýдут слýшать мýзыку

Because of this close similarity to English, students tend to quickly learn (and perhaps learn too well) this tense. You will have few problems with it, but be prepared for the second part, the perfective future, covered later in this chapter.

CONVERSATION PRACTICE

Планы на лето

The following people have plans for the summer. Compose sentences stating what they will be doing at their summer destination, choosing from the list of verbs below. Use imperfective future for all of them.

Example: В Крыму́ Ната́ша бу́дет купа́ться в мо́ре.
(In the Crimea Natasha will go swimming in the sea.)

изуча́ть англи́йский язы́к	to study English
танцева́ть и слу́шать му́зыку	to dance and listen to music
отдыха́ть на пля́же	to relax on the beach
чини́ть свою́ ста́рую маши́ну	to repair his old car
жа́ловаться на всё	to complain about everything
занима́ться альпини́змом	to go mountain climbing
преподава́ть тео́рию му́зыки	to teach music theory
путеше́ствовать	to travel
сиде́ть и спле́тничать	to sit and gossip
ходи́ть по магази́нам	to go shopping
пить во́дку весь день	to drink vodka all day

1. Алекса́ндр/заво́д

2. его́ жена́ А́нна/Евро́па

3. их дочь Ири́на/А́льпы

4. их сын Дми́трий/дискоте́ка

5. ста́рая ба́бушка Васили́са/до́ма

6. глухо́й де́душка Ака́кий/до́ма

7. Профе́ссор Ле́нсон/консервато́рия

8. Мада́м Бовари́/Пари́ж

9. И́горь Самсо́нов/Нью-Йо́рк

10. Катери́на Ива́новна/Ита́лия

11. Бори́с Никола́евич/у себя́ в кабине́те

Perfective

This verb tense has no correlate in English. The perfective future expresses the opinion of the speaker that the action mentioned will end successfully or produce a result. Remember, since the future has not yet happened, we cannot know with certainty that this will be so. The speaker is merely expressing his or her conviction and attitude regarding a future event.

Since the perfective future focuses on completion or the production of a result, the perfective future, as well as the perfective past, verb will often sound incomplete without a direct object. The phrase **Я прочитаю** would translate as *I will get read,* which is just as incomplete in English. With its proper complement, however, a complete thought would be expressed in **Я прочитаю эту статью,** translated as *I will get that article read.*

The perfective future is formed by conjugating the perfective infinitive. It is extremely difficult for English speakers to become accustomed to this structure. Since they are still in the process of learning the difference between imperfective and perfective infinitives, native speakers of English do not easily discriminate between the present tense and the perfective future: because they are hearing a conjugated verb, they hear only the present tense. It is slightly easier to form and use the perfective.

Some verbs do not form perfective future. These are verbs that express actions and cannot, or normally do not, lead to results. Such verbs are **жить, играть, заниматься, сидеть, бояться,** among others.

Consider these two paradigms of perfective future:

Прочитать	**Написать**
я прочитаю книгу	я напишу доклад
ты прочитаешь книгу	ты напишешь доклад
он/она прочитает книгу	он/она напишет доклад
мы прочитаем книгу	мы напишем доклад
вы прочитаете книгу	вы напишете доклад
они прочитают книгу	они напишут доклад

Both of these verbs, **прочитать** and **написать,** sound somehow incomplete without the addition of the direct object. Without it your listener is left wondering what will be read or written, since the notion of accomplishment is so strongly emphasized by using this aspect.

Perfective verbs, both past and future, must be used with a sequence of actions because logically the earlier verb(s) must be completed before the later verb(s). To practice this principle, try the following exercise.

TEST FOR MASTERY 1, PART 1

In the left-hand column are activities that must be accomplished before the subject proceeds to go to the places listed in the right-hand column. Form sentences of this type with this information. Change your subjects so that you can practice conjugation at the same time.

Example: Когда́ Джон напи́шет докла́д, он пойдёт на собра́ние. (When/After John writes the report, he will go to the meeting.)

написа́ть докла́д	собра́ние
пообе́дать	кино́
помы́ть посу́ду	гастроно́м
вы́учить но́вые слова́	уро́к
приня́ть душ	спать
встать	ва́нная
встре́тить дру́га	музе́й
купи́ть но́вую маши́ну	дере́вня
вы́ключить телеви́зор	кабине́т
пригото́вить обе́д	столо́вая
сде́лать всё	спа́льня

TEST FOR MASTERY 1, PART 2

For practice you might want to change all of the sentences above into the perfective past tense.

Example: Когда Джон написал доклад, он пошёл на собрание. (After John wrote the report, he went to the meeting.)

Imperative Mode

The formation of the imperative in Russian has a series of straightforward rules that admit very few exceptions.

Formation

First, take the third-person plural of the verb and remove the last two letters:

читáют	мóют	кýрят	готóвят	плáчут
читá-	мо-	кур-	готóв-	плач-

If what remains ends in a vowel, simply add the letter **й.** This is the imperative form. If what remains ends in a consonant, then check the stress of the first-person singular. If the first-person singular is stressed on the end, add the letter **и.** If the first-person singular is stressed on the stem, add the letter **ь.**

The imperatives of the above verbs are therefore **читáй! мой! не курú! готóвь! не плачь!** These forms of the imperative are used when addressing **ты.** When addressing someone or a group as **вы,** add the particle **-те: читáйте! мóйте! не курúте! готóвьте! не плáчьте!**

Reflexive verbs also follow these rules:

Infinitive	Imperative	English
Занимáться	Занимáйся!	Study!
Боя́ться	Не бóйтесь!	Don't be afraid!
Одéться	Одéнься!	Get dressed!
Смея́ться	Не смéйтесь!	Don't laugh!

The only exceptions to these rules are as follows:

1. Verbs whose imperfective/perfective pairs end in **-авать** and **-ать** form their imperative not according to the above rules but from the infinitive stem: **вставáй! давáй! узнавáй! передавáй! дай! узнáй! передáй!**

2. The verbs **встать, есть,** and **лечь** form the imperatives **встань, ешь,** and **ляг** (the expected soft sign in this last verb is missing).

3. There are a few verbs that by their nature do not form imperatives. Two very common ones are **éздить** and **вúдеть.** Instead of these verbs, prefixed verbs with the stem **-езжать** and **смотри!** are used.

4. In verbs such as **пить,** whose present-tense stems consist of a single consonant plus a soft sign, the imperative is formed by adding the fleeting vowel **е,** after which the soft sign changes to **й: пьют → пь → пеь → пей.**

Aspect with Imperative

1. A single command to one person generally uses a perfective verb. It suggests that you strongly want this one action completed, producing the desired

result. However, if you are extending an invitation or offering a suggestion rather than issuing an order, the imperfective verb is normally used. Consider the following:

Imperfective	**English**	**Perfective**	**English**
Сади́тесь, пожа́луйста.	Sit down, please. (Have a seat.)	Сядь!	Sit! (to a dog)
Бери́те кусо́к то́рта.	Take (have) a piece of cake.	Возьми́те торт и понеси́те его́ в столо́вую.	Take the cake and bring it to the dining room.
Входи́те, пожа́луйста.	Come in, please.	Войди́те в кабине́т, па́па ско́ро бу́дет.	Go into the den, dad will be there right away.

2. The imperfective is normally used when there is no reference to a result and/or you are focusing on the action itself, especially if you are focusing on how or where the action should be performed rather than on the result.

Чита́йте гро́мче!	Read more loudly!
Бери́те кни́ги в библиоте́ке.	(You should) borrow books from the library.
Иди́те ме́дленнее!	Walk slower.
Чита́йте э́тот расска́з до́ма.	Read this story at home.
Одева́йся тепло́—на у́лице хо́лодно.	Dress warmly—it's cold outside.

3. The imperfective is used to convey urgency: **Спеши́те! Уже́ во́семь часо́в** (*Hurry up, it's already eight o'clock!*). This is the sense that is intended when a command has to be repeated, especially when that command was originally issued in the perfective:

Опусти́ моне́ту!	Put the coin in! (to a child who wanted to drop the coin into the fare box of a tram himself)
Ну, чего́ ты стои́шь? Опуска́й!	Well, what are you waiting for? Drop it in!
Закро́й окно́.	Close the window.
Ну, закрыва́й!	Well? Close it already!

Прочита́йте второ́е предложе́ние.	Read the second sentence.
Ну, чита́йте!	Well, go on! (Get started!)

In all three examples, the speaker switches aspect to emphasize the fact that you should at least begin the action—forget about the results for the time being.

Aspect with Negative Imperative

If you do not want the action performed, the imperfective imperative is normally the choice:

Не открыва́й окно́.	Don't open the window.
Не буди́ ребёнка.	Don't wake the baby.
Не говори́ ей об э́том—она́ уже́ зна́ет.	Don't tell her—she already knows.
Не пиши́ уро́ки карандашо́м.	Don't do your homework with a pencil.

If the negative imperative, however, includes a sense of warning—*be careful that you don't*—then the perfective is normally used. Compare:

Imperfective	English	Perfective	English
Не тро́гай мои́ ве́щи.	Don't touch my things.	Не тронь плиту́!	Don't touch the stove!
Не говори́ ему́ об э́том.	Don't bother telling him.	Не скажи́ ему́ об э́том—э́то секре́т.	(Make sure you) don't tell him! It's a secret.
Не па́дай ду́хом. (idiom)	Don't lose hope. (Don't let your spirits fall.)	Не упади́—здесь ско́льзко.	Don't fall—it's slippery.

The first example especially illustrates the difference between denying permission and conveying a warning. If you can add to your English thought the idea "*Be careful you don't*" or "*Make sure you don't,*" then you must use the perfective imperative.

TEST FOR MASTERY 2

Mom is giving the orders, but you tell her, "*I don't feel like it.*" Note that her command is given in the perfective (because she wants it done, obviously), but you answer in the imperfective, because the impersonal expression **мне не хо́чется** refers to the action of the verb. If you need help understanding the commands, refer to the answer key for translations.

Example: Пригото́вь уро́ки! → Мне не хо́чется гото́вить уро́ки.

1. Вы́неси му́сор!

2. Ляг спать!

3. Убери́ твою́ ко́мнату!

4. Встань!

5. Закро́й дверь!

6. Съешь о́вощи!

7. Вы́пей молоко́!

8. Помо́й ру́ки!

9. Наде́нь пальто́!

10. Вы́сморкайся!

TEST FOR MASTERY 3

Mom is giving orders, but now you're in a good mood and are willing to obey immediately. Tell her so, saying that you will do it right away.

Example: Пригото́вь уро́ки! → Хорошо́. Я сейча́с их пригото́влю

1. Вы́неси му́сор!

2. Ляг спать!

3. Убери́ твою́ ко́мнату!

4. Встань!

5. Закро́й дверь!

6. Съешь о́вощи!

7. Вы́пей молоко́!

8. Помо́й ру́ки!

9. Наде́нь пальто́!

10. Вы́сморкайся!

ANSWER KEY

Conversation Practice

1. На заво́де Алекса́ндр бу́дет чини́ть свою́ ста́рую маши́ну.

2. В Евро́пе его́ жена́ А́нна бу́дет путеше́ствовать.

3. На А́льпах их дочь Ири́на бу́дет занима́ться альпини́змом.

4. На дискоте́ке их сын Дми́трий бу́дет танцева́ть и слу́шать му́зыку.

5. До́ма ста́рая ба́бушка Васили́са бу́дет сиде́ть и спле́тничать.

6. До́ма глухо́й де́душка Ака́кий бу́дет жа́ловаться на всё.

7. В консервато́рии Профе́ссор Ле́нсон бу́дет преподава́ть тео́рию му́зыки.

8. В Пари́же Мада́м Бо́вари бу́дет ходи́ть по магази́нам.

9. В Нью-Йо́рке И́горь Самсо́нов бу́дет изуча́ть англи́йский язы́к.

10. В Ита́лии Катери́на Ива́новна бу́дет отдыха́ть на пля́же.

11. У себя́ в кабине́те Бори́с Никола́евич бу́дет пить во́дку весь день.

Test for Mastery 1, Part 1

1. Когда́ я пообе́даю, я пойду́ в кино́.

2. Когда́ Ма́ша помо́ет посу́ду, она́ пойдёт в гастроно́м.

3. Когда́ Са́ша вы́учит но́вые слова́, он пойдёт на уро́к.

4. Когда́ вы при́мете душ, вы пойдёте спать.

5. Когда́ О́льга вста́нет, она́ пойдёт в ва́нную.

6. Когда́ мы встре́тим дру́га, мы все пойдём в музе́й.

7. Когда́ я куплю́ но́вую маши́ну, я пое́ду в дере́вню.

8. Когда́ па́па вы́ключит телеви́зор, он пойжёт в кабине́т.

9. Когда́ мы пригото́вим обе́д, мы все пойдём в столо́вую.

10. Когда́ ма́ма сде́лает всё, она́ пойдёт в спа́льню.

Test for Mastery 1, Part 2

1. пообе́дал(а), пошёл/пошла́

2. помы́ла, пошла́

3. вы́учил, пошёл

4. при́няли, пошли́

5. вста́ла, пошла́

6. встре́тили, пошли́

7. купи́л(а), пое́хал(а)

8. вы́ключил, пошёл

9. пригото́вили, пошли́

10. сде́лала, пошла́

Test for Mastery 2

1. (Take out the garbage!) Мне не хо́чется выноси́ть му́сор.

2. (Go to sleep!) Мне не хо́чется ложи́ться спать.

3. (Clean up your room!) Мне не хо́чется убира́ть ко́мнату.

4. (Get up!) Мне не хо́чется встава́ть.

5. (Close the door!) Мне не хо́чется закрыва́ть дверь.

6. (Eat your vegetables!) Мне не хо́чется есть о́вощи.

7. (Drink your milk!) Мне не хо́чется пить молоко́.

8. (Wash your hands!) Мне не хо́чется мыть ру́ки.

9. (Put on your coat!) Мне не хо́чется надева́ть пальто́.

10. (Blow your nose!) Мне не хо́чется сморка́ться.

Test for Mastery 3

1. вы́несу

2. ля́гу

3. уберу́

4. вста́ну

5. закро́ю

6. съем

7. вы́пью

8. помо́ю

9. наде́ну

10. вы́сморкаюсь

<u>11</u> The Dative Case (continued)

Дательный падеж (продолжение)

Useful Vocabulary

The Telephone

брать / взять трубку	to pick up the receiver
набира́ть / набра́ть но́мер	to dial the / a number
ждать гудка́	to wait for a dial tone
ре́зкий гудок	busy signal
ве́шать / пове́сить трубку	to hang up the receiver
телефо́н-автома́т	pay phone
опуска́ть / опусти́ть моне́ту	to drop in the coin
ме́лочь	change
жето́н	token
телефо́нная ка́рточка	calling card
попа́сть не туда́	to get a wrong number
набра́ть не тот но́мер	to dial the wrong number
подходи́ть / подойти́ к телефо́ну	to answer the telephone
звони́ть / позвони́ть	to call
дозвони́ться	to reach
разгова́ривать	to talk, converse
болта́ть	to chat
перезвони́ть	to call back

Какóй твой телефóн?	What's your telephone number?
Мóжно + асс.	May I spcak with X?
Позовúте, пожáлуйста, + асс.	May I speak with X?
Попросúте, пожáлуйста, + асс.	May I speak with X?
Чтó-нибудь передáть?	May I take a message?

CONVERSATION PRACTICE

Телефóн

Дéйствующие лúца

Лéна: студéнтка в МГУ
Пéтя: аспирáнт Филологúческого факультéта
Áлик: хúмик, рабóтает в чáстной лаборатóрии

Сцéна: в библиотéке

ЛЕ́НА:	Пéтя! Мне надоéло читáть и занимáться. Давáй пойдём на дискотéку сегóдня вéчером.
ПÉТЯ:	Тúше, Лéна! Э́то тебé не футбóльный матч, а библиотéка!
Л:	Я извиняюсь. Но у меня прекрáсная идéя! Пойдём сегóдня вéчером на дискотéку. Мы мóжем танцевáть до утрá. Давáй забýдем про всё э́то.
П:	Я соглáсен. Я ни странúчку бóльше читáть не могý. Но не хóчешь приглaсúть Áлика? Навéрно, емý совсéм скýчно в э́той тёмной и мáленькой лаборатóрии.
Л:	Договорúлись. Где ближáйший телефóн-автомáт?
П:	У глáвного вхóда. У тебя мéлочь есть?
Л:	Нет, но жетóн у меня есть. Пошлú позвонúть!

Сцéна: на ýлице
(Лéна берёт трýбку, опускáет жетóн, и ждёт гудкá. Потóм онá набирáет нóмер.)

Л:	Никтó не подхóдит. (Онá ждёт.)
ЖÉнский гóлос:	Слýшаю вас!
Л:	Попросúте, пожáлуйста, Алексáндра Михáйловича.
Ж:	Здесь нет никакóго Алексáндра Михáйловича. Вы не тудá попáли.
Л:	Извинúте, пожáлуйста.

П:	Что́ случи́лось—ты оши́блась но́мером?
Л:	Очеви́дно, да. Я опя́ть перезвоню́.

(Ле́на второ́й раз набира́ет но́мер.)

Мужско́й го́лос:	Алло́!
Л:	До́брый день. Бу́дьте добры́, позови́те, пожалуйста, Алекса́ндра Миха́йловича.
М:	Сейча́с, позову́.

(че́рез мину́ту)

М:	Его́ нет сего́дня. Он заболе́л и пошёл домо́й. Что́-нибудь ему́ переда́ть?
Л:	Спаси́бо, нет. Я ему́ перезвоню́ домо́й.

(вешает тру́бку)

Л:	Ну, Петь. А́лик бо́лен—бе́дное дитя́!
П:	Да, мне жаль его́.
Л:	Зна́ешь что? Мне бо́льше не хо́чется танцева́ть. Дава́й лу́чше зайдём к А́лику домо́й.
П:	Договори́лись. Мне то́же не до дискоте́к. Пошли́.

(Ухо́дят все.)

The Telephone

Dramatis personae
Lena: a student at Moscow State University
Petya: a graduate student in the Languages Department
Alik: a chemist working in a private laboratory

Scene: at the library

LENA:	Petya! I'm sick of reading and studying. Let's go to the disco tonight.
PETYA:	Shhh, Lena. What do you think this is, a soccer game? It's a library!
L:	I apologize. But I have a great idea. Let's go to a discotheque tonight. We can dance until morning. Let's forget about all of this.

P:	I agree. I can't read a single page more. But wouldn't you like to invite Alik? He's probably bored in his small, dark laboratory.
L:	Agreed. Where's the nearest pay phone?
P:	At the main entrance. Do you have change?
L:	No, but I have a token. Let's go make the call.

Scene: on the street

(Lena picks up the receiver, deposits her token, and waits for the dial tone. Then she dials the number.)

L:	No one's answering. (She waits.)
WOMAN'S VOICE:	May I help you?
L:	May I speak with Alexander Mikhailovich?
W:	There's no Alexander Mikhailovich here. You dialed the wrong number.
L:	Excuse me, please.
P:	What happened? Did you get the number wrong?
L:	Apparently so. I'll try again.

(Lena dials a second time.)

MAN'S VOICE:	Hello?
L:	Good afternoon. Would you be so kind as to call Alexander Mikhailovich to the phone?
M:	I'll get him right away.

(after a minute)

M:	He's not here today. He got sick and went home. Can I take a message?
L:	No, thanks. I'll call him at home.

(hangs up)

L:	Well, Pete. Alik's sick, poor baby.
P:	Yes, I feel sorry for him.
L:	You know what? I don't feel like dancing any more. Let's go visit Alik instead.
P:	OK. I don't feel like going to a discotheque either. Let's go.

(Exeunt omnes.)

Conversation Comments

How to Say "Hello"

Most Russians answer the phone with **«Алло»**, pronounced either with a soft or a hard *l*. **«Слушаю»** or **«Слушаю вас»**, which do not sound as casual as their literal translation ("*I'm listening to you*"), are also frequently heard. This response may correspond to "*May I help you?*" Some people answer the phone with a simple **«Да»**. In general, the telephone conversation of most Russians is exceedingly brief, even curt, when compared with our own. They dispense with many of the niceties and don't feel the need to provide excuses as to why they must hang up. Do not be offended if you are suddenly faced with a dead line!

Никто не Подходит

This phrase is translated literally as "*No one's approaching*," meaning that no one is coming to the telephone.

How to Ask for Someone

By far the easiest way to ask for someone is to use the word **можно** plus the accusative case, which conveys, "*May I speak with X?*": **Мо́жно Бо́рю, пожа́луйста? Мо́жно Софи́ю Семёновну?**

Another way to ask for someone is to use **попроси́те** or **позови́те** (*ask* or *call*) plus the accusative of the person wanted: **Попроси́те к телефо́ну Ива́на Фёдоровича, пожа́луйста.**

To ask **«Бо́ря до́ма?»** ("*Is Borya home?*") is possible but is much more rarely used than it is in English.

Wrong Number

If you get a wrong number, someone will tell you that **«Вы не туда́ попа́ли»** ("*You arrived not there*") or **«Вы оши́блись но́мером»** ("*You made a mistake with the number*"). Apologize and hang up.

Бу́дьте Добры *or* Бу́дьте Любезны

These expressions translate as "*Would you be so kind as to*" and are rather formal—and very polite—in tone. Lena is being ultrapolite, since she is calling Alik at his place of employment.

Taking a Message

«Что-нибудь переда́ть?» literally translates as "*Something to convey?*" and basically means "*May I take a message?*"

More Uses of the Dative Case

A previous chapter covered several common uses of the dative case: as indirect object, the object of certain prepositions, and to express a person's age. There are many further uses of this case, the most widely used in spoken Russian.

Certain Verbs

Here is a list of verbs, by no means complete, that take dative case, listed in alphabetical order:

ве́рить / пове́рить	to believe
зави́довать / позави́довать	to envy
запреща́ть / запрети́ть	to forbid
звони́ть / позвони́ть	to call, telephone
меша́ть / помеша́ть	to annoy, bother, get in the way
обеща́ть / пообеща́ть	to promise
отвеча́ть / отве́тить	to answer
позволя́ть / позво́лить	to allow, permit
помога́ть / помо́чь	to help
принадлежа́ть	to belong
ра́доваться / обра́доваться	to rejoice
разреша́ть / разреши́ть	to allow, permit
сле́довать / после́довать	ought to, should
сове́товать / посове́товать	to advise
удивля́ться / удиви́ться	to be surprised
улыба́ться / улыбну́ться	to smile

Examples

Не на́до зави́довать бога́тому челове́ку.	You shouldn't envy a rich person.
Позво́льте (разреши́те) мне предста́вить вам Наста́сью Фили́пповну.	Allow me to present to you Nastasya Filippovna.
Я тебе́ обеща́ю, что всё сде́лаю до за́втра.	I promise you that I will get everything done before tomorrow.
Вам сле́довало бы так не говори́ть.	You shouldn't have talked like that.
Младе́нец вдруг улыбну́лся ма́ме.	The baby suddenly smiled at his mother.
Я звони́ла ему́ весь день.	I tried calling him all day.

На́ша Ю́лия Я́ковлевна помога́ет бе́дным и голо́дным.	Our Yulia Yakovlevna helps the poor and the hungry.
Что́ вы посове́туете мне де́лать?	What do you advise me to do?
Я удиви́лась его́ наха́льству.	I was astonished at his insolence.

Impersonal Verbs

каза́ться / показа́ться	to seem, appear
надоеда́ть / надое́сть	to be fed up with, sick of
нездоро́виться	to feel sick
нра́виться / понра́виться	to like
приходи́ться / прийти́сь	to have to
спа́ться	to fall asleep
хвата́ть / хвати́ть	to be enough, to suffice
хоте́ться	to feel like

Examples

Мне ка́жется, что ты прав.	It seems to me that you're right.
Нам надое́ло занима́ться.	We're sick of studying.
Мне нездоро́вится.	I don't feel well.
Как вам нра́вятся мои́ но́вые ту́фли?	How do you like my new shoes?
Вам придётся ждать.	You will have to wait.
Ему́ не спи́тся.	He can't fall asleep.
Нам не хвата́ет хле́ба.	We don't have enough bread.
Мне не хо́чется танцева́ть.	I don't feel like dancing.

Impersonal Expressions

мо́жно	one may, it is permitted
нельзя́	one may not, it is forbidden
жаль	feel sorry for
пора́	it's time

Examples

Ма́ма, мне мо́жно ходи́ть в кино́?	Mom, may I go to the movies?
Здесь нельзя́ кури́ть.	Smoking is not allowed here.
Мне жаль его́.	I feel sorry for him.
Нам пора́ идти́ домо́й.	It's time for us to go home.

Subjective Feelings

Мне жа́рко (*I'm hot*) / **хо́лодно** (*cold*) / **ску́чно** (*bored*) / **ве́село** (*happy*) / **гру́стно** (*sad*) / **сты́дно** (*ashamed*).

Expressing Necessity

The synonymous short adjectives **на́до** and **ну́жно** plus an infinitive are used to express necessity:

Мне на́до занима́ться.	I have to study.
Тебе́ ну́жно встре́тить Са́шу на вокза́ле.	You have to meet Sasha at the train station.
Ему́ на́до бы́ло пойти́ домо́й.	He had to go home.
Андре́ю ну́жно бу́дет позвони́ть в больни́цу.	Andrei will have to call the hospital.

The word **необходи́мо** is used the same way. It conveys a stronger degree of necessity than **на́до/ну́жно.**

Needing

In Russian, the expression is reversed: the thing that is needed is the grammatical subject of the sentence and stands in the nominative case. The short adjective **ну́жен** agrees with the subject in gender and number. The person who needs is in the dative case:

Мне ну́жен но́вый велосипе́д.	I need a new bicycle.
Ему́ нужна́ была́ но́вая маши́на.	He needed a new car.
Вам не ну́жно бы́ло ра́дио?	Didn't you need a radio?
Тебе́ ну́жны бу́дут де́ньги.	You will need money.
А́нне ну́жен бу́дет план го́рода.	Anna will need a map of the city.

NOTE: Because these sentences have a grammatical subject—that is, a word that appears in the nominative case—the verb in the past tense will agree in gender and number with that subject. The auxiliary in the future tense will agree in number only.

Negative Pronouns

These pronouns, with the stress on the first syllable, differ from the negative pronouns prefixed in **ни-** that must be used with a negated verb. Their basic meaning is "*There is no X for someone to Y.*" Consider these examples:

Мне не́где жить.	I have nowhere to live. (There is nowhere for me to live.)
Ему́ не́когда отдыха́ть.	He has no time to relax.
Бори́су не́ с кем разгова́ривать.	Boris has no one to talk to.
Ли́зе не́чего де́лать.	Liza has nothing to do.
Им не́куда бы́ло пое́хать.	They had nowhere to go.

The following sentence, interestingly, has two complements in the dative case, for separate reasons. **Ей** is dative because of **не́кому**; **не́кому** is dative because it is governed by the verb **звони́ть**: **Ей не́кому звони́ть** (*She has no one to call/ There is no one for her to call*).

Note that **не́кого** and **не́чего** have a full declension, except for the nominative case. Note also that if a preposition is required, it is inserted between the prefix and the stem. See the third example above.

Interrogative Pronouns Plus the Infinitive

Что́ мне де́лать?	What am I to do?
Где им жить?	Where are they (supposed) to live?
Что́ мне бы́ло сказа́ть?	What was I supposed to say?

> **NOTE:** Since the expressions in the sections "Impersonal Expressions," "Subjective Feelings," "Expressing Necessity," "Negative Pronouns," and "Interrogative Pronouns" are impersonal, the past tense is formed with the neuter **бы́ло** and the future tense with the third-person singular **бу́дет**. These auxiliaries have no effect on the aspect of the infinitive that follows.

TEST FOR MASTERY

Fill in the blanks with the correct word that governs the dative case.

1. Ма́ме _____ но́вая кастрю́ля. (needs)

2. Тебе́ _____ занима́ться до́ма. (will have to)

3. Мне _____ без тебя. (was bored)

4. Я _____ ему до после́дней ка́пли кро́ви! (envy)

5. Мне _____ тебя́. (sorry)

6. Как вам _____ Москва́? (like)

7. На про́шлой неде́ле ему́ не _____. (sleep)

8. Нельзя́ _____ э́тому челове́ку. (believe)

9. Мне _____ идти́ домо́й. (it's time)

10. Он мне _____ быть до́ма к пяти́. (promised)

11. Не _____ мне! Я о́чень занята́! (bother)

12. Больно́му _____ кури́ть. (is not allowed)

Test for Mastery

1. нужна́

2. на́до бу́дет / ну́жно бу́дет

3. бы́ло ску́чно

4. зави́дую

5. жаль

6. нра́вится

7. спало́сь

8. ве́рить

9. пора́

10. обеща́л

11. меша́й

12. нельзя́

12 The Genitive Case

Родительный падеж

Useful Vocabulary

Verbs

боя́ться	to be afraid of
избега́ть	to avoid
тре́бовать	to demand, require
жела́ть	to wish (somebody something)
пуга́ться	to be scared by
достига́ть	to achieve
заслу́живать	to deserve
ко́нчиться	to be out of

Adverbs of Quantity

ско́лько	how much?
мно́го	a lot, many
не́сколько	several, a few
ма́ло	(very) few
немно́го	some, a few
сто́лько	how many!

Food

бухáнка	loaf	помидóры	tomatoes
ветчинá	ham	рис	rice
винó	wine	сáхар	sugar
водá	water	соль	salt
горóх	peas	сосíски	hot dogs
икрá	caviar	суп	soup
конфéты	candy	сыр	cheese
конья́к	cognac	торт	cake
лук	onions	хлеб	bread
мáсло	butter	чай	tea
мёд	honey	чеснóк	garlic
óвощи	vegetables	шоколáд	chocolate
пéрец	pepper		

Other

отдéл	department

CONVERSATION PRACTICE

В гастронóме

Девушка:	Слýшаю вас!
Покупатель:	Скажи́те, пожáлуйста, сегóдня у вас есть фрáнцýзский сыр?
Д:	К сожалéнию, сегóдня у нас нет фрáнцýзского сы́ра. Но голлáндский сыр у нас есть.
П:	Хорошó. Дáйте, пожáлуйста, три́ста грамм голлáндского сы́ра.
Д:	Чтó ещё?
П:	Чёрная икрá у вас есть?
Д:	Нет. Чёрной икры́ сегóдня нет. У нас есть тóлько крáсная икрá.
П:	Сто грамм крáсной икры́. А у вас бéлый хлеб есть?
Д:	Нет, бéлый хлеб кóнчился. Но у нас есть чёрный хлеб.
П:	Тогдá дáйте две бухáнки чёрного хлéба.
Д:	Вот, пожáлуйста.
П:	Насчёт овощéй . . . У вас есть картóфель?
Д:	Нет, картóфеля нет. Но у нас есть горóх, лук, рис, помидóры.
П:	Полкилó горóха, килó помидóров, и 400 грамм ри́са.

Д:	Что́ ещё?
П:	Две́сти грамм ма́сла, две больши́е колбасы́, и лук.
Д:	У нас сего́дня нет колбасы́.
П:	В тако́м слу́чае, да́йте соси́ски, 500 грамм.
Д:	И ско́лько лу́ка?
П:	Кило́ лу́ка, пожа́луйста.
Д:	Вот лук. Ещё?
П:	Да. Я хочу́ печь шокола́дный торт для моего́ сы́на. За́втра бу́дет его́ день рожде́ния. У вас есть хоро́ший шокола́д?
Д:	Да. Сего́дня у нас есть вку́сный швейца́рский шокола́д.
П:	Да́йте коро́бку швейца́рского шокола́да.
Д:	Пожа́луйста.
П:	Скажи́те, где у вас продаю́т вино́ и конья́к?
Д:	Там, нале́во—в ви́нном отде́ле.
П:	Большо́е спаси́бо.
Д:	До свида́ния. И жела́ем сча́стья и здоро́вья ва́шему сы́ну на день рожде́ния! И прия́тного аппети́та!

At the Grocery

Girl:	May I help you?
Customer:	Tell me, do you have any French cheese today?
G:	Unfortunately, we don't have any French cheese today. But we do have Dutch cheese.
C:	Okay. Please give me 300 grams of Dutch cheese.
G:	What else?
C:	Do you have any black caviar?
G:	No, we don't have any today. We have only red caviar.
C:	One hundred grams of red caviar. Do you have white bread?
G:	No, we're out of white bread. But we have black bread.
C:	Then give me two loaves of black bread.
G:	There you go.
C:	As for vegetables . . . Do you have any potatoes?
G:	No, we don't have any potatoes. But we have peas, onions, rice, and tomatoes.
C:	Half a kilo of peas, a kilo of tomatoes, and 400 grams of rice.
G:	What else?
C:	Two hundred grams of butter, two large sausages, and onions.
G:	We don't have sausage today.
C:	In that case give me hot dogs, 500 grams.

G:	And how many onions?
C:	A kilo of onions, please.
G:	Here are your onions. Anything else?
C:	Yes. I want to bake a chocolate cake for my son. It's his birthday tomorrow. Do you have any good chocolate?
G:	Yes. Today we have delicious Swiss chocolate.
C:	Give me a box of Swiss chocolate.
G:	There you go.
C:	Tell me, where are wine and cognac sold here?
G:	Over there to the left, in the Wine Department.
C:	Thank you very much.
G:	Good-bye. And we wish your son happiness and health for his birthday. And bon appetit!

Conversation Notes

1. You will notice the frequency of the word **пожа́луйста** throughout the above transaction. Besides meaning *please,* it means *you're welcome* and serves as a linguistic oil between customer and clerk.

2. In the phrases **Да́йте, пожалуйста** and **Скажи́те, пожалуйста,** you will notice the absence of the indirect pronoun object *me.* Russians tend not to use references to the self as a subject if not necessary, although English cannot dispense with them. The proper translations here are *Tell me, please* and *Give me, please.*

3. The Russian expression for *We're out of X* uses the verb **ко́нчиться** with an active subject: **молоко́ ко́нчилось** (we're out of milk), **во́дка ко́нчилась** (we're out of vodka), **горо́х ко́нчился** (we're out of peas), **соси́ски ко́нчились** (we're out of hot dogs), and so forth.

4. Most vegetables in English are plural: *Go to the store and buy onions, peas, potatoes, carrots,* and so forth. In Russian, most vegetables are singular. In order to refer to one piece of a particular kind of vegetable, a new diminutive noun is formed: **карто́шка** (a potato), **морко́вка** (a carrot), and so forth.

CONVERSATION PRACTICE 1

Change all the adjectives you can find in the conversation above to other adjectives. Make French cheese American cheese and so on.

The Genetive Case

The genitive case is the second most widely used case in Russian, both in frequency and in terms of reasons for using it. It can express possession, absence or nonexistence, partitive meaning, quantity or number, and comparison and convey many English phrases with the preposition *of* (*the capture of Kabul*/**Взя́тие Кабу́ла**). And, as with most other cases in Russian, the genitive is governed by certain verbs and a wide range of prepositions.

Forms and Endings

Singular Nouns and Adjectives

The endings for the genitive singular are as follows:

	Nouns	**Adjectives**
Masculine	-а / -я	-ого / -его
Neuter	-а / -я	-ого / -его
Feminine	-ы / -и	-ой / -ей

NOTE: The alternate endings represent instances where either a spelling rule or the principle of softness will apply.

1. Masculine and neuter soft nouns take the ending **-я: Игорь/Игоря, слова́рь/словаря́, музе́й/музе́я, пла́тье/пла́тья, зда́ние/зда́ния.** Feminine soft nouns, including those that end in a soft sign, take the ending **и: ку́хня/ку́хни, Же́ня/Же́ни, ле́кция/ле́кции, тетра́дь/тетра́ди.**

2. Feminine nouns whose stems end in one of the consonants belonging to the seven-letter spelling rule (**ж, ч, ш, щ, к, г, х**) must take the ending **-и: кни́га/кни́ги, да́ча/да́чи, Ма́ша/Ма́ши, библиоте́ка/библиоте́ки.**

3. For adjectives, either the five-letter spelling rule or the principle of softness will apply, depending on the adjective. The adjectives **хоро́ший, ста́рший,** and **мла́дший** are three of the most common adjectives you know that are governed by the spelling rule. Examples of soft adjectives are **после́дний** (last), **вчера́шний** (yesterday's), **зде́шний** (local), **у́тренний** (morning), **и́скренний** (sincere), **ве́рхний** (upper), and **си́ний** (dark blue). In fact, except for the group described in the next paragraph, the adjective **ка́рий** (brown or hazel as applied to eyes) is the only commonly used soft adjective in Modern Russian that does not end in **-ний.**

There is also a fairly large group of widely used adjectives that belongs to the so-called mixed declension. These adjectives, most of which are derived from the names of animals, take the ending **-ьего,** adding a soft sign to the stem before the soft ending. Some examples of adjectives of this type are **ли́сий,** as in **ли́сий мех** (fox fur); **соба́чий,** as in **соба́чья жизнь** (a dog's life); **пти́чий,** as in **пти́чье гнездо́** (bird's nest); **коро́вий,** as in **коро́вье молоко́** (cow's milk). Examples of the few not derived from animals' names are **бо́жий,** as in **бо́жий свет** (God's light, daylight); **вдо́вий,** as in **вдовий дом** (the widow's house), **ба́бий,** as in **ба́бье ле́то** (Indian summer, literally *grandmother's summer*), and the utterly common adjective **тре́трий,** as in **тре́тья страни́ца** (the third page).

Pronouns and Possessive Pronoun–Adjectives

Nominative	Genitive	Nominative	Genitive
мой, моё	моего́	наш, на́ше	на́шего
твой, твоё	твоего́	ваш, ва́ше	ва́шего
моя́	мое́й	на́ша	на́шей
твоя́	твое́й	ва́ша	ва́шей
э́тот, э́то	э́того	э́та	э́той
кто	кого́	что	чего́

As you can see, the singular forms for *my* and *your* are soft and will naturally take the soft endings **-его** and **-ей.** The plural pronouns *our* and *your* take the same endings as the singular because the five-letter spelling rule is operative.

TEST FOR MASTERY 1

Put the following adjective–noun combinations into the genitive case. For extra practice, identify which phrases include exceptions due to spelling rules or softness.

1. изве́стный а́втор
2. ру́сская балери́на
3. све́жий хлеб
4. швейца́рский шокола́д
5. мла́дший брат
6. вчера́шняя газе́та
7. коро́вье молоко́
8. пти́чий ры́нок
9. ле́тнее у́тро
10. ва́ше моро́женое
11. после́дний ру́сский царь
12. брита́нская короле́ва

13. мой лу́чший друг

14. твоя́ сестра́ На́дя

15. у́тренняя заря́дка

16. афга́нский ковёр (*rug*)

17. цветно́й телеви́зор

18. англи́йксий язы́к

19. апельси́новый сок

20. си́нее пальто́

Expressing Possession

Possession as expressed by the genitive case corresponds to the English use of *'s* in the singular and *s'* in the plural or a prepositional phrase using *of*. Thus, while in English, depending on style and context, we may say either *the son of my best friend* or *my best friend's son*, Russian allows only the former: **сын моего́ лу́чшего дру́га.** (You may occasionally find a different word order that is similar to English usage, but this is considered nonstandard and is used for a special reason, either poetic or idiosyncratic. You may also occasionally hear Russian émigrés living in America use this word order, no doubt due to the influence of English.)

TEST FOR MASTERY 2

Take any item from the first group and compose a sentence saying that it belongs to someone from the second group:

Example: Э́то кабине́т президе́нта. (This is the president's office.)

1. гита́ра	мой мла́дший брат
2. да́ча	сестра́ Же́ня
3. рома́н	э́тот рок-музыка́нт
4. компью́тер	моя́ ста́ршая сестра́
5. подру́га	ру́сский программи́ст
6. жена́	э́тот францу́зский писа́тель

There are certain nouns in Russian that form their own possessives. These are formed from nouns denoting members of the family and proper names, especially diminutives. Thus, instead of saying literally *the room of my mom,* a Russian is more likely to say *Mom's room,* using the possessive form of *mom.*

These words are formed as follows:

1. From masculine nouns that end in a consonant, add **-ов:**

Noun	Possessive	English
Ива́н	Ива́нов дом	Ivan's house
оте́ц	отцо́в кабине́т	father's study
Пётр	Пе́тров день	St. Peter's Day
Ахилле́с	ахилле́сова пята́	Achilles' heel

Adjectives of this type are now considered to be archaic, but many of them still occur in certain fixed expressions, often of mythological or Biblical origin: **ада́мово я́блоко** (Adam's apple), **но́ев ковче́г** (Noah's ark), **чёртова дю́жина** (a baker's dozen, literally, a devil's dozen), **ка́инова печа́ть** (the mark of Cain), **пи́ррова побе́да** (Pyrrhic victory), **ви́ттова пля́ска** (St. Vitus' dance), and **дамо́клов меч** (the sword of Damocles). In the above meanings, these adjectives are not capitalized.

2. From masculine and feminine nouns, including nicknames ending in **-а/-я,** drop the vowel ending and add **-ин:**

Noun	Possessive	Example	English
Ва́ня	Ва́нин	Ва́нина маши́на	Vanya's car
ма́ма	ма́мин	ма́мино пальто́	mom's coat
сестра́	се́стрин	се́стрина ко́мната	(my) sister's room
На́дя	На́дин	На́дин муж	Nadya's husband
Зо́я	Зо́ин	Зо́ины игру́шки	Zoë's toys
па́па	па́пин	па́пины боти́нки	dad's shoes
де́душка	де́душкин	де́душкин шарф	grandfather's scarf
жена́	же́нин	же́нин компью́тер	(my) wife's computer

A handful of adjectives of this type are slightly irregular. The two most common are **муж/му́жнин** (husband's) and **брат/бра́тнин** (brother's). Remember that these adjectives are colloquial. Also note that because of their colloquial nature, such adjectives are rarely declined, that is, they almost never appear in the oblique cases (genitive, dative, instrumental, and prepositional).

Укра́ли ма́мин кошелёк!	Mom's wallet was stolen!
Ва́нина неве́ста о́чень краси́вая.	Vanya's fiancée is very pretty.

Нельзя́ туда́ входи́ть! Э́то па́пина ко́мната. — Don't go in there! That's dad's room.

Соба́ка съе́ла Ка́тины ту́фли. — The dog ate Katya's shoes.

Family Names

As you may have noticed, this type of adjective is the source of Russian surnames. The expression **Ива́нов сын** (Ivan's son) simply dropped the word *son* and left the modern surname *Ivanov*. A similar phenomenon took place with feminine nouns, resulting in surnames ending in **-ин**, such as **Пу́шкин, Бороди́н,** and **Ле́нин.**

In Modern Russian, last names in **-ин** and **-ов** most certainly do decline. They are examples of the mixed declension, which includes elements of nouns and adjectives. Masculine last names are declined like nouns, except for the instrumental, which uses the adjective ending **-ым.** Feminine names are declined like **э́та**—the nominative and accusative have noun endings and the oblique cases have adjective endings. Plural surnames have adjective endings, except for the nominative case.

	Masculine	Feminine	Plural
Nominative	Петро́в	Петро́ва	Петро́вы
Accusative	Петро́ва	Петро́ву	Петро́вых*
Genitive	Петро́ва	Петро́вой*	Петро́вых*
Prepositional	Петро́ве	Петро́вой*	Петро́вых*
Dative	Петро́ву	Петро́вой*	Петро́вым*
Instrumental	Петро́вым*	Петро́вой*	Петро́выми*

* indicates adjectival endings.

TEST FOR MASTERY 3

Change the words in parentheses to the correct forms of the names. Remember that first names are treated as nouns.

1. Вы зна́ете (Anna Petrova)? Она́ бы́вшая жена́ (of Aleksei Petrov).

2. Мы с (the Petrovs, [*use instrumental case*]) ча́сто хо́дим в кино́.

3. Переда́йте приве́т (to the Petrovs)!

4. (Vanya Petrov) всегда́ ску́чно у ро́дственников на пра́здниках.

5. Сестра́ (of Masha Petrova)—это моя́ лу́чшая подру́га.

6. Э́то кварти́ра (of our neighbor, Ivan Antonovich Petrov).

More *of* Phrases

Certain expressions using the preposition *of* will use the genitive case in Russian:

цвет мое́й но́вой маши́ны	the color of my new car
цена́ чёрного хле́ба	the price of dark bread
наступле́ние весны́	the coming of spring
вопро́с большо́й ва́жности	a question of great importance
досто́ин внима́ния	worthy of attention
за́пах све́жей капу́сты	the smell of fresh cabbage

There are, however, certain expressions involving geographical place names that, tempting though it may be to use the genitive case, are rendered idiomatically into Russian by means of adjectives. Some examples are:

брита́нская короле́ва	the queen of England
граф Пари́жский	the count of Paris
Пеннсильва́нский университе́т	the University of Pennsylvania

On the other hand, some phrases that use adjectives in English wind up to be genitive expressions in Russian. Consider the following:

колбаса́ пе́рвого со́рта	first-class sausage
защи́та диссерта́ции	dissertation defense
проду́кция высо́кого ка́чества	high-quality production
студе́нт пе́рвого ку́рса	a first-year student (freshman)
второ́й курс ру́сского языка́	second-year Russian

There are even more misleading *of* phrases in English. For instance, *the director of the factory* is translated into Russian as **руководи́тель заво́дом,** using instrumental instead of genitive case, because the verb **руководи́ть** governs the instrumental. The only conclusion to be drawn from such evidence is to look before you leap, to read widely, and to make sure you get a native speaker to edit your work.

Expressing Quantity

Partitive Genitive

The idea of partitive corresponds to the English understanding of *some,* which is usually not translated into Russian. Compare these two sentences: **Дайте хлеба, пожалуйста** (*Give me some bread, please*) and **Передайте хлеб** (*Pass the bread*).

Here are some additional examples of partitive genitive:

Она не ела, только выпила чая.	She didn't eat. She just drank some tea.
Он наносил воды.	He brought some water.
Она нарвала цветов.	She picked some flowers.
Хочешь торта?	Would you like some cake?
Мама! (Я) Хочу шоколада.	Mom, I want some chocolate.

There is another ending in the genitive case for masculine words that are used in a partitive meaning. This form is gradually disappearing from use, although you will still see it in texts and hear it from older native speakers. Here are some of the most commonly used nouns that take a partitive ending in **-у/-ю**:

Partitive	English	Partitive	English	Partitive	English
чаю	tea	коньяку	cognac	шуму	noise
сахару	sugar	мёду	honey	сыру	cheese
шёлку	silk	мелу	chalk	чесноку	garlic
луку	onions	перцу	pepper	гороху	peas
рису	rice	народу	people	клею	glue
табаку	tobacco	супу	soup	шоколаду	chocolate

Remember, the meaning must be partitive to use this ending. In addition, adjectives are not used with partitives in **-у.** Compare **стакан чаю** (a glass of tea)[1] and **стакан крепкого чая** (a glass of strong tea).

Measures

This concept also includes any of the normal measures of commodities:

кило сахара	a kilo of sugar
чашка чая	a cup of tea

---

[1] Russians drink tea in glasses rather than cups.

буха́нка хле́ба	a loaf of bread
200 грамм икры́	200 grams of caviar
метр шёлка	a meter of silk
полкило́ ма́сла	half a kilo of butter
ба́нка мёда	a jar of honey
буты́лка вина́	a bottle of wine
кусо́к сы́ра	a piece of cheese
ба́нка ко́ка-ко́лы	a can of coke
стака́н воды́	a glass of water

TEST FOR MASTERY 4

Choose one measure of quantity from the first group and one commodity from the second group to form phrases of your own. The answer section contains possible combinations.

Measure of Quantity	**Commodity**
1. метр (*meter*)	са́хар (*sugar*)
2. кусо́к (*piece*)	ко́ка-ко́ла (*coke*)
3. кило́ (*kilo*)	вино́ (*wine*)
4. полкило́ (*half a kilo*)	ма́сло (*butter*)
5. буха́нка (*loaf*)	шёлк (*silk*)
6. литр (*liter*)	чай (*tea*)
7. буты́лка (*bottle*)	икра́ (*caviar*)
8. грамм (*gram*)	мёд (*honey*)
9. стака́н (*glass*)	хлеб (*bread*)
10. ба́нка (*jar, can*)	молоко́ (*milk*)
	сыр (*cheese*)
	вода́ (*water*)

To make the exercise more challenging, use one of the following adjectives (or choose one of your own) with your combinations, for example, **буха́нка све́жого**

хлеба (*a loaf of fresh bread*): **свéжий, ѝмпотрный, каспѝйский, холóдный, францýзский, китáйский, хорóший, дорогóй, дешёвый, минерáльный.**

Adverbs of Measure

There are numerous words expressing measure that take the genitive, either singular or plural. Among the most common are **скóлько** (how many/much?), **мнóго** (a lot, many), **нéсколько** (a few), **стóлько** (how many, so many!), **немнóго** (not many, a few), **мáло** (few, little).

Numbers

Numbers are the bane of the existence of every student of Russian. On the surface, it seems to make little sense that numbers may take nominative singular, genitive singular, or genitive plural, but there is an order to this madness. The idea of using the genitive case after numbers arises because a number describes a certain measure or quantity. A clue to this meaning may be seen in English when we use a pronoun after a number instead of a noun. Compare: *I bought two magazines* and *I bought two of them.* In the second instance, the preposition *of* is required (it is not possible to say, **I bought two them*) and indicates the underlying idea of a part of many, a quantity, an amount. So without further ado, let us plunge into the maze of Russian numbers.

The Number One
The number one and all its compounds—such as 21, 171, 291, 2,071, and so on—takes a singular adjective and noun. (Note: The number 11 is not included in this rule.)

The number one will agree in gender with the noun following it.

двáдцать одѝн нóвый студéнт	21 new students
стó однá глýпая собáка	101 silly dogs
ты́сяча однá арáбская ночь	1,001 Arabian nights
вóсемьдесят однó стрáнное слóво	81 odd words

The Numbers Two, Three, and Four
Two, three, and four and all their compounds—such as 42, 394, 7,863—depend on the gender of the noun.

If the noun is masculine or neuter, the noun will be in the genitive singular but the adjective will be in the genitive plural. For these nouns, the word **два** is used in examples.

For feminine nouns, which use the form **две,** the noun is also in the genitive singular but adjectives are in the nominative plural. It is worth mentioning at this point that in addition to nominative plural adjectives, you will see forms in the genitive plural, the same as with masculine and neuter nouns. This usage has recently been characterized as old-fashioned, but the student would be well advised to learn this variant because it appears widely throughout Russian literature and is practiced by educated—though elderly—native speakers. It is also one way to mark the noun as genitive singular rather than nominative plural. Refer to the following examples: **две ми́лые сестры́, две ми́лых сестры́; две ску́чные ле́кции, две ску́чных ле́кции.** In the first grouping, regardless of whether the adjective is nominative plural or genitive singular, the Russian native speaker knows that the noun **сестры́** is genitive singular because the stress falls on the last syllable. In the second set of examples, however, the stress on the noun **ле́кции** does not distinguish between nominative plural and genitive singular forms. Therefore, **ску́чные ле́кции** sounds somehow more logical and less jarring to the ear than **ску́чных ле́кции,** which mixes singular and plural forms.

For all nouns after the numbers five and above, including the teens, use genitive plural for both adjective and noun. To generate these forms, we must unfortunately introduce the endings of the dreaded genitive plural. See page 205 and following.

Zero Quantity or Negation

The idea of negation or nothingness is closely tied to the genitive case. There are two primary ways in which this is expressed in Russian:

1. *Not having.* Recall that the idiomatic expression for possession involves reversing the English construction. The Russian says, in effect, "*By me there is X.*"

У меня́ есть соба́ка.	I have a dog.
У него́ есть брат.	He has a brother.
У мое́й сестры́ есть де́ти.	My sister has children.

To negate these sentences, replace **есть** with the negative particle **нет** followed by the genitive case.

2. *Nonexistence.* There are two ways that nonexistence can be translated: **В э́том го́роде нет музе́я** can be rendered into English as *There is no museum in this city* or as *This city has no museum.*

You will often hear the genitive case used for the direct object of a negated verb instead of the accusative case, although this usage is not obligatory. The tendency is to use accusative for something very specific and the genitive for something nonspecific or unreal. Compare **Он не ждёт жены́** (*He is not waiting for a wife*) with **Он не ждёт жену́** (*He is not waiting for his wife*).

CONVERSATION PRACTICE 2

Answer the statements by saying that you, unfortunately, do not have the item in question.

Example: У меня́ есть большо́й дом. → А у меня́ нет большо́го до́ма.

1. У меня́ есть ми́лая до́чка.

2. У меня́ есть дорога́я маши́на.

3. У меня́ есть краси́вая жена́.

4. У меня́ есть у́мный сын.

5. У меня́ есть золото́е кольцо́.

6. У меня́ есть но́вый ру́сский слова́рь.

7. У меня́ есть биле́т на конце́рт.

8. У меня́ есть попуга́й (*parrot*) и крокоди́л.

9. У меня́ есть большо́й бассе́йн.

10. У меня́ есть вре́мя.

Verbs That Take the Genitive Case

Some verbs invariably require the genitive case. Among them are the following:

боя́ться	to be afraid of
жела́ть	to wish (someone something)
избега́ть	to avoid
каса́ться	to concern
пуга́ться	to be scared by

достига́ть	to (try to) attain, achieve
заслу́живать	to earn, merit, deserve
тре́бовать	to demand, require

Prepositions Requiring Genitive Case

The following is an alphabetical list of the most commonly used prepositions governing the genitive case. Their meanings and an example of use are included. See the appendix for a full list.

Preposition	English	Example	English
без	without	Она́ чита́ет без акце́нта.	She reads without an accent.
вме́сто	instead of	Она́ пошла́ в апте́ку вме́сто ма́мы.	She went to the drugstore instead of mom.
вокру́г	round, around	путеше́ствовать вокру́г Земли́.	to travel around the Earth.
для	for	Э́то пода́рок для тебя́.	This present is for you.
до	before (temporal)	Сде́лайте э́то до собра́ния.	Get this done before the meeting.
	up to (spatial)	Мы дое́хали до го́рода.	We drove as far as the city.
из	from (opposite of **в**): various meanings	Она́ идёт из библиоте́ки.	She's coming from the library.
		Он из большо́й семьи́.	He is from a large family.
		Ма́ма сде́лала э́то из любви́.	Mom did this out of love.
кро́ме	besides, but	Все кро́ме меня́ бы́ли на собра́нии.	Everyone but me was at the meeting.
ми́мо	past, along	Мы шли ми́мо большо́го до́ма.	We walked past a big building.
насчёт	regarding, about, on the subject of	Я хочу́ поговори́ть с администра́тором насчёт стола́.	I would like to speak with the manager about a table.
о́коло	near, nearby; approximately	Мы живём о́коло па́рка.	We live near the park.
		Там бы́ло о́коло пятидесяти студе́нтов.	There were about fifty students there.

Preposition	English	Example	English
от	from (opposite of **к**): various meanings	Я получи́ла письмо́ от сестры́.	I got a letter from my sister.
		Она́ живёт недалеко́ от меня́.	She lives not far from me.
		Она́ идёт от ба́бушки.	She is coming from grandmother's.
по́сле	after	По́сле войны́ они́ жи́ли в Ми́нске.	After the war they lived in Minsk.
про́тив	against	Я про́тив его́ предложе́ния.	I am against his suggestion.
ра́ди	for the sake of	Сде́лай э́то ра́ди дете́й!	Do this for the sake of the children!
с (со)	from (opposite of **на**)	Па́па прихо́дит с рабо́ты.	Daddy's coming home from work.
	since	Он у́чится здесь с на́чала сентября́.	He has been studying here since the beginning of September.
	off (the surface)	Она́ взяла́ газе́ту со стола́.	She took the newspaper off the table.
среди́	among, with	Э́тот певе́ц о́чень популя́рен среди́ молодёжи.	This singer is very popular with young people.
у	near; with various idioms	Она́ стои́т у две́ри и ждёт.	She is standing by the door waiting.
		У меня́ есть кенгуру́.	I have a kangaroo.
		У меня́ боли́т зуб.	My tooth hurts.
		Дени́са ещё живёт у роди́телей.	Denise still lives with her parents (at her parents').

TEST FOR MASTERY 5

Replace the English translation with the correct form of the verb or preposition.

1. Э́тот ребёнок (is afraid of) больши́х соба́к.

2. Почему́ ты ещё живёшь (with) роди́телей?

3. (After) заня́тий мы все пойдём домо́й.

4. Порá голосовáть (*to vote*). Кто за, кто (against).

5. Вáся остановѝлся и взял карандáш (from) пóла.

6. Чтó (concerns) меня,[2] я бýду сидéть дóма.

7. Он говорѝт по-рýсски почтѝ (without) акцéнта.

8. Мáма, когдá ты вернёшься (from) пóчты?

9. (After) ýжина мы бýдем слýшать мýзыку.

10. В э́том ромáне (approximately) пятисóт странѝц.

11. Пáпа! Для (who) э́тот большóй мѝшка?

12. Я (wish) вам успéха!

13. Он (from) Áнглии.

14. Нáдо (to avoid) жѝра и слáдостей.

15. Автóбус идёт (past) моегó дóма.

Introduction to Genitive Plural Endings

The difficulty with genitive plural endings is that there are so many of them—four to be precise—and that each gender uses more than one.

	-ов	**-ев**	**-ей**	**-ø**
Masculine	студéнтов	музéев	писáтелей	солдáт
Neuter	(облакóв*)	плáтьев	морéй	слов
Feminine	—	—	ночéй	книг

* This type of neuter genitive plural is very rare.

Let's begin with the easier categories, feminine and neuter nouns.

Feminine Nouns

The overwhelming majority of feminine nouns in Russian take a zero ending in the genitive plural. This means that the last vowel is dropped, leaving the stem of the word. Examples:

---

[2] *As far as I am concerned.*

Nominative Singular	Genitive Plural
кни́га	книг
кассе́та	кассе́т
газе́та	газе́т
библиоте́ка	библиоте́к
ла́мпа	ламп
подру́га	подру́г

Fleeting Vowels

If, after removing the final vowel, you should be left with a consonant cluster, that is, two or more consonants that ordinarily do not occur in word-final position in Russian, it may be necessary to insert what is known as a fleeting vowel. In most instances, the fleeting vowel will be **-o-**. The five-letter spelling rule might require you to use **-e-**. Last, you will occasionally come across nouns whose final letters do not include the consonant **-к-**. For these nouns, use **-e-** as the fleeting vowel. There are, unfortunately, exceptions to this rule as well. To give one example, **кухня** becomes **кухонь.**[3]

Nominative Singular	Genitive Plural
блу́зка	блу́зок
студе́нтка	студе́нток
ло́жка	ло́жек
ру́чка	ру́чек
сосна́	со́сен
пе́сня	пе́сень[3]
ма́йка	ма́ек[4]

The noun **сестра́** (and, of course, **медсестра́**) uses the unpredictable fleeting vowel **ё,** thus producing the genitive plural **сестёр.**

What Is the Stem? What Is the Ending?

There are instances where you will be tempted to drop the final vowel instead of dropping the final vowel sound. It is important to resist this impulse and remember that you are dropping only the vowel sound while retaining the stem of the word. In other words, you are dropping the **a** of the ending, not the last letter **я.**

---

[3] The soft sign at the end of this word will be explained in the following section.

[4] This is an example of the need for a soft fleeting vowel.

To understand what is happening, let's take some feminine nouns ending in **-ия** and express the letter **я** of the suffix as the combination **йа.** Then drop the last letter, which is now also the same thing as the last vowel sound, and you will arrive at the correct genitive plural form.

Nominative Singular	Expanded Form	Genitive Plural	English
ле́кция	ле́кцийа	ле́кций	lecture, class
лаборато́рия	лаборато́рийа	лаборато́рий	lab
фами́лия	фами́лийа	фами́лий	last name
профе́ссия	профе́ссийа	профе́ссий	profession

A similar phenomenon can be observed with feminine nouns in a consonant plus **я.** For example, a feminine noun such as **неде́ля** must show in the genitive plural that the stem is soft. This is done orthographically by adding a soft sign.[5] **Кухня** is another noun of this type.

Feminine Nouns in a Soft Sign

All feminine nouns in a soft sign remove the soft sign and add **-ей.** There are no exceptions, but you must remember that the nouns **мать** and **дочь** lengthen their stems in the oblique cases, thus becoming in the genitive plural **матере́й** and **дочере́й.** There is another noun, **ку́рица** (chicken), that does the opposite, that is, it shortens, rather than lengthens, its stem in the plural. Nonetheless, the genitive plural is formed regularly by dropping the final vowel: **ку́рица** is **ку́ры** in the nominative plural and **кур** in the genitive plural.

NOTE: Masculine nouns that end in the vowel **a** are declined like feminine nouns: **мужчи́на/мужчи́н, де́душка/де́душек,** and so forth. Several nouns have exceptional endings: **ю́ноша/ю́ношей, дя́дя/дя́дей.**

Feminine Nouns in a Soft Sign Plus -я

Nouns of this type, such as **статья́** (article), are combination fleeting vowel–zero ending genitive plurals: **стате́й.**

---

[5] There are certain words where the soft sign is not added. **Спа́льня** (bedroom), for example, becomes **спа́лен; башня** (tower), **ба́шен, пе́сня** (song), **пе́сен.** For these types of nouns, checking a good Russian dictionary such as Ozhegov is recommended.

Use the following words in combination with a noun expressing measure (such as **мно́го, не́сколько**) or a number (five and above, including teens and numbers ending in a zero) to produce phrases using the genitive plural. Some possible combinations are given in the answer section.

1. продавщи́ца	14. исто́рия
2. фи́рма	15. шко́льница
3. поликли́ника	16. ночь
4. же́нщина	17. ко́мната
5. рекла́ма	18. специа́льность
6. балала́йка	19. колбаса́
7. пиани́стка	20. ры́ба
8. кома́нда	21. де́вушка
9. балери́на	22. галере́я
10. ро́к-гру́ппа	23. пье́са
11. ло́дка	24. соба́ка
12. ма́рка	25. рука́
13. ша́пка	26. спецшко́ла

Neuter Nouns

Like feminine nouns, neuter nouns are formed with relative ease: drop the final vowel sound. You should be able to produce the genitive plural of the following nouns without any further comment:

ле́то	сло́во	ме́сто
кольцо́	окно́	письмо́
чудо́вище	учи́лище	лека́рство
мне́ние	упражне́ние	оконча́ние

Reading across, the correct forms are **лет, слов, мест, коле́ц, о́кон, пи́сем, чудо́вищ, учи́лищ, лека́рств,**[6] **мне́ний, упражне́ний, оконча́ний.**

---

[6] Believe it or not, Russians have no trouble pronouncing this consonant cluster. The genitive plural of **лека́рство** is, indeed, **лека́рств.**

Among the zero-ending group are the ten relatively rare neuter nouns that end in **-мя.** Only two are commonly used: **и́мя/имён** and **вре́мя/времён.**

The remainder of neuter nouns take one of three endings:

1. Most neuter nouns in a soft consonant plus **е** take the ending **-ей.** Two common examples of this relatively small category are the words **по́ле/поле́й** and **мо́ре/море́й.**

2. Some neuter nouns whose irregular nominative plural ending is an unstressed **-ья** take **-ьев.** For example: **де́рево/дере́вья/дере́вьев, перо́/пе́рья/пе́рьев,** and **крыло́/кры́лья/кры́льев.** We may also include in this group the noun **пла́тье/пла́тья/пла́тьев,** although strictly speaking the nominative plural is not irregular.

Other neuter nouns whose regular nominative plural is unstressed **-ья,** such as **ожере́лье/ожере́лья,** form their genitive plural with the insertion of a weak fleeting vowel: **ожере́лье/ожере́лья/ожере́лий** (necklace), **копьё/ко́пья/ко́пий** (spear).

3. There is less than a handful of neuter nouns whose genitive plural is formed irregularly with **-ов.** Two commonly used ones are **о́блако/облако́в** (cloud) and **очко́/очко́в** (point, as in the score of a game). Another is **остриё/остриёв** (point or spike).

Summary

All feminine nouns in **-а** and almost all neuter nouns in **-о** have a zero ending in the genitive plural. Remember to insert a fleeting vowel if necessary:

Nominative Singular	Genitive Plural	English
ла́па	лап	paw
сло́во	слов	word
ка́рта	карт	map
ви́за	виз	visa
ме́сто	мест	place, spot
маши́на	маши́н	car
окно́	о́кон	window
ку́кла	ку́кол	doll

Remember to remove only the final sound in nouns that end in **-ия** and **-ие:**

Nominative Singular	Genitive Plural	English
заня́тие	заня́тий	lesson
церемо́ния	церемо́ний	ceremony
аллерги́я	аллерги́й	allergy
настрое́ние	настрое́ний	mood
реше́ние	реше́ний	decision
коме́дия	коме́дий	comedy

To remind you of how this operates, watch what happens below:

Nominative Singular	Expanded Form	Genitive Plural	English
мне́ние	мне́нийэ	мне́ний	opinion
упражне́ние	упражне́нийэ	упражне́ний	exercise

ANSWER KEY

Test for Mastery 1

1. изве́стного а́втора
2. ру́сской балери́ны
3. све́жего хле́ба
4. швейца́рского шокола́да
5. мла́дшего бра́та
6. вчера́шней газе́ты
7. коро́вьего молока́
8. пти́чьего ры́нка
9. ле́тнего у́тра
10. ва́шего моро́женого
11. после́днего ру́сского царя́
12. брита́нской короле́вы
13. моего́ лу́чшего дру́га
14. твое́й сестры́ На́ди
15. у́тренней заря́дки
16. афга́нского ковра́
17. цветно́го телеви́зора
18. англи́йского языка́
19. апельси́нового со́ка
20. си́него пальто́

A. Exceptions Due to Spelling Rules

3. све́жего
5. мла́дшего

10. ва́шего

13. лу́чшего

B. Exceptions Due to Softness

6. вчера́шней

7. коро́вьего

8. пти́чьего

9. ле́тнего

11. после́днего

13. моего́

14. твое́й

15. у́тренней

20. си́него

Test for Mastery 2

1. Э́то гита́ра мое́й ста́ршей сестры́.

2. Э́то да́ча мое́й сестры́ Же́ни.

3. Э́то рома́н э́того францу́зского писа́теля.

4. Э́то компью́тер ру́сского программи́ста.

5. Э́то подру́га э́того ро́к-музыка́нта.

6. Э́то жена́ моего́ мла́дшего бра́та.

Test for Mastery 3

1. А́нну Петро́ву, Алексе́я Петро́ва

2. с Петро́выми

3. Петро́вым

4. Ва́не Петро́ву

5. Ма́ши Петро́вой

6. на́шего сосе́да, Ива́на Анто́новича Петро́ва

Test for Mastery 4

1. метр и́мпортного шёлка

2. кусо́к францу́зского сы́ра

3. кило́ са́хара

4. полкило́ све́жей икры́ (!)

5. буха́нка францу́зского хле́ба

6. литр холо́дной ко́ка-ко́лы

7. две буты́лки минера́льной воды́

8. две́сти грамм ма́сла

9. стака́н све́жего молока́

10. ба́нка хоро́шего мёда

11. буты́лка дешёвого грузи́нского вина́

12. сто грамм кита́йского ча́я

Conversation Practice 2

1. А у меня́ нет ми́лой до́чки.

2. А у меня́ нет дорого́й маши́ны.

3. А у меня́ нет краси́вой жены́.

4. А у меня́ нет у́много сы́на.

5. А у меня́ нет золото́го кольца́.

6. А у меня́ нет но́вого ру́сского словаря́.

7. А у меня́ нет биле́та на конце́рт.

8. А у меня́ нет попуга́я и крокоди́ла.

9. А у меня́ нет большо́го бассе́йна.

10. А у меня́ нет вре́мени.

Test for Mastery 5

1. бои́тся
2. у
3. По́сле
4. про́тив
5. с

6. каса́ется
7. без
8. с
9. По́сле
10. о́коло

11. кого́
12. жела́ю
13. из
14. избега́ть
15. ми́мо

Test for Mastery 6

1. ма́ло продавщи́ц
2. 5 фирм
3. не́сколько поликли́ник
4. мно́го же́нщин
5. 10 рекла́м
6. ско́лько балала́ек?
7. 6 пиани́сток
8. ско́лько кома́нд?
9. мно́го балери́н
10. не́сколько ро́к-гру́пп
11. ско́лько ло́док?
12. мно́го ма́рок
13. 5 ша́пок

14. ско́лько исто́рий?
15. 26 шко́льниц
16. не́сколько ноче́й
17. мно́го ко́мнат
18. 7 специа́льностей
19. 10 колба́с
20. 12 рыб
21. не́сколько де́вушек
22. 15 галере́й
23. ско́лько пьес?
24. 8 соба́к
25. мно́го рук
26. не́сколько спецшко́л

13 The Genitive Plural

Родительный падеж множественного числа

Useful Vocabulary

City Life

зда́ние	building
библиоте́ка	library
музе́й	museum
кинотеа́тр	movie theater
магази́н	store
це́рковь	church
рестора́н	restaurant
кафе́	cafe
теа́тр	theater
гастроно́м	charcuterie
университе́т	university
стадио́н	stadium
кла́дбище	cemetery
гости́ница	hotel
парк	park
у́лица	street
проспе́кт	prospect, avenue
Тверска́я улица	Tverskaya Street

Ста́рый Арба́т	Old Arbat
метро́	subway
авто́бус	bus
тролле́йбус	trolley
такси́	taxi
ста́нция метро́	subway station
остано́вка авто́буса	bus stop
стоя́нка такси́	taxi station
о́пера	opera
бале́т	ballet
цирк	circus
футбо́льный матч	soccer game
вы́ставка	exhibit
конце́рт	concert
достопримеча́тельности	sights
Кремль	the Kremlin
Большо́й теа́тр	the Bolshoi Theater
ГУМ	G.U.M. (department store)
Парк им. Го́рького	Gorky Park
па́мятник Пу́шкину	the Pushkin Monument
рестора́н «Ара́гви»	Aragvi Restaurant
Кита́йгород	Chinatown
Новоде́вичье кла́дбище	Novodevichy Cemetery
Лу́жники	Luzhniki sports complex
Кра́сная пло́щадь	Red Square
Мавзоле́й Ле́нина	Lenin's Tomb
Храм Васи́лия Бдаже́нного	St. Basil's Cathedral

Reading

Экску́рсия по Москве́

Экскурсово́д:	Здра́вствуйте! Добро́ пожа́ловать в Москву́! Вы здесь в пе́рвый раз?
Господи́н Браун:	Здра́вствуйте! Да, я в Москве́ в пе́рвый раз. Я не о́чень хорошо́ говорю́ по-ру́сски. Говори́те ме́дленно, пожа́луйста.
Э:	Коне́чно. Что вы уже́ зна́ете о Москве́?
ГБ:	Я почти́ ничего́ не зна́ю о ва́шем го́роде.

Э:	Ну, вот. Москва—старе́йший и красиве́йший го́род. Он был осно́ван в двена́дцатом ве́ке Ю́рием Долгору́ким. В Москве́ всё есть: мно́го высо́ких зда́ний, краси́вых па́рков, изве́стных теа́тров, интере́сных музе́ев, замеча́тельных рестора́нов, хоро́ших кафе́, ста́рых церкве́й, удо́бных гости́ниц.
ГБ:	И я хочу́ всё посмотре́ть!
Э:	Прекра́сно! Я вам покажу́ все достопримеча́тельности на́шего го́рода. Начнём с Кра́сной пло́щади. Там, впереди́, вы уви́дите Храм Васи́лия Блаже́нного. Он был постро́ен при Ива́не Гро́зном, в шестна́дцатом ве́ке. Э́то одна́ из са́мых краси́вых церкве́й в ми́ре. Там, сле́ва—э́то ГУМ: Городско́й универса́льный магази́н. ГУМ оди́н из са́мых больши́х магази́нов в ми́ре.
ГБ:	Как «Ме́йсиз» у нас?
Э:	Да, как в ва́шем «Ме́йсиз», в ГУ́Ме есть мно́го това́ров.
ГБ:	Мо́жно туда́ заходи́ть? Мне на́до купи́ть не́сколько сувени́ров для мое́й семьи́.
Э:	К сожале́нию, у нас вре́мени нет. Там спра́ва нахо́дится Кремль и Мавзоле́й Ле́нина. В э́том мавзоле́е похоро́нен В.И. Ле́нин, пе́рвый вождь сове́тской Росси́и.
ГБ:	Как интере́сно!
Э:	За на́ми изве́стный Проспе́кт Ма́ркса, и ря́дом, Мане́жная пло́щадь. По э́тим у́лицам ка́ждый день е́здят ты́сячи маши́н, авто́бусов, такси́.
ГБ:	Зна́ете что? Я как раз на́чал чу́вствовать за́пах све́жей капу́сты! Здесь ря́дом нет хоро́ших рестора́нов?
Э:	Да, на э́той же у́лице два отли́чных рестора́на: «Ара́гви» нахо́дится на пло́щади Пу́шкина, а о́чень вку́сный кита́йский рестора́н немно́жко да́льше. Е́сли мест нет в «Ара́гви», мы пойдём туда́.
ГБ:	Ну, пошли́! Я умира́ю с го́лоду!

Tour of Moscow

Tour Guide:	Hello! Welcome to Moscow! Are you here for the first time?
Mr. Brown:	Hello! Yes, I am in Moscow for the first time. I don't speak Russian very well. Speak slowly, please.

G: Of course. What do you know about Moscow already?

B: I know almost nothing about your city.

G: Well, then. Moscow is a very old and very beautiful city. It was founded in the twelfth century by Yuri Dolgoruky. Moscow has everything: many tall buildings, beautiful parks, famous theaters, interesting museums, marvelous restaurants, good cafes, old churches, and comfortable hotels.

B: And I want to see it all!

G: Wonderful! I will show you all the sights of our city. Let's begin with Red Square. Straight ahead you will see the Cathedral of St. Basil. It was built during the reign of Ivan the Terrible, in the sixteenth century. It is one of the most beautiful churches in the world. There on the left is G.U.M.—the City Department Store. G.U.M. is one of the biggest stores in the world.

B: Like our Macy's?

G: Yes, like your Macy's, G.U.M. has many kinds of goods.

B: Can we stop in? I have to buy some souvenirs for my family.

G: Unfortunately, we don't have any time. There on the right is the Kremlin and Lenin's Mausoleum. Lenin, the first leader of Soviet Russia, is buried in this mausoleum.

B: How interesting!

G: Behind us is the famous Marx Prospect and next to it, Manège Square. Thousands of cars, buses, and taxis drive up and down these streets every day.

B: You know what? I just caught the scent of fresh cabbage. Aren't there any good restaurants nearby?

G: Yes, there are two excellent restaurants on this very street. The Aragvi is on Pushkin Square, and a very good Chinese restaurant is a little farther. If there are no tables in the Aragvi, we'll go there.

B: Well, let's go! I'm dying of hunger!

READING EXERCISE

See if you can find all the words in the above Russian section that are in the genitive case. Refer to the passage in the answer key to compare your answers.

The Genitive Plural

Without doubt, the genitive plural is a source of great anxiety and confusion among students, and not without reason. There are four different endings for nouns, and they are used with all three genders, but in different environments. The conventional approach to learning these endings proceeds according to gender. While comprehensive and logical, this method leaves many students stuttering while they try to calculate the correct answer and in fact takes much time to master. The analysis below relies on recognizing the morphology, or underlying structure, of the word and quickly frees the student to attempt (usually correctly) the genitive plural of most Russian nouns. Of course, a complete summary of exceptional forms will be found later in this chapter.

It is said that somewhere in its declension, each Russian noun will appear with the so-called zero ending (or base form). For most masculine nouns, it is the nominative singular. For the majority of feminine and neuter nouns, the zero ending is found in the genitive plural.

Masculine nouns already appear in their base form. Most of them have no special ending except for the soft sign, which is, phonetically speaking, part of the stem. Note that the fairly large group of masculine nouns in **-а**, such as **па́па** (papa), **Ва́ня** (Vanya), **де́душка** (grandfather), **сирота́** (orphan), **ю́ноша** (teenage boy), and **ми́шка** (teddy bear) are conjugated like feminine nouns and do not belong to the zero-ending category.

Feminine and neuter nouns find their zero-ending form in the genitive plural.

Noun Endings

Masculine

For masculine zero-ending nouns, except those ending in **ь, ж, ч, ш, щ,** the genitive plural ending is **-ов** (or **-ев** for masculines that end in **-й,** such as **музе́й** and **геро́й**). Examine the following table to see the formation of this type of masculine nouns in the genitive plural:

Nominative Singular	Genitive Plural	English
журна́л	журна́лов	magazine
штат	шта́тов	state
дом	домо́в	house
го́род	городо́в	city
компью́тер	компью́теров	computer

Nominative Singular	Genitive Plural	English
спортсме́н	спортсме́нов	athlete
музе́й	музе́ев	museum
трамва́й	трамва́ев	streetcar
санато́рий	санато́риев	sanatorium
мавзоле́й	мавзоле́ев	mausoleum
слу́чай	слу́чаев	instance, case
бой	боёв	battle, fight
кафете́рий	кафете́риев	cafeteria
оте́ц	отцо́в	father
купе́ц	купцо́в	merchant
кана́дец	кана́дцев	Canadian
ме́сяц	ме́сяцев	month

The last two examples above illustrate the five-letter spelling rule, which states that an unstressed **o** may not be written after **ж, ч, ш, щ,** and **ц.** The rule does not apply to **оте́ц** or **купе́ц,** since they are end-stressed nouns.

Masculine nouns that end in a soft sign or the letters **ж, ч, ш, щ** (which were once soft in the early history of Russian) take the ending **-ей.** Feminine nouns in a soft sign also take this ending.

Nominative Singular	Genitive Plural	English
царь	царе́й	tsar
тетра́дь	тетра́дей	notebook
каранда́ш	карандаше́й	pencil
врач	враче́й	doctor
рубль	рубле́й	ruble
дверь	двере́й	door
нож	ноже́й	knife
мышь	мыше́й	mouse
плащ	плаще́й	cloak

Feminine

Feminine nouns that end in a consonant plus **a** or **я** drop the vowel sound but retain the soft sign as a mark of softness if the stem so requires.

Nominative Singular	Genitive Plural	English
кни́га	книг	book
газе́та	газе́т	newspaper

Nominative Singular	Genitive Plural	English
ла́мпа	ламп	lamp
ка́рта	карт	map
маши́на	маши́н	car
река́	рек	river
учи́тельница	учи́тельниц	(female) teacher
жена́	жён	wife
геро́йня	геро́йнь	heroine
неде́ля	неде́ль	week
бу́ря	бурь	storm

Very often you will be faced with what seems to us an unpronounceable stem because of the likelihood that feminine nouns contain a feminizing suffix. In these cases the principle of the fleeting vowel comes into play. The noun **студе́нтка,** for example, would become the unwieldy **студе́нтк** without its last vowel, unpronounceable even for a Russian. Therefore, a fleeting vowel is inserted before the **к: студе́нток.** Other examples of feminines with fleeting vowels are:

Nominative Singular	Genitive Plural	English
ку́кла	ку́кол	doll
де́вушка	де́вушек	girl, girlfriend
ви́лка	ви́лок	fork
су́мка	су́мок	purse
дере́вня	дереве́нь	village
ку́хня	ку́хонь	kitchen
сва́дьба	сва́деб	wedding
копе́йка	копе́ек	kopek
балала́йка	балала́ек	balalaika
сестра́	сестёр[1]	sister

The fleeting vowel is usually **o** but may appear as **e** because of the five-letter spelling rule or because of softness within the stem.

The word **копе́йка** (kopek), like **балала́йка,** is an interesting case in the formation of the genitive plural. Watch what happens:

копе́йка → копе́йк → копе́йок → копе́ёк → копе́ек

---

[1] Accept the genitive plural form **cестёр** without explanation, and you will be a happier person for it.

After the vowel **a** drops, there remains the stem **копе́йк.** This word, however pronounceable to the American tongue, is somehow lacking in Russian and needs an inserted (fleeting) vowel. When **o** is inserted, the resulting combination contracts from **йо** to **ё.** However, the stress on this word is fixed on the stem, and therefore the vowel **ё** changes to **e,** since **ё** can be pronounced as [yo] only when it is stressed.

In a similar manner, **сва́дьба** (wedding) inserts a fleeting vowel, but because of the soft sign in the stem, the vowel appears as **e,** since again the stress is on the stem of the word. These operations happen in a flash of a second in the mind of a native speaker:

сва́дьба → сва́дьб → сва́дьоб → сва́дёб → сва́деб

Feminine nouns that end in **-ия** also appear in the zero ending in the genitive plural, but there is one adjustment that must be made before proceeding, and that is you must expand the letter **я** into its constituent parts: **йа.** Once this is done, the final vowel sound (**a**) may be dropped and the true (soft) root remains. Consider the following:

Nominative Singular	Genitive Plural	English
ле́кция	ле́кций	lesson
симфо́ния	симфо́ний	symphony
фо́бия	фо́бий	phobia
рели́гия	рели́гий	religion
коме́дия	коме́дий	comedy
фами́лия	фами́лий	last name
интона́ция	интона́ций	intonation
сту́дия	сту́дий	studio, workshop
а́рмия	а́рмий	army

The genitive plural of words such as **иде́я** (idea), **галаре́я** (gallery), **ше́я** (neck), and **змея́** (snake) behave the same way. Their forms are **иде́й, галере́й, ше́й,** and **змей.**

In the case of some end-stressed feminine nouns that end in **-ья,** they, too, drop this suffix and replace it with **-ей,** but the process is slightly different. Consider the example **семья́** (family):

семья́ → семьйа́ → семьй → ?

What happens in this case is that, like feminines in **-ия, семья́** takes a zero ending, but then we wind up with the ungainly form seen in step three above, **семьй.** This is an unpronounceable word to the Russian tongue, so what is needed, as in the group above, is a fleeting vowel. And since the **м** is soft, the fleeting vowel will be **e.** The genitive plural of words of this type, therefore, is **семéй.** Other nouns of this type are **свинья́** (pig), **судья́** (judge; this word is masculine, even when it refers to a woman), **статья́** (article), and **скамья́** (bench).

There are some nouns with this ending whose stress falls on the stem. In the genitive plural, their ending is **-ий,** since the vowel is in a weak position (unstressed). One example of this type is the word **гóстья/гóстий** (female guest). It is best to check a dictionary for the correct form.

Neuter

Neuter nouns form their genitive plural in a fashion identical to feminine nouns above. Some nouns simply drop the last vowel:

Nominative Singular	Genitive Plural	English
слóво	слов	word
мéсто	мест	place
вéко	век	eyelid
я́блоко	я́блок	apple
лицó	лиц	face
одея́ло	одея́л	blanket
болóто	болóт	swamp
тéло	тел	body
колесó	колёс[2]	wheel
óзеро	озёр	lake
óтчество	óтчеств[3]	patronymic

Many more neuter nouns need a fleeting vowel to form the genitive plural:

---

[2] If there is an irregularity in the nominative plural, the new stem will be followed throughout the plural declension, including the genitive plural. **Колёс** and **озёр** are based on their nominative plural forms **колёса** and **озёра.**

[3] Yes, Russians can pronounce this word.

Nominative Singular	Genitive Plural	English
окно́	о́кон	window
письмо́	пи́сем	letter
кольцо́	коле́ц	ring
око́шко	око́шек	window
бревно́	брёвен	log
сукно́	су́кон	cloth
полоте́нце	полоте́нец	sheet
пятно́	пя́тен	spot, stain

The largest category of neuter nouns, however, consists of nouns in **-ие.** Hundreds upon hundreds of these nouns form their genitive plural in the same way that feminine nouns in **-ия** do: they expand their ending to **-ийэ** before dropping the final vowel sound **э:**

Nominative Singular	Genitive Plural	English
зда́ние	зда́ний	building
упражне́ние	упражне́ний	exercise
мне́ние	мне́ний	opinion
зва́ние	зва́ний	rank, title
де́йствие	де́йствий	action, act
усло́вие	усло́вий	condition
изда́ние	изда́ний	edition
колеба́ние	колеба́ний	fluctuation, vacillation
прича́стие	прича́стий	participle
откры́тие	откры́тий	discovery

Summary

Gender	Stem Ending	Genitive Plural	Example
Masculine	zero	**-ов**	**домо́в**
	ц or **й**	**-ев**	**музе́ев**
	ж, ч, ш, щ	**-ей**	**враче́й**
	soft sign	**-ей**	**рубле́й**
Feminine	consonant + **а** or **я**	zero	**стран**
	vowel + **я**	zero	**ле́кций**
	soft sign	**-ей**	**ноче́й**
Neuter	consonant + **о**	zero	**слов**
	vowel + **e**	zero	**зда́ний**

Adjective Endings

Adjective endings offer none of the complications that nouns do. There is only one ending in the genitive plural, which needs to be adjusted, naturally, for the spelling rule or softness: **-ых/-их.** Some examples are **но́вых, ру́сских, после́дних, ску́чных, америка́нских, си́них, хоро́ших.**

Remember that there are nouns that are derived from adjectives. They will be declined like adjectives. This includes words such as **больно́й** (patient), **взро́слый** (adult), **гости́ная** (living room), **живо́тное** (animal), **насеко́мое** (insect), and also proper surnames in the form of adjectives, such as **Достое́вский** and **Толсто́й: Мы бы́ли у Толсты́х в Я́сной Поля́не** (*We were at the Tolstoy's place at Yasnaya Polyana*).

TEST WARM-UP

Here are words you have mostly not seen before. See how many of them you can correctly form in the genitive plural before you try the Test for Mastery that follows.

пласти́нка	це́рковь	та́нец	дере́вня
маши́на	откры́тие	ба́бушка	стол
кабине́т	диск	фи́зик	ры́ба
спа́льня	во́йско	подру́га	существо́
спи́чка	до́ллар	библиоте́ка	лицо́
поня́тие	страни́ца	де́ло	ковбо́й
гастроно́м	кольцо́	учи́тель	
диплома́т	зверь	ору́дие	

ANSWERS TO WARM UP

пласти́нок	церкве́й	та́нцев	дереве́нь
маши́н	откры́тий	ба́бушек	столо́в
кабине́тов	ди́сков	фи́зиков	ры́б
спа́лень	во́йск	подру́г	суще́ств
спи́чек	до́лларов	библиоте́к	лиц
поня́тий	страни́ц	де́л	ковбо́ев
гастроно́мов	коле́ц	учителе́й	
диплома́тов	звере́й	ору́дий	

TEST FOR MASTERY 1

Change the words in parentheses to the correct form of the genitive plural.

1. Ско́лько у вас (но́вый дом) в э́том го́роде?

2. К сожале́нию, у нас сего́дня ма́ло (кра́сный помидо́р).

3. В э́той шко́ле мно́го (у́мная учени́ца).

4. Ско́лько (жи́тель) в э́той дере́вне?

5. В э́той гости́нице 1000 (больша́я ко́мната).

6. Там во дворе́ игра́ют де́сять (шу́мный шко́льник).

7. В э́том кио́ске продаю́т мно́го (интере́сная газе́та).

8. Ско́лько (ле́то), ско́лько (зима́)![4]

9. В ру́сской грамма́тике сто́лько (сло́жное пра́вило)!

10. 10 (до́ллар) 95 (цент).

11. У меня́ нет (кра́сный каранда́ш).

12. В э́том рома́не сли́шком мно́го (страни́ца)!

TEST FOR MASTERY 2

The phrase **оди́н из . . .** is a frequently used way of expressing high degree in sentences such as *This is one of the longest rivers in the world.* This exercise will test two grammatical elements. The word *one* will agree in Russian with the gender of the singular noun that is the focus of the sentence. The words following **из** will be in the genitive plural. Form sentences from the following words, according to the model.

Example: Миссиси́пи / дли́нный / река́ / мир: / Миссиси́пи—одна́ из са́мых дли́нных рек в ми́ре. (The Mississippi is one of the longest rivers in the world.)

1. «Война́ и мир» / интере́сный рома́н / мир

2. Филаде́льфия / ста́рый го́род / Аме́рика

---

[4] Literally, *How many summers, how many winters!* This expression is used to indicate a long time, for instance, since people have seen each other.

3. Ма́гда / моя́ трудолюби́вая (*industrious*) студе́нтка

4. Сан-Франци́ско / краси́вый го́род / США

5. Наполео́н / вели́кий генера́л на́шей э́ры

6. Пу́шкин / изве́стный поэ́т / мир

7. Оста́нкино бы́ло / высо́кое зда́ние / Росси́я

8. Во́лга / дли́нная река́ / Евро́па

9. А́нна Каре́нина / сло́жное лицо́ (*character*) / ру́сская литерату́ра

10. «Двена́дцать сту́льев» / смешна́я кни́га / на́ша бибилоте́ка

11. «Достопримеча́тельности» / дли́нное сло́во / ру́сский язы́к

12. «Ферра́ри» / дорога́я маши́на / мир

13. Санскри́т / ста́рый язы́к / мир

14. Ре́пин / тала́нтливый худо́жник / на́ша страна́

15. Моя́ сестра́ / успе́шная певи́ца / э́та гру́ппа

Numbers

As you may recall from previous chapters, the genitive case is closely related to concepts of number and quantity. Here are the complete rules for use of the genitive case after numbers with adjectives and nouns.

- The numeral **один/одно/одна** and all compounds containing it, except for 11, will be followed by the nominative singular of both adjective and noun.

- For masculine and neuter nouns, the numerals **два, три,** and **четыре** and all compounds containing them, except for 12, 13, and 14, will be followed by the genitive plural for adjectives and genitive singular for nouns.

- For feminine nouns, the numerals **две, три,** and **четыре** and all compounds containing them, except for 12, 13, and 14, will be followed by the nominative plural for adjectives and genitive singular for nouns.

- All remaining numerals, including the teens and all numbers that end in zero, require the genitive plural of both adjective and noun.

MATH PROBLEMS[5]

Special Vocabulary

зараба́тывать/зарабо́тать	to earn
сто́ит	(it) costs
заболе́ть	to get sick
всё-таки	all the same
вы́играть	to win
никако́й	none, no kind of
нельзя́	it is not possible, you can't

Solve the following math problems:

1. Джо́н зараба́тывает пять до́лларов в час. Сего́дня он рабо́тал пять часо́в. Ско́лько «Сни́керсов»[6] мо́жет он купи́ть, е́сли оди́н «Сни́керс» сто́ит два до́ллара пятьдеся́т це́нтов?

2. Мэ́ри зараба́тывает семь до́лларов пятьдеся́т це́нтов в час. Ско́лько «Сни́керсов» мо́жет она́ купи́ть, е́сли она́ рабо́тает три часа́?

3. У Джо́на двена́дцать «Сни́керсов». Ско́лько часо́в он рабо́тал?

4. Мэ́ри хо́чет купи́ть три́дцать «Сни́керсов». Ско́лько часо́в ей на́до бу́дет рабо́тать?

5. Джон заболе́л, но всё-таки хо́чет де́вять «Сни́керсов». Ско́лько часо́в Мэ́ри на́до бу́дет рабо́тать, что́бы купи́ть де́вять «Сни́керсов» Джо́ну, е́сли она́ сама́ хо́чет три «Сни́керса» для себя́?

6. Джон хо́чет купи́ть двена́дцать «Сни́керсов». Мэ́ри то́же хо́чет купи́ть двена́дцать. Кому́ на́до бу́дет бо́льше рабо́тать? На ско́лько часо́в бо́льше?

7. Мэ́ри вы́играла сто рубле́й на Ло́тто. Ско́лько «Сни́керсов» мо́жет она́ купи́ть за э́ти де́ньги?

8. На День Свято́го Валенти́на Джон хо́чет купи́ть Мэ́ри сто «Сни́керсов». Ско́лько часо́в ему́ на́до бу́дет рабо́тать?

---

[5] With apologies to the late Alexander Lipson of Cornell University
[6] Snickers bars became enormously popular in Russia after 1990.

Exceptions

The first category of exceptions to the rules on genitive plural formation has to do with nouns that are different in the plural in some essential way.

Masculine and Neuter Nouns with an Irregular Plural in -ья

1. If the stem is stressed, the genitive plural is formed by replacing this ending with **-ьев**:

Nominative Singular	Nominative Plural	Genitive Plural
бра́т	бра́тья	бра́тьев
ли́ст	ли́стья	ли́стьев
сту́л	сту́лья	сту́льев
пру́т (twig)	пру́тья	пру́тьев
су́к (bough)	су́чья	су́чьев
де́рево	дере́вья	дере́вьев
перо́	пе́рья	пе́рьев

2. If the ending is stressed, the genitive plural is formed by replacing this ending with **-ей**:

Nominative Singular	Nominative Plural	Genitive Plural
муж	мужья́	муже́й
сын	сыновья́	сынове́й
друг	друзья́	друзе́й
князь	князья́	князе́й
де́верь (brother-in-law)	деверья́	девере́й

Masculine Nouns with Other Irregular Plurals

1. Singular nouns in **-ёнок** with a plural in **-ята** and singular nouns in **-ин** with a plural in **-е** take a zero ending:

Nominative Singular	Nominative Plural	Genitive Plural
котёнок	котя́та	котя́т
поросёнок	порося́та	порося́т
гусёнок	гуся́та	гуся́т
англича́нин	англича́не	англича́н
болга́рин	болга́ре	болга́р
славяни́н	славя́не	славя́н

2. Nouns that are hard in the singular and soft in the plural (including those nouns whose stems change) have a genitive plural in zero or **-ей**:

Nominative Singular	Nominative Plural	Genitive Plural
сосе́д	сосе́ди	сосе́дей
чёрт	че́рти	чертéй
ребёнок	де́ти	детéй
человéк	лю́ди	людéй
у́хо	у́ши	ушéй
колéно	колéни	колéней
плечó	плéчи	плеч

Masculine Nouns with a Zero Ending in the Genitive Plural

These nouns are quite common in Russian and need to be memorized. Some have to do with military rank, some with measures, some with nationalities. Occasionally in conversational Russian you will hear the zero ending with vegetables and fruit. This is quite common, but the standard form has the regular ending **-ов.**

Nominative Singular/ Genitive Plural	English	Nominative Singular/ Genitive Plural	English
солдáт	soldier	грузи́н	Georgian
партизáн	partisan	башки́р	Bashkir
раз	time, occasion	ампéр	ampere
боти́нок	shoe	герц	Hertz
глаз	eye	вольт	volt
сапóг	boot	грамм	gram
чулóк	stocking	арши́н	arshin

The word **человéк** is also the form used in the genitive plural when used with numbers, **скóлько,** and **нéсколько.** For all other occasions requiring the genitive plural, use the form **людéй.**

NOTE: You may have noticed that almost all the exceptions have to do with masculine nouns.

Pluralia Tantum Nouns

There are many common nouns that ordinarily occur only in the plural. For these the genitive plural form must be memorized. Some of the most common are:

Nominative Plural	Genitive Plural	English
брю́ки	брюк	trousers
воро́та	воро́т	gate
вы́боры	вы́боров	election
де́ньги	де́нег	money
джу́нгли	джу́нглей	jungle
дрова́	дров	firewood
духи́	духо́в	perfume
кавы́чки	кавы́чек	quotation marks
кани́кулы	кани́кул	vacation
коньки́	конько́в	skates
ку́дри	ку́дрей	curls
но́жницы	но́жниц	scissors
обо́и	обо́ев	wallpaper
очки́	очко́в	eyeglasses
по́хороны	похоро́н	funeral
роди́тели	роди́телей	parents
са́ни	са́ней	sleigh
сли́вки	сли́вок	cream
стихи́	стихо́в	verse
су́мерки	су́мерек	twilight
су́тки	су́ток	24-hours
счёты	счётов	abacus
хло́поты	хлопо́т	troubles
хло́пья	хло́пьев	flakes
черни́ла	черни́л	ink
ша́хматы	ша́хмат	chess
щи	щей	cabbage soup
я́сли	я́слей	nursery school

Neuter nouns have few exceptions. The most common is **о́блако/о́блака/ облако́в,** instead of the expected **облак** (cloud).

Feminine nouns have no exceptional forms.

CHALLENGER

Here is a brain-wracking puzzle. Place the following words into their correct box in the graph, and then fill out the row. The words as given below are in various forms. It is your job to figure out where to place them.

далласа́нин, пингвиня́та, вождя́, Че́хов, господи́н, россия́не, воробьи́, знамён, тата́рин, черни́ла, ку́дри, дрова́, лоб, па́лец, хло́пья, по́хороны, молока́, ту́фля, коро́ль, рог, сена́тор, пера́, плечо́, у́хо, ска́зка, сва́дьбы, облака́, глаз, се́рдце, око́шко.

Nominative Singular (кто/что)	**Genitive Singular** (кого́/чего́)	**Nominative Plural**	**Genitive Plural**

ANSWER KEY

Reading Exercise

Экскурсово́д:	Здра́вствуйте! Добро́ пожа́ловать в Москву́! Вы здесь в пе́рвый раз?
Господи́н Бра́ун:	Здра́вствуйте! Да, я в Москве́ в пе́рвый раз. Я не о́чень хорошо́ говорю́ по-ру́сски. Говори́те ме́дленно, пожа́луйста.
Э:	Коне́чно. Что вы уже́ зна́ете о Москве́?
ГБ:	Я почти́ ничего́ не зна́ю о ва́шем го́роде.
Э:	Ну, вот. Москва́—старе́йший и красиве́йший го́род. Он был осно́ван в двена́дцатом ве́ке Ю́рием Долгору́ким. В Москве́ всё есть: мно́го <u>высо́ких зда́ний</u>, <u>краси́вых па́рков</u>, <u>изве́стных теа́тров</u>, <u>интере́сных музе́ев</u>, <u>замеча́тельных рестора́нов</u>, <u>хоро́ших кафе́</u>, <u>ста́рых церкве́й</u>, <u>удо́бных гости́ниц</u>.
ГБ:	И я хочу́ всё посмотре́ть!
Э:	Прекра́сно! Я вам покажу́ все достопримеча́тельности <u>на́шего го́рода</u>. Начнём с <u>Кра́сной пло́щади</u>. Там, впереди́, вы уви́дите Храм <u>Васи́лия Блаже́нного</u>. Он был постро́ен при Ива́не Гро́зном, в шестна́дцатом ве́ке. Э́то одна́ из <u>са́мых краси́вых церкве́й</u> в ми́ре. Там, сле́ва—э́то ГУМ: Городско́й Универса́льный Магази́н. ГУМ оди́н из <u>са́мых больши́х магази́нов</u> в ми́ре.
ГБ:	Как «Ме́йсиз» у нас?
Э:	Да, как в ва́шем «Ме́йсиз», в ГУ́Ме есть мно́го <u>това́ров</u>.
ГБ:	Мо́жно туда́ заходи́ть? Мне на́до купи́ть не́сколько <u>сувени́ров</u> для <u>мое́й семьи́</u>.
Э:	К сожале́нию, у нас <u>вре́мени</u> нет. Там спра́ва нахо́дится Кремль и Мавзоле́й <u>Ле́нина</u>. В э́том мавзоле́е похоро́нен В.И. Ле́нин, пе́рвый вождь <u>сове́тской Росси́и</u>.
ГБ:	Как интере́сно!
Э:	За на́ми изве́стный Проспе́кт <u>Ма́ркса</u>, и ря́дом, Мане́жная пло́щадь. По э́тим у́лицам ка́ждый день е́здят ты́сячи <u>маши́н</u>, <u>авто́бусов</u>, <u>такси́</u>.
ГБ:	Зна́ете что? Я как раз на́чал чу́вствовать за́пах <u>све́жей капу́сты</u>! Здесь ря́дом нет <u>хоро́ших рестора́нов</u>?

Э: Да, на э́той же у́лице два <u>отли́чных рестора́на</u>: «Ара́гви»
           нахо́дится на пло́щади <u>Пу́шкина</u>, а о́чень вку́сный
           кита́йский рестора́н немно́жко да́льше. Éсли <u>мест</u> нет в
           «Ара́гви», мы пойдём туда́.
ГБ: Ну, пошли́! Я умира́ю с <u>го́лоду</u>!

Test for Mastery 1

1. но́вых домо́в

2. кра́сных помидо́ров

3. у́мных учени́ц

4. жи́телей

5. больши́х ко́мнат

6. шу́мных шко́льников

7. интере́сных газе́т

8. лет, зим

9. сло́жных пра́вил

10. до́лларов, це́нтов

11. кра́сных карандаше́й

12. страни́ц

Test for Mastery 2

1. «Война́ и мир»—оди́н из са́мых интере́сных рома́нов в ми́ре.

2. Филаде́льфия—оди́н из са́мых ста́рых городо́в в Аме́рике.

3. Ма́гда—одна́ из мои́х са́мых трудолюби́вых студе́нток.

4. Сан-Франци́ско—оди́н из са́мых краси́вых городо́в в США.

5. Наполео́н—оди́н из са́мых вели́ких генера́лов на́шей э́ры.

6. Пу́шкин—оди́н из са́мых изве́стных поэ́тов в ми́ре.

7. Оста́нкино бы́ло одно́ из са́мых высо́ких зда́ний в Росси́и.

8. Во́лга—одна́ из са́мых дли́нных рек в Евро́пе.

9. А́нна Каре́нина—одно́ из са́мых сло́жных лиц в ру́сской литерату́ре.

10. «Двена́дцать сту́льев»—одна́ их са́мых смешны́х книг в на́шей библиоте́ке.

11. «Достопримеча́тельности»—одно́ из са́мых дли́нных слов в ру́сском языке́.

12. «Ферра́ри»—одна́ из са́мых дороги́х маши́н в ми́ре.

13. Санскри́т—оди́н из са́мых ста́рых языко́в в ми́ре.

14. Ре́пин—оди́н из са́мых тала́нтливых худо́жников в на́шей стране́.

15. Моя́ сестра́—одна́ из са́мых успе́шных певи́ц в э́той гру́ппе.

Math Problems

1. Де́сять.

2. Де́вять.

3. Шесть часо́в.

4. Де́сять часо́в.

5. Четы́ре часа́.

6. Джо́ну. На два часа́ бо́льше.

7. Никаки́х. Нельзя́ купи́ть «Сни́кероы» за рубли́!

8. Пятьдеся́т.

CHALLENGER

Nominative Singular (кто/что)	Genitive Singular (кого́/чего́)	Nominative Plural	Genitive Plural
далласа́нин	далласа́нина	далласа́не	далласа́н
пингвинёнок	пингвинёнка	**пингвиня́та**	пингвиня́т
вождь	**вождя́**	вожди́	вожде́й
Че́хов	Че́хова	Че́ховы	Че́ховых
господи́н	господи́на	господа́	госпо́д
россия́нин	россия́нина	**россия́не**	россия́н
воробе́й	воробья́	**воробьи́**	воробьёв
зна́мя	зна́мени	знамёна	**знамён**
тата́рин	тата́рина	тата́ры	тата́р
(no singular)	(no singular)	**черни́ла**	черни́л
(no singular)	(no singular)	**ку́дри**	кудре́й

Nominative Singular (кто/что)	Genitive Singular (кого/чего)	Nominative Plural	Genitive Plural
(no singular)	(no singular)	**дрова́**	дров
лоб	лба	лбы	лбов
па́лец	па́льца	па́льцы	па́льцев
(no singular)	(no singular)	**хло́пья**	хло́пьев
(no singular)	(no singular)	**по́хороны**	похоро́н
молоко́	**молока́**	(no plural)	(no plural)
ту́фля	ту́фли	ту́фли	ту́фель
коро́ль	короля́	короли́	короле́й
рог	ро́га	рога́	рого́в
сена́тор	сена́тора	сена́торы	сена́торов
перо́	**пера́**	пе́рья	пе́рьев
плечо́	плеча́	пле́чи	плеч
у́хо	у́ха	у́ши	ушей
ска́зка	ска́зки	ска́зки	ска́зок
сва́дьба	**сва́дьбы**	сва́дьбы	сва́деб
о́блако	о́блака	**облака́**	облако́в
глаз	гла́за	глаза́	глаз
се́рдце	се́рдца	сердца́	серде́ц
око́шко	око́шка	око́шки	око́шек

14 The Instrumental Case

Творительный падеж

Useful Vocabulary

Professions

адвока́т	lawyer
антропо́лог	anthropologist
архите́ктор	architect
библиоте́карь	librarian
био́лог	biologist
води́тель авто́буса	bus driver
врач	doctor, physician
генера́л	general
журнали́ст	journalist
инжене́р	engineer
кинозвезда́	movie star
лётчик	pilot
меха́ник	mechanic
милиционе́р	policeman (in Russia)
педаго́г	educator
перево́дчик	translator
писа́тель	writer
пожа́рник	firefighter

профе́ссор	professor
психо́лог	psychologist
секрета́рь	secretary
такси́ст	taxi driver
учёный	scientist, scholar
фи́зик	physicist
хи́мик	chemist

Verbs

рабо́тать	to work (as)
служи́ть	to work (as) (white collar)
стать	to become
быть	to be
лечи́ть	to treat or cure (by means of)

Transportation

авто́бус	bus
велосипе́д	bicycle
маши́на	car
метро́	subway
мотоци́кл	motorcycle
по́езд	train (long distance)
самолёт	airplane
такси́	taxi
трамва́й	tram
тролле́йбус	trolley
электри́чка	commuter train

VOCABULARY PRACTICE

This exercise lists famous people, some of them in English so that you can recognize them. Say who they are, employing an adjective describing their nationality and another adjective of your choice.

1. Frank Lloyd Wright

2. Си́гмунд Фрейд

3. Ма́рия Монтессо́ри

4. John Dewey

5. А.С. Пу́шкин

6. Наполео́н

7. Мадо́нна

8. Ма́ргарет Мид

9. А́льберт Эйнште́йн

10. Кларк Кент

11. F. Lee Bailey *or* Alan Dershowitz

12. Ralph Kramden

13. Mr. Goodwrench

14. Louis Pasteur

15. Чарлз Да́рвин

CONVERSATION PRACTICE

Кем ты хо́чешь стать?

БА́БУШКА: Ва́нечка! Кем ты хо́чешь стать? Пожа́рником? Милиционе́ром? Космона́втом?

ВА́НЯ: Ба́бушка! Ты же зна́ешь, что бу́дущим ле́том я око́нчу университе́т!

Б: Да, дорого́й, я забы́ла. Тогда́ наве́рное ты хо́чешь быть лётчиком, и́ли президе́нтом на́шей страны́, и́ли больши́м капитали́стом?

В: Да нет! По́сле оконча́ния университе́та я хочу́ поступи́ть в аспиранту́ру. Я бу́ду занима́ться и́ли биоло́гией, и́ли микробиоло́гией, и́ли биохи́мией.

Б: А по́сле аспиранту́ры?

В: А по́сле аспиранту́ры я бу́ду рабо́тать био́логом.

Б: А почему́ ты не хо́чешь учи́ться на врача́?

В: Потому́ что я не интересу́юсь медици́ной.

Б: Ну, так что ж. Е́сли ты дово́лен свое́й жи́знью, э́то са́мое гла́вное.

В: Я согла́сен с тобо́й. Быть счастли́вым—э́то всё.

Б: Ну, Ва́ня, мне пора́. Сего́дня ве́чером мы с твое́й ма́мой идём на конце́рт.

В: А как вы туда́ е́дете—авто́бусом или трамва́ем?

Б: Мы е́дем на метро́. На такси́ сли́шком до́рого, а авто́бусом сли́шком ме́дленно.

В: Поня́тно. Ну, всего́ хоро́шего, ба́бушка!

Б: (*не́жным го́лосом*) Мы все горди́мся тобо́й, Ва́нечка. Ты бу́дешь по́льзоваться больши́м успе́хом во что бы то ни ста́ло.

В: Я счита́ю э́то больши́м комплиме́нтом!

Б: Пока́, Ва́ня!
В: До свида́ния, ба́бушка!

Find all of the words in the instrumental case in the dialogue above. See the answer key to check that you got them all.

What Do You Want to Be (When You Grow Up)?

GRANDMA: Vanya! What do you want to be someday? A firefighter? A police officer? An astronaut?

VANYA: Grandma! You know that next summer I'm graduating from the university!

G: Yes, dear, I forgot. Then you probably want to be a pilot or the president of our country, or a big capitalist.

V: Of course not! After I graduate I want to go to graduate school. I want to study either biology or microbiology or biochemistry.

G: And after graduate school?

V: After graduate school I will work as a biologist.

G: And why don't you want to study to be a doctor?

V: Because I'm not interested in medicine.

G: Well, OK. If you are satisfied with your life, that's the most important thing.

V: I agree with you. Being happy is everything.

G: Well, Vanya, I have to go. Your mother and I are going to a concert tonight.

V: How are you getting there, by bus or tram?

G: We're taking the subway. The taxi is too expensive, and the bus is too slow.

V: Right. Have a nice time, grandma.

G: (*in a tender voice*) We are all proud of you, Vanya. You will be very successful, no matter what.

V: I consider that a big compliment!

G: Bye, Vanya!

V: Good-bye, Grandma!

Noun Endings

The endings of the instrumental case are as follows:

Masculine and Neuter	-ом/-ем
Feminine	-ой/-ей[1]
Plural	-ами/-ями

Remember, of course, to apply the five-letter spelling rule if necessary: **с отцо́м,** but **с ме́сяцем.**

There are several exceptions in the instrumental plural. They are **людьми́, детьми́, дочерьми́, лошадьми́, дверьми́.**[2]

Adjective Endings

Masculine and Neuter	-ым/-им
Feminine	-ой/-ей[3]
Plural	-ыми/-ими

The second endings for masculine, neuter, and plural adjectives are used when required by the seven-letter spelling rule and the feminine alternate ending when required by the five-letter spelling rule. All three alternate endings are used, of course, when the stem of the adjective is soft.

Uses

As an Instrument or Means

The instrumental case is so called because one among its many uses is to express the notion that something is being used as an instrument or means.

---

[1] There is an expanded form for feminine nouns—**-ою/-ею**—that will be encountered in poetry and the literary language, but these alternative endings, which were widespread throughout the nineteenth century, are gradually disappearing.

[2] The regular forms **лошадя́ми** and **дверя́ми** are also acceptable.

[3] See footnote 1.

писа́ть пра́вой или ле́вой руко́й	to write with your right or left hand
смотре́ть глаза́ми и слу́шать уша́ми	to look with your eyes and hear with your ears
есть суп ло́жкой	to eat soup with a spoon
есть пи́ццу рука́ми	to eat pizza with your hands
ре́зать бума́гу но́жницами	to cut paper with scissors
стреля́ть ружьём	to shoot with a gun
руби́ть капу́сту ножо́м	to chop cabbage with a knife.
мыть ру́ки мы́лом и горя́чей водо́й	to wash your hands with soap and hot water
скрежета́ть зуба́ми	to grind your teeth

English usually uses the preposition *with* in such cases, but this can lead to confusion in Russian, which does not use a preposition in this meaning.

Russian uses the instrumental case with certain verbs and parts of the body where English uses a direct object. Some examples of this usage are:

кача́ть голово́й	to shake your head
маха́ть руко́й	to wave your hand
пожа́ть плеча́ми	to shrug your shoulders
трясти́ кулако́м	to shake your fist
ударя́ть ного́й	to kick your leg/foot

Means of Transportation

This usage is synonymous with using **на** with the prepositional case.

Он е́дет на рабо́ту авто́бусом.	He goes to work by bus.
Туда́ на́до е́хать то́лько самолётом.	You can get there only by plane.

На plus the prepositional case must be used for the indeclinable nouns **метро́** and **такси́.**

Manner

Она́ говори́т ти́хим го́лосом.	She speaks in a quiet voice.

The Second of a Double Direct Object

Его вы́брали президе́нтом.	He was elected president.
Её назна́чили дире́ктором.	She was appointed director.
Я призна́л себя́ вино́вным.	I admitted my guilt. (I recognized myself as guilty.)
Все счита́ют его́ тала́нтливым.	Everyone considers him talented.
Я нахожу́ э́ту о́перу бана́льной.	I find this opera banal.

Time Expressions

The most common time expressions that are used in the instrumental refer to times of the day and seasons of the year: **у́тром** (in the morning), **днём** (in the afternoon), **ве́чером** (in the evening), **но́чью** (at night), **весно́й** (in the spring), **ле́том** (in the summer), **о́сенью** (fall), **зимо́й** (in the winter).

Some examples of the use of these expressions are **бу́дущим ле́том** (next summer), **вчера́ ве́чером** (last night), **сего́дня у́тром** (this morning), **про́шлой о́сенью** (last fall), **за́втра днём** (tomorrow afternoon).

With Certain Verbs

The instrumental is optional after the past and future tenses of the verb **быть.** If it is used, it indicates a temporary rather than a permanent or intrinsic condition. Thus, you may say either **Она́ была́ тала́нтливой актри́сой** or **Она́ была́ тала́нтливая актри́са.** But you must say only **Она́ была́ ру́сская.**

After the infinitive form of **быть,** the instrumental is required: **Кем ты хо́чешь быть?**

The instrumental is required after all forms of the verb **стать.**

After the two verbs **рабо́тать** and **служи́ть** the instrumental is used when you wish to indicate that someone works *as* something: **Ива́н Петро́вич рабо́тает хи́миком.**

Among the other verbs that take instrumental are **явля́ться** (to be, in formal writing), **вы́глядеть** (to look like), **каза́ться** (to seem), **оказа́ться** (to turn out to be), and **оста́ться** (to remain).

По́сле сме́рти роди́телей Ка́тя оста́лась сирото́й.	After the death of her parents, Katya was left an orphan.
Э́тот рома́н ка́жется мне о́чень сло́жным.	This novel seems complicated to me.

Он оказа́лся успе́шным бизнесме́ном.

He turned out to be a successful businessman.

With Certain Prepositions

C *(with)*

One way to test for the need or absence of a preposition is to see whether your sentence works with the opposite preposition **без** (without). If it does, then in most cases you will need the preposition **c** to express *with* in Russian. Compare **Он ходи́л на конце́рт с О́льгой** with **Он ходи́л на конце́рт без О́льги**.

Here are some examples of the use of the preposition **c:**

Мы с бра́том ходи́ли в кино́.[4]	My brother and I went to the movies.
Она́ живёт ря́дом со мно́й.	She lives next door to me.
Я пью чай с лимо́ном и с са́харом.	I drink tea with lemon and sugar.
Он согла́сен со мно́й.	He agrees with me.
Что́ бу́дет с на́шим сы́ном?	What's going to happen to our son?
О́ля ходи́ла на конце́рт с Ва́ней.	Olga went to the concert with Vanya.
Он до́лго говори́л с милиционе́ром.	He talked with the policeman for a long time.
Я о́чень люблю́ пирожки́ с гриба́ми.	I love mushroom pirozhki.
С удово́льствием!	With pleasure! *or* I'd love to! (*as a response to an invitation*)

Note that this is also the way that Russians express how food is filled or what it comes with. In English we use an adjective phrase: *a ham sandwich, meat pirozhki,* or *mushroom soup.* In Russian you use the preposition **c: бутербро́д с ветчино́й, пирожки́ с мя́сом, суп с гриба́ми.**

За

This preposition has three meanings that are used with the instrumental case:

1. *for,* in the sense of *going for, to fetch*

Он пошёл в магази́н за молоко́м.	He went to the store for milk.
Она́ пошла́ за ружьём.	She went for (to get) the rifle.

---

[4] **Мы с X** is the idiomatic Russian expression for *X and I.*

2. in a spatial sense meaning *behind:* **Бáбушка сидúт за гаражóм и пьёт вóдку** (*Grandma is sitting behind the garage drinking vodka*).

3. *at:* **Он сидúт за столóм и занимáется** (*He is sitting at the table studying*).

Мéжду *(between)*

Онá сидúт мéжду Вúктором и Ларúсой.	She sits between Victor and Larisa.
Мéжду нáми я считáю Кáтю ужáсной сплéтницей.	Between us, Katya's an awful gossip.
Лáтвия нахóдится мéжду Эстóнией и Литвóй.	Latvia is located between Estonia and Lithuania.

Над *(over, above; on; at)*

Над нáми летáют тóлько птúцы.	Only birds fly over us.
Онá рабóтает над диссертáцией.	She's working on her dissertation.
Почемý ты всегдá смеёшься нáдо мной?	Why are you always laughing at me?

Под *(below, underneath, nearby)*

Твоú тýфли стоя́т под столóм.	Your shoes are under the table.
Онú живýт под Москвóй.	They live in the Moscow suburbs.
Сверхчеловéк живёт под вúдом журналúста Клáрка Кéнта.	Superman lives under the guise of the journalist Clark Kent.

Перед *(spatially in front of; temporally right before)*

Давáйте встрéтимся перед Большúм теáтром.	Let's meet in front of the Bolshoi Theater.
Нáдо помы́ть рýки перед обéдом.	One should wash one's hands before dinner.

In the opinion of many who study and teach Russian, one of the most memorable pieces of verse of the modern age was composed by Alexander Lipson for his brilliant Russian grammar[5] as a mnemonic device for learning instrumental prepositions:

---

[5] Lipson, Alexander, *A Russian Course,* part 2 (Columbus, Ohio: Slavica, 1981).

Ме́жду сту́лом и столо́м
Ре́жет Же́ня нос ножо́м
Пе́ред бра́том и отцо́м.
Э́то о́чень стра́нный дом.

Between the chair and the table
Zhenya is cutting his nose with a knife
In front of his brother and his father.
This is a very strange house.

TEST FOR MASTERY 1

Match the people in column A with a noun in column B that they might have been, and then state what they became (column C). Feel free to substitute your own ideas for the suggestions in column B, and use adjectives freely.

Example: В мо́лодости Хи́лари Кли́нтон была́ <u>официа́нткой</u>, но она́ переду́мала и ста́ла адвока́том.

A	B	C
1. Мадо́нна	меха́ник	больша́я кинозвезда́
2. Екатери́на II	продаве́ц(вщи́ца)	мэр Нью-Йо́рка
3. Достое́вский	хулига́н(ка)	наш пе́рвый президе́нт
4. А́льберт Э́йнштейн	зану́да (*a bore*)	цари́ца Росси́и
5. Г. Вашингто́н	фе́рмер	знамени́тый учёный
6. Ива́н Па́влов	убро́щик(щица) (*janitor*)	вели́кий психо́лог
7. Ру́ди Джулья́ни	плохо́й студе́нт	изве́стный писа́тель

TEST FOR MASTERY 2

Compose sentences that express the season(s) during which people engage in various sports. Use the verb supplied with the activity. Choose your own names. If the activity may be enjoyed year round, use the expression **кру́глый год** (this is in the accusative case). Note: The verb **занима́ться** takes the instrumental case.

Model: Ди́ма пла́вает на мо́ре   (Dima swims in the sea only in
             то́лько ле́том.   the summer.)

1. фехтова́ние   fencing (занима́ться)

2. ката́ться на лы́жах   to ski

3. ката́ться на во́дных лы́жах   to water-ski

 4. ката́тся на велосипе́де   to go bike riding

 5. пла́вать в бассе́йне   to swim in a pool

 6. игра́ть в те́ннис   to play tennis

 7. гуля́ть в па́рке   to walk in the park

 8. фигу́рное ката́ние   figure skating (занима́ться)

 9. гимна́стика   gymnastics (занима́ться)

10. ката́ться на ро́ликах   to go roller-skating

11. бе́гать на стадио́не   to run at the stadium

12. е́здить верхо́м   to go horseback riding

13. ката́ться на конька́х   to go ice-skating

14. игра́ть в хокке́й   to play hockey

15. йо́га   yoga (занима́ться)

TEST FOR MASTERY 3

Place the words in parentheses into the instrumental case. For help, see the answer key for translations of the sentences. Be sure you know why the instrumental is required.

1. Ла́твия расположе́на ме́жду (Литва́) и (Эсто́ния).

2. За (го́ры) нахо́дится ма́ленькая дере́вня.

3. (Что) ты пи́шешь? Я пишу́ иногда́ (ру́чка), иногда́ (каранда́ш).

4. Все счита́ют его́ (спосо́бный инжене́р).

5. Пе́тя лю́бит пирожки́ с (грибы́), с (мя́со), и с (рис), но он не лю́бит пирожки́ с (капу́ста).

6. В мо́лодости я рабо́тал (официа́нт), а тепе́рь я служу́ (секрета́рь).

7. Ма́ша хо́чет стать (больша́я кинозвезда́).

8. Она́ говори́ла мне э́тот секре́т (шо́пот).

9. Перед (прави́тельство) стои́т о́страя пробле́ма.

10. Когда́ я не́рвничаю, я скрежещу́ (зу́бы).

11. —(Что́) вы занима́етесь?—Я рабо́таю (архите́ктор).

12. Соба́ка игра́ет с (ко́шка) под (стол).

13. (Ле́то) мы е́здили в Теха́с. Туда́ мы е́хали (самолёт), а обра́тно (по́езд).

14. Ва́ня пошёл на по́чту за (ма́рки).

ANSWER KEY

Vocabulary Practice

1. Э́то изве́стный америка́нский архите́ктор.

2. Э́то знамени́тый австри́йский психо́лог.

3. Э́то изве́стный италья́нский педаго́г.

4. Э́то изве́стный америка́нский библиоте́карь.

5. Э́то замеча́тельный ру́сский писа́тель.

6. Э́то знамени́тый францу́зский генера́л.

7. Э́то плоха́я америка́нская кинозвезда́.

8. Э́то изве́стный америка́нский антропо́лог.

9. Э́то потряса́ющий неме́цкий фи́зик.

10. Э́то кро́ткий (*meek*) америка́нский журнали́ст.

11. Э́то изве́стный америка́нский адвока́т.

12. Э́то бе́дный америка́нский води́тель авто́буса.

13. Э́то у́мный америка́нский меха́ник.

14. Э́то знамени́тый францу́зский врач.

15. Э́то изве́стный англи́йский био́лог.

Reading Exercise

БА́БУШКА: Ва́нечка! <u>Кем</u> ты хо́чешь стать? <u>Пожа́рником</u>? <u>Милиционе́ром</u>?
<u>Космона́втом</u>?

ВА́ня: Ба́бушка! Ты же зна́ешь, что <u>бу́дущим ле́том</u> я око́нчу университе́т!

Б: Да, дорого́й, я забы́ла. Тогда́ наве́рное ты хо́чешь быть <u>лётчиком</u>, и́ли <u>президе́нтом</u> на́шей страны́, и́ли <u>больши́м капитали́стом</u>?

В: Да нет! По́сле оконча́ния университе́та я хочу́ поступи́ть в аспиранту́ру. Я бу́ду занима́ться и́ли <u>биоло́гией</u>, и́ли <u>микробиоло́гией</u>, и́ли <u>биохи́мией</u>.

Б: А по́сле аспиранту́ры?

В: А по́сле аспиранту́ры я буду́ рабо́тать <u>биологом</u>.

Б: А почему́ ты не хо́чешь учи́ться на врача́?

В: Потому́ что я не иетересу́юсь <u>медици́ной</u>.

Б: Ну так что ж. Если ты дово́лен <u>свое́й жи́знью</u>, э́то са́мое гла́вное.

В: Я согла́сен с <u>тобо́й</u>. Быть <u>счастли́вым</u>—это всё.

Б: Ну, Ва́ня, мне пора́. Сего́дня <u>ве́чером</u> мы с <u>твое́й ма́мой</u> идём на конце́рт.

В: А как вы туда́ е́дете—<u>авто́бусом</u> и́ли <u>трамва́ем</u>?

Б: Мы е́дем на метро́. На такси́ сли́шком до́рого, а <u>авто́бусом</u> сли́шком ме́дленно.

В: Поня́тно. Ну, всего́ хоро́шего, ба́бушка!

Б: (*нежным голосом*) Мы все горди́мся <u>тобо́й</u>, Ва́нечка. Ты бу́дешь по́льзоваться <u>больши́м успе́хом</u> в жи́зни, во что́ бы то ни ста́ло.

В: Я счита́ю э́то <u>больши́м комплиме́нтом</u>!

Б: Пока́, Ва́ня!

В: До свида́ния, ба́бушка!

Test for Mastery 1

1. В мо́лодости Мадо́нна была́ настоя́щей хулига́нкой, но она́ ста́ла большо́й кинозвездо́й.

2. Когда́ она́ была́ ма́ленькой, Екатери́на II была́ плохо́й студе́нткой, но она́ ста́ла цари́цей Росси́и.

3. В мо́лодости Достое́вский рабо́тал убо́рщиком, но он стал изве́стным писа́телем.

4. Когда́ он был ма́леньким, А́льберт Эйнште́йн рабо́тал меха́ником, но он стал знамени́тым учёным.

5. В мо́лодости Вашингто́н был фе́рмером, но он стал на́шим пе́рвым президе́нтом.

6. Когда́ он был ма́леньким, Ива́н Па́влов рабо́тал продавцо́м, но он стал вели́ким психо́логом.

7. В мо́лодости Ру́ди Джулья́ни был больши́м зану́дой, но он стал мэ́ром Нью-Йо́рка.

Test for Mastery 2

1. Ка́тя занима́ется фехтова́нием зимо́й и весно́й.

2. И́горь ката́ется на лы́жах то́лько зимо́й.

3. Та́ня ката́ется на во́дных лы́жах то́лько ле́том.

4. Серёжа ката́ется на велосипе́де весно́й, ле́том, и о́сенью.

5. А́ня пла́вает в бассе́йне кру́глый год.

6. Ва́ся игра́ет в те́ннис ле́том.

7. Ли́за гуля́ет в па́рке весно́й и о́сенью.

8. Са́ша занима́ется фигу́рным ката́нием зимо́й.

9. О́ля занима́ется гимна́стикой кру́глый год.

10. Же́ня ката́ется на ро́ликах весно́й, ле́том, и о́сенью.

11. Со́ня бе́гает на стадио́не весно́й и о́сенью.

12. Фе́дя е́здит верхо́м ле́том.

13. Ната́ша ката́ется на конька́х то́лько зимо́й.

14. Де́нис игра́ет в хокке́й то́лько зимо́й.

15. И́ра занима́ется йо́гой кру́глый год.

Test for Mastery 3

1. Литво́й, Эсто́нией

2. гора́ми

3. Чем, ру́чкой, карандашо́м

4. спосо́бным инжене́ром

5. гриба́ми, мя́сом, ри́сом, капу́стой

6. официа́нтом, секретарём

7. большо́й кинозвездо́й

8. шо́потом

9. прави́тельством

10. зуба́ми

11. Чем, архите́ктором

12. ко́шкой, столо́м

13. ле́том, самолётом, по́ездом

14. ма́рками

Test for Mastery 3 Translation

1. Latvia is situated between Lithuania and Estonia.

2. Beyond the mountains there is a small village.

3. What are you writing with? Sometimes I write with a pen and sometimes with a pencil.

4. Everyone considers him a capable engineer. (Everyone thinks that he is a capable engineer.)

5. Petya likes mushroom pirozhki, meat pirozhki, and rice pirozhki, but he doesn't like cabbage pirozhki.

6. In my youth I worked as a waiter, but now I work as a secretary.

7. Masha wants to become a big movie star.

8. She told me this secret in a whisper.

9. The administration is faced with a critical problem. (*Lit*. Before the administration stands a critical problem.)

10. When I'm nervous I grind my teeth.

11. What do you do? I work as an architect.

12. The dog is playing with the cat under the table.

13. In the summer we went to Texas. We went there by plane but returned by train.

14. Vanya went to the post office for stamps.

15 Verbs of Motion

Глаголы движения

Students of Russian have been known to wring their hands and sweat profusely in their many attempts to master Russian verbs of motion. It is widely known that a shelf's worth of books have been written on the subject, and, indeed, there is no denying that verbs of motion are a complex and Byzantine topic. These verbs, however, cannot only be mastered, they can be conquered in a relatively painless way, so that ninety-five percent of the time the student will be able to choose the correct form of the verb.

Probably the most daunting fact is that there are so many ways to translate the simple verb *to go* in Russian. A speaker will distinguish between going on foot, by vehicle, by plane, or by boat. You may also *crawl, climb, run,* or *shuffle.* Any one of these verbs may be rendered into English as *go.* Which to choose?

Intransitive Verbs of Motion

Imperfective		Perfective	English
Indeterminate (multidirectional)	**Determinate (unidirectional)**		
ходи́ть	идти́	пойти́	to go (on foot)
е́здить	е́хать	пое́хать	to go (by vehicle)
лета́ть	лете́ть	полете́ть	to fly
пла́вать	плыть	поплы́ть	to swim, sail
бе́гать	бежа́ть	побежа́ть	to run

Imperfective		Perfective	English
Indeterminate (multidirectional)	**Determinate (unidirectional)**		
броди́ть*	брести́	побрести́	to stroll, shuffle
по́лзать*	ползти́	поползти́	to crawl
ла́зить*	лезть	поле́зть	to climb

* These verbs are less commonly used and will not be covered in this chapter.

Let's begin with two simple but essential criteria that Russians use to characterize what they mean when they say *go*.

1. Russians distinguish between going on your own two feet and going by vehicle—any ground vehicle (bicycle, skateboard, golf cart, bus, paddy wagon, elevator), as long as you are riding or being driven.

2. Russians specify the type of action—whether it is a one-time, one-direction action, or whether it is multiple or habitual.

It is this latter principle that needs to be understood, learned, and remembered, and the best way to do this is by comparing a few Russian sentences with the English translations.

Ходи́ть vs. Идти́

Ходи́ть		Идти́	
я хожу́	мы хо́дим	я иду́	мы идём
ты хо́дишь	вы хо́дите	ты идёшь	вы идёте
он хо́дит	они́ хо́дят	она идёт	они́ иду́т

Both of these verbs mean *to go*, both give the present tense when conjugated, both are imperfective, and both specify *by foot*. Wherein lies the difference? Let's compare several pairs of sentences and see how their translations differ.

Indeterminate	English	Determinate	English
Я ча́сто хожу́ в теа́тр.	I often go to the theater.	Я иду́ в теа́тр сего́дня ве́чером.	I am going to the theater tonight.
Он хо́дит ме́дленно.	He walks slowly.	Он идёт домо́й.	He is going home.

Indeterminate	English	Determinate	English
Ребёнок ужé хóдит.	The child already walks.	Ребёнок идёт к мáтери.	The child is walking to his mother.
Сáша хóдит на занятия три рáза в недéлю.	Sasha goes to school three days a week.	Сáша идёт на занятия сегóдня ýтром.	Sasha is going to school this morning.
Мои дéти не хóдят в шкóлу.	My children don't go to school.	Мои дéти идýт в шкóлу через 5 минýт.	My children are going to school in 5 minutes.
Мы почти никогдá не хóдим в кинó.	We almost never go to the movies.	Мы идём в кинó сегóдня днём.	We are going to the movies this afternoon.
Кудá вы хóдите кáждый вéчер пóсле ýжина?	Where do you go every evening after dinner?	Кудá вы идёте сейчáс?	Where are you going now?
Почемý ты так быстро хóдишь?	Why do you walk so fast?	Кудá ты так быстро идёшь?	Where are you rushing to?

As you can see, the sentences in the indeterminate column all translate the forms of **ходи́ть** as *go* or *walk*. Similarly, the forms of **идти́** in the determinate column are all translated as *am/is/are going*. This is one way that you can check yourself: If the verb you need calls for an *-ing* form, you can be fairly sure that you need a determinate verb of motion.

Indeterminate verbs of motion, by process of elimination, are used for everything else where *go* (on foot) is needed. The following sentences illustrate further uses for the indeterminate verb **ходи́ть.** No destination is specified in any of these sentences. The action of walking is emphasized.

Мать хóдит по кóмнате с больным ребёнком в рукáх.	The mother is walking around the room with a sick child in her arms.
Мой муж óчень лю́бит ходи́ть по гóроду вéчером.	My husband likes to walk around the city in the evening.
Тури́сты хóдят по Крáсной плóщади.	The tourists are walking around Red Square.

TEST FOR MASTERY 1

Fill in the blanks with the appropriate verb of motion for going on foot. You are provided with the correct forms to make the exercise a bit easier. The indeterminate verb is listed first. Try to articulate your reasons for choosing one form over another.

1. Жéня, куда́ ты _____? (хо́дишь / идёшь)

2. Я _____ в библиоте́ку ка́ждый день. (хожу́ / иду́)

3. Вот наконе́ц _____ наш авто́бус! (хо́дит / идёт)

4. Па́па _____ по ко́мнате, говори́т про себя́ (*to himself*). (хо́дит / идёт)

5. Я о́чень люблю́ _____ по го́роду. (ходи́ть / идти́)

6. Э́тот ребёнок ещё не _____. (хо́дит / идёт)

7. Почему́ э́тот по́езд _____ так ме́дленно? (хо́дит / идёт) (*Be careful with this one!*)

8. Дождь _____ как из ведра́ (*as out of a bucket*). (хо́дит / идёт)

9. Ты ча́сто _____ в кино́? (хо́дишь / идёшь)

10. Куда́ она́ так бы́стро _____? (хо́дит / идёт)

11. Лю́ди _____ по у́лице на рабо́ту. (хо́дят / иду́т)

12. Почему́ вы не _____ на рабо́ту? (хо́дите / идёте) Вы больны́?

Éздить vs. Éхать

Éздить		Éхать	
я е́зжу	мы е́здим	я е́ду	мы е́дем
ты е́здишь	вы е́здите	ты е́дешь	вы е́дете
она́ е́здит	они́ е́здят	он е́дет	они́ е́дут

These verbs behave in exactly the same ways as **ходи́ть** and **идти́** above, except they have the additional meaning of going by vehicle. Their meanings, therefore, can be extended to mean *ride* or *drive*.

Indeterminate	English	Determinate	English
Я ча́сто е́зжу в Босто́н.	I often go to Boston.	За́втра я е́ду в Босто́н.	I am going to Boston tomorrow.
Он е́здит ме́дленно.	He drives slowly.	Он е́дет домо́й.	He is driving home.

Indeterminate	English	Determinate	English
Са́ша е́здит на рабо́ту ка́ждый день.	Sasha drivcs to work every day.	Чсрсз час Са́ша сдст на рабо́ту.	Sasha is going to work in an hour.
Мы почти́ никогда́ не е́здим за́ город.	We almost never go out of town.	За́втра мы е́дем в дере́вню.	Tomorrow we're going to the countryside.
Я люблю́ е́здить в Крым.	I like to go to the Crimea.	В ма́рте я е́ду в Крым.	In March I am going to the Crimea.

As in the previous section, all the verbs in the determinate column express the present progressive tense in English (*am/are/is going*).

TEST FOR MASTERY 2

Fill in the blanks with the appropriate verb of motion for going by vehicle. Again, you are provided with the correct forms to make the exercise a bit easier. The indeterminate verb is listed first. Try to articulate your reasons for choosing one form over another.

1. А́ня, куда́ ты _____ ка́ждое ле́то? (е́здишь / е́дешь)

2. Я _____ на рабо́ту ка́ждый день. (е́зжу / е́ду)

3. Дава́й _____ на о́перу на такси́. (е́здим / е́дем)

4. Мы о́чень лю́бим _____ по го́роду. (е́здить / е́хать)

5. Ка́ждый день фе́рмеры _____ в го́род. (е́здят / е́дут)

6. Куда́ вы _____? (е́здите / е́дете)

7. На бу́дущей неде́ле мы _____ во Фдори́ду. (е́здим / е́дем)

8. Ба́бушка никогда́ не _____ туда́. (е́здила / е́хала)

9. Ты ча́сто _____ за́ город? (е́здишь / е́дешь)

10. Куда́ она́ так бы́стро _____? (е́здит / е́дет)

11. Почему́ наш тролле́йбус так ме́дленно _____? (е́здит / е́дет)

12. Ко́ля _____ к Ната́ше в дере́вню раз в ме́сяц. (е́здит / е́дет)

Reading Exercise

The following short dialogue between a father and son at the zoo illustrates the use of indeterminate verbs of motion. There is, however, one determinate verb of motion in the text. See if you can find it.

В зоопа́рке[1]

—Па́па, ра́зве бе́лые медве́ди пла́вают?

—Пла́вают. И о́чень хорошо́! Посмотри́, как бы́стро плывёт э́тот медве́дь.

—А почему́ они́ пла́вают, они́ ведь не ры́бы.

—Они́ должны́ пла́вать, потому́ что они́ живу́т на льди́нах в Ледови́том океа́не.

—Вот интере́сно! Они́ и хо́дят, и бе́гают, и пла́вают. Мо́жет быть, они́ и лета́ют как пти́цы?

—Не говори́ глу́постей.

—Ну и что же . . . Ведь самолёты то́же не пти́цы, а лета́ют.

—Самолёты стро́ят лю́ди. И лета́ют на них лю́ди.

—И ещё медве́ди е́здят на велосипе́дах, да? Я ви́дел, когда́ ходи́л с ма́мой в цирк.

—Да, е́здят. Но то́лько в ци́рке их специа́льно э́тому у́чат.

At the Zoo

"Dad, do white bears swim?"

"Yes, they do. And they swim well! Look how fast that bear is swimming."

"But why do they swim? They're not fish, after all."

"They have to swim because they live on ice floes in the Arctic Ocean."

---

[1] The following dialogue has been adapted from *Русский язык для иностранных студентов* by Kostomarov, Polovnikova, and Shvedova (Moscow, 1977).

"That's interesting! So they walk and run and swim. Maybe they also fly like birds?"

"Don't be silly."

"Well, all right. But airplanes are not birds, and they fly."

"Airplanes are built by people. And people fly on them."

"And bears also ride bicycles, right? I saw them when I went to the circus with mama."

"Yes, they do. But only in the circus, and they are specially trained to do this."

Analysis

The use of the indeterminate verb of motion is the focus of this dialogue from the child's very first question, *"Do white bears swim?"* The idea of *swimming* as an activity is of prime interest. *Yes, bears (can) swim.* The father immediately follows up by adding that they swim well, putting emphasis on the manner of the action. Later, the father mentions that bears have to swim, and again, the emphasis is on general necessity rather than a specific goal. They live on ice floes and therefore must know how to swim. The child then muses on the characteristics of the bear's locomotion: it walks and runs and swims—and perhaps flies? These four verbs are all indeterminate, that is, they do not specify any direction or time but rather define the type of motion typical to bears. The child then says, *"Airplanes fly,"* again using the indeterminate verb: people walk, planes fly. They are not flying to any place in particular. They simply have the ability to fly. The same applies to people who fly in planes. They fly back and forth, here and there, at various times. Last, the child inquires as to whether bears ride bicycles. Again, this is an indeterminate verb mentioning only the bear's ability to perform this action. No goal or time is specified.

Did you find the one determinate verb of motion? It is in the second line of the dialogue, when the father says, *"Look how fast that bear is swimming* (плывёт)!" The reasons for using this verb are quite specific and differ from the criteria for choosing indeterminate verbs. The context here—*Look! The bear is swimming (toward us)*—specifies one time (the present) and one direction (no matter where precisely the bear is swimming, he is swimming in one direction—forward). Second, the English translation uses the present progressive form of the verb, and ninety-nine percent of English present progressive verbs (the *-ing* form of the verb) will be rendered in Russian by the determinate verb.

Transitive Verbs of Motion

Imperfective		Perfective	English
Indeterminate (multidirectional)	**Determinate (unidirectional)**		
води́ть	вести́	повести́	to lead
носи́ть	нести́	понести́	to carry
вози́ть	везти́	повезти́	to transport

Анекдоты[2]

The following well-known children's jokes will illustrate verbs of motion in practice. The verbs of motion have been underlined so that you can quickly locate them.

1. —Скажи́те, пожа́луйста, почему́ вы <u>пла́ваете</u> в костю́ме и шля́пе?
   —Я <u>пла́ваю</u>? Это *вы* <u>пла́ваете</u>, дорого́й мой, а я тону́!

2. —Неуже́ли ты ве́ришь му́жу, что он <u>е́здит</u> лови́ть ры́бу? Ведь он ни ра́зу не пойма́л ни одно́й ры́бы.
   —Поэ́тому я и ве́рю ему́.

3. Одна́жды в Екатеринбу́рге две стару́шки се́ли в по́езд. В ваго́не они́ сиде́ли и разгова́ривали.
   —Куда́ вы <u>е́дете</u>?—спроси́ла одна́.
   —Я <u>е́ду</u> в Москву́, к сы́ну.
   —А я—во Владивосто́к, к до́чери.
   —Смотри́те, кака́я тепе́рь замеча́тельная те́хника,—сказа́ла пе́рвая стару́шка.—Мы сиди́м в одно́м ваго́не, а <u>е́дем</u> в ра́зные сто́роны!

4. —Ты опя́ть <u>идёшь</u> в теа́тр? Ведь мы уже́ <u>ходи́ли</u> на э́ту пье́су.
   —Да, но я <u>ходи́ла</u> не в э́том пла́тье.

5. До́ктор Бра́ун утеша́ет пацие́нта:
   —Пове́рьте мне, вам ничто́ не угрожа́ет. Про́сто вам необходи́м све́жий во́здух. Я бы посове́товал бо́льше <u>ходи́ть</u>, дви́гаться. Кто́ вы по профе́сии?
   —Я почтальо́н.

---

[2] The forms of the jokes that appear here have been adapted from *Verbs of Motion in Russian* by L. Muravyova (Moscow, 1975).

6. Ми́ша пришёл домо́й и сказа́л ма́ме:

—Ты бу́дешь дово́льна, ма́ма, я сего́дня сэконо́мил: я не сел на авто́бусе, а всю доро́гу <u>бежа́л</u> за ним.

—Ну что ж. На сле́дующий раз <u>беги́</u> за такси́, ты сэконо́мишь гора́здо бо́льше.

Jokes

1. "Tell me, please, why are you swimming in a suit and hat?"
   "I'm swimming? No, it's you who are swimming. I'm drowning!"

2. "Do you really believe your husband when he says he goes fishing? After all, he's never caught a single fish."
   "That's exactly why I believe him."

3. Once upon a time in Yekaterinburg, two old ladies got onto a train. In the car they sat and talked.
   "Where are you going?" asked one of them.
   "I am going to Moscow to my son's place."
   "And I'm going to my daughter's in Vladivostok."
   "Look what wonderful technology we have today," said the first lady. "We are sitting in the same train but are going in different directions!"

4. "You're going to the theater again? But we've already gone to that play."
   "Yes, but I didn't go in this dress."

5. Dr. Brown is trying to soothe a patient:
   "Believe me, nothing is threatening you. But you must get fresh air. I would advise you to walk more, to move about. What do you do for a living?"
   "I'm a mailman."

6. Misha came home and said to his mother:
   "You'll be pleased, mom. I saved money today. I didn't take the bus but ran after it the entire way."
   "So what. Next time run after a taxi. You'll save much more."

Prefixed Verbs of Motion

Prefixed verbs of motion are considerably easier than their nonprefixed cousins. Because of their similarities, however, they may confuse what you have already learned about the nonprefixed forms. Forget the latter for now. It will all come together later.

Unlike nonprefixed verbs of motion, the prefixed forms behave like most Russian verbs—they have only one imperfective and one perfective form. The formation of these verbs turns out to be extremely simple: When you add the prefix to the indeterminate verb of motion, you form the new, prefixed *imperfective* verb. When the prefix is added to the determinate verb of motion, the new, prefixed *perfective* verb of motion is formed. As you might suspect, however, nothing in Russian is that simple. In this case, you must beware of those indeterminate verbs that change their stems ever so slightly but just enough to add confusion to the mix.

From the table below, note that the stems for prefixation of *to go by vehicle, to run, to swim, to stroll, to crawl,* and *to climb* are stressed on the last syllable, whereas nonprefixed indeterminate verbs are stressed on the stem. This tip should help a great deal in keeping such similar words separate.

Second, pay special attention to the verbs *to go by vehicle, to swim, to stroll,* and *to climb* because they contain one consonant mutation and three vowel mutations from one form to the other, much the same way as English changes vowels from present to past to participle forms: *sing, sang, sung.*

Last, note that, except for the verb **ходить,** all of the remaining verbs are first conjugation and are conjugated like **рабо́тать.**

Base Forms

Original Indeterminate Verb	Secondary Imperfective	Secondary Perfective
ходить	ходить	-йти*
е́здить	-езжа́ть*	е́хать
бе́гать	-бега́ть*	бежа́ть
лета́ть	лета́ть	лете́ть
пла́вать	-плыва́ть*	плыть
броди́ть	-бреда́ть*	брести́
по́лзать	-ползá́ть*	ползти́
ла́зить	-лезá́ть*	лезть

* These verb forms do not exist without a prefix.

As far as the perfective forms of prefixed verbs, only **-йти** is irregular. All the rest are identical to the nonprefixed determinate verb of motion.

Remember the following irregularities, which were introduced in the previous lesson on verbs of motion. They are the same as for nonprefixed determinate forms.

1. The verb **éхать** has the present tense stem **-ед,** with the stem stressed.

2. The verb **бежáть** is an irregular verb in Russian. Its forms are **бегу́, бежи́шь, бежи́т, бежи́м, бежи́те, бегу́т.**

3. The verb **лете́ть** is regular second conjugation, with a consonant mutation in the first-person singular.

4. The verb **плыть** has the present tense stem **-плыв-.**

5. The verbs **брести́** and **ползти́** have the stems **-бред-** and **-полз-** and are end stressed.

6. The verb **лезть** has the stem **-лез-** and is stem stressed.

Prefixes

При-

This prefix means *arriving, coming, entering.*

The prepositions that follow this verb are the same as for the other verbs of motion: **в** and **на.** You may, however, also add that someone is arriving from a place, as in the fourth example below. In this case, the appropriate preposition will be either **из** or **с.** You will also see the preposition **к** in the meaning *toward.*

Па́па пришёл домо́й в 11 часо́в.	Dad came home at 11 o'clock.
Когда́ вы прие́хали в Аме́рику?	When did you arrive in (come to) America?
Авто́бус всегда́ прихо́дит во-время.	The bus always arrives on time.
Она́ прие́дет в Босто́н из Ло́ндона за́втра.	She will arrive in Boston from London tomorrow.
Во ско́лько прилета́ет самолёт?	At what time is the plane arriving?
Теплохо́д приплыва́ет к бе́регу.	The ship is sailing toward the shore.
За́втра к нам приезжа́ют го́сти.	Guests are coming to visit us tomorrow.

у-

Meaning *leaving* or *departing,* this is the antonymous prefix of **при-.** Again, the prepositions following may indicate departure *to* or *from.* The implication of this prefix is not being here. Thus, the reply to the last question tacitly conveys the information that she is gone for the day.

Он улетáет из Бостóна.	He is leaving Boston.
Он улетáет в Парúж.	He is leaving for Paris.
Он улетáет из Бостóна в Парúж.	He is leaving Boston for Paris.
Онú уéхали из Мúнска.	They left Minsk (are no longer here).
—Мóжно Мáрию Петрóвну?	"May I speak with Maria Petrovna?"
—Онá ужé ушлá. Онá бýдет зáвтра.	"She left. (She's gone.) She'll be in tomorrow."

The following joke illustrates the differences in position with two prefixed verbs of motion:

—Что случúлось? Почемý ты не пошёл в шкóлу?	"What happened? Why didn't you go to school?"
—Ты ведь говорúла, мáма, что óчень беспокóишься за меня, когдá я ухожý кудá-нибудь.	"But mom, you said that you worry a lot about me when I go out somewhere."

The first verb of motion, **пошёл,** indicates the mother's surprise that the child is still home and not gone or away as was expected. The sentence is similar to asking the child, *"Why aren't you at school?"* The point is that the child should not be at home. The child's response, using the verb **ухожý** (imperfective, present tense) points to going away from home and being away, no matter the destination.

в-

This prefix is spelled **во-** in front of **-йти** and **въ-** in front of soft vowels. It uses the prepositions **в** and **на** and/or **из** and **с** and **к** for people. The meaning of this prefix is *in* or *into.* By extension, you may translate forms of this verb as *enter.* Consider the following examples:

Маши́на въе́хала в гара́ж.	The car entered (drove into) the garage.
Грузови́к въезжа́ет на стро́йку.	The truck is entering the construction site.
В ко́мнату вбежа́ли де́ти.	The children ran into the room.
Ма́ша вошла́ в огоро́д.	Masha went into the garden.
Они́ вхо́дят к администра́тору.	They are coming in to see the manager.

Вы-

This prefix expresses the meaning *out of, out* (from inside), *exiting*. Use the prepositions **из** or **на,** but use **от** for people.

Де́ти вы́бежали из мо́ря.	The children ran out of the water.
Он в возмуще́нии вы́шел от дире́ктора.	He came out of the boss's office angry.
Та́ня вы́шла из ко́мнаты.	Tanya came out of her room.
Он вы́шел на не́сколько мину́т.	He stepped out for a few minutes.
Арти́сты вы́шли на сце́ну.	The performers came out on stage.

Read the text that follows, paying special attention to the verbs of motion with the prefixes **вы-** and **в-:**

Я **выхожу́** у́тром во дво́р и де́лаю заря́дку на све́жем во́здухе. Ещё ра́но, но во двор **выбега́ют** де́ти на́ших сосе́дей. Мла́дшие **выво́зят** ма́ленькую теле́жку с игру́шками.

Ста́рший сын **выво́зит** из гаража́ свой мотоци́кл. Он сади́тся на мотоци́кл и **выезжа́ет** за воро́та. Мла́дшие бра́тья **выбега́ют** за ним на у́лицу со свое́й теле́жкой. Я **вхожу́** в дом. Навстре́чу мне **выхо́дит** на́ша сосе́дка и **выно́сит** ковёр, чтобы почи́стить его́. В э́тот моме́нт её ста́рший сын **въезжа́ет** во двор на мотоци́кле и за ним с у́лицы **вбега́ют** мла́дшие де́ти и **ввозят** теле́жку. Я открыва́ю дверь и **вхожу́** в свою́ кварти́ру.

(In the morning I go out into the yard and do my exercises in the fresh air. It's still early, but our neighbors' children run out into the yard. The younger ones bring out their little wagon with their toys.

The older son takes his motorcycle out of the garage. He gets on the motorcycle and drives out the gates. His younger brothers run out after him onto the street with their wagon. I go into the house. My neighbor is coming out to meet me and is carrying out a rug to clean it. At that moment her older son drives into the yard with his motorcycle, and the children run in after him and bring in their wagon. I open the door and go into my apartment.)

The difference between the prefixes **при-** and **в-** is one of specificity: **При-** is much more general, arriving here in a large, perhaps nameless place. **В-,** on the other hand, usually cannot be used without specifying (or strongly implying) the place. If you knock on the door and someone inside says, **«Войди́те!»**, it is clear that you are permitted to enter the room.

The differences between **у-** and **вы-** are similarly understood. The general meaning of **у-** is *gone, left, away.* Compare the following two sentences, which are different replies to the question **«Мо́жно Ива́на Ива́новича?»** (*"May I speak to Ivan Ivanovich?"*): **«Его́ нет. Он ушёл»** (*"He's not here. He left"*) as opposed to **«Его́ нет. Он вы́шел на не́сколько мину́т»** (*"He's not here. He stepped out for a few minutes"*). The first reply implies that he is gone for the day. The second, on the other hand, implies that he will be back.

Под-

This prefix is spelled **подо-** in front of **-йти** and **подъ-** in front of soft vowels and has the meaning *approaching, up to, toward, as far as.* The difference between this prefix and the prefix **при-** is that the latter implies entering or going into an area, whereas with **под-** the subject goes up to a border but does not cross over it.

The only preposition that is generally used with verbs prefixed in **под-** is **к** (**ко**).

A typical start to a joke may begin something like this: **Ко мне́ подошёл оди́н па́рень . . .** (*So this guy walked up to me . . .*). Other examples are **Докла́дчик подошёл к микрофо́ну и на́чал говори́ть** (*The speaker approached the microphone and began to speak*) and **Мы подлета́ли к Пари́жу но́чью** (*It was night when we approached Paris*).

От- (ото-, оть-)

This is the opposite prefix of **под-.** It indicates *away, off, from.* The differences between this prefix and **у-** and **вы-** is that this prefix indicates motion away from a border or limit. The preposition used with these verbs is **от** (**ото**).

—Никола́й, подойди́ к окну́ и посмотри́, что́ случи́лось на у́лице.
    Никола́й ме́дленно подхо́дит к окну́ и выгля́дывает на у́лицу.

Через мину́ту он отхо́дит от окна́ и лени́во сади́тся в кре́сло.

—Так в чём же де́ло?!

—Ничего́ осо́бенного. Грузови́к сверну́л в переу́лок.

—Отку́да же тако́й шум?

—Там не́ было переу́лка,—споко́йно отвеча́ет Никола́й.

("Nikolai, go to the window and see what happened on the street."

Nikolai slowly goes up to the window and looks out onto the street. After a minute he walks away from the window and lazily sits down in his chair.

"So what's going on?"

"Nothing special. A truck turned into an alley."

"So what's all the noise about?"

"There was no alley there," said Nikolai calmly.)

Пере-

This prefix means *across, through*. With intransitive verbs of motion, the preposition **через** (across) is optional.

Мы перешли́ (через) у́лицу.	We crossed the street.
Они́ перее́хали (через) мост и пое́хали да́льше.	They crossed the bridge and drove on.

С- (со-, съ-)

This prefix has the form **съ** before soft vowels and has the meaning *off, down from*. The verb is followed by the preposition **с** plus the genitive case.

Ка́тя сошла́ с ле́стницы.	Katya got down from the ladder.
Бума́га слете́ла со стола́.	The paper flew off the table.

TEST FOR MASTERY 3

Fill in the blanks with the correct verb of motion.

1. Когда́ зелёный свет гори́т, мо́жно _____ через у́лицу. (to cross)

2. Она́ _____ к нему́ и сказа́ла «До́брый день». (walked up to)

3. Когда́ вы с семьёй _____ в Аме́рику? (came to)

4. Он _____ в ко́мнату и сня́л пальто́. (entered)

5. —Где Ива́н Бори́сович?—Он _____ на не́сколько мину́т. (stepped out)

6. —А мо́жно Мари́ю Ива́новну?—Она́ уже́ _____ домо́й. (left)

7. Ви́тя уже́ _____? (arrived)

8. _____ от окна́! (move away from)

9. Си́ма! Я так ра́да тебя́ ви́деть! _____, пожа́луйста! (come in)

10. Ма́ша! Что́ ты де́лаешь?! Ты с ума́ _____?!! (gone out of)

Анекдоты

The following jokes or stories come from the versions that appear in L. Muravyova's *Verbs of Motion in Russian.* These little vignettes are well known, especially among children. They are silly in tone, like the English riddle "Why did the chicken cross the road?" and are not meant to be taken seriously. All of them, however, illustrate the wide use of both prefixed and nonprefixed verbs of motion.

The verbs of motion in these jokes have been underlined so that you can quickly locate them. Included are transitive verbs of motion (*taking, bringing,* and so forth.).

Марк Твен был изве́стен свое́й рассе́яностью. Одна́жды, когда́ он <u>е́хал</u> в по́езде, в купе́ <u>вошёл</u> контролёр. Твен стал иска́ть биле́т во всех карма́нах, но безуспе́шно. Наконе́ц контролёр, кото́рый знал писа́теля в лицо́, сказа́л:

—Ла́дно, не беспоко́йтесь. Предъяви́те свой биле́т, когда́ я <u>бу́ду идти́</u> обра́тно. А е́сли вы его́ не найдёте, то́же не беда́. Это ме́лочь. . . .

—Нет, уж, кака́я там ме́лочь,—запротестова́л Твен.—Я обяза́тельно до́лжен найти́ э́тот прокля́тый биле́т, ина́че как я узна́ю, куда́ я <u>е́ду</u>!

(Mark Twain was well known for his absentmindedness. Once when he was riding in a train, the conductor entered the car. Twain started to look for his ticket in all his pockets, but without success. Finally the conductor, who knew Twain by sight, said:

"OK, don't worry. Show me your ticket when I come back. And if you don't find it, it's no big deal. It's nothing."

"No, what do you mean, nothing?" Twain began in protest. "I absolutely have to find that damned ticket, or else how will I know where I'm going?")

На приёме жена́ замеча́ет, что её муж то и де́ло <u>подхо́дит</u> к сто́йке со спиртны́ми напи́тками.

—Послу́шай,—говори́т она́, <u>отводя́</u> его́ в сто́рону,—ты уже́ в девя́тый раз <u>подхо́дишь</u> к сто́йке. Что́ о тебе́ лю́ди поду́мают?

—О, не беспоко́йся,—успока́ивает её муж.—Я ка́ждый раз говорю́, что беру́ бока́л для тебя́.

(At a reception, a wife notices that her husband keeps going up to the table with alcoholic drinks.

"Listen," she says, taking him aside, "You're going to that table for the ninth time. What will people think of you?"

"Oh, don't worry," her husband says, calming her down. "Every time I go up I say that I'm getting a glass for you.")

В рестора́н <u>зашли́</u> лев и кро́лик.

—Я го́лоден. Да́йте мне сала́т,—сказа́л кро́лик.

—А ваш прия́тель не го́лоден?—спроси́л официа́нт.

—Глу́пый вопро́с,—сказа́л кро́лик.—Е́сли бы он был го́лоден, я бы не сиде́л здесь.

(A lion and a rabbit walked into a restaurant.

"I'm hungry. Give me a salad," said the rabbit.

"And your friend—isn't he hungry?" asked the waiter.

"That's a stupid question," said the rabbit. "If he were hungry, I wouldn't be sitting here.")

В кафе́ <u>захо́дит</u> пожило́й мужчи́на и сади́тся за сто́лик. К нему́ <u>подбега́ет</u> официа́нт и не о́чень ве́жливо заявля́ет:

—Э́тот стул за́нят.

—Ну что́ ж,—говори́т посети́тель,—в тако́м слу́чае забери́те его́ и <u>принеси́те</u> мне друго́й.

(An elderly man walks into a café and sits down at a table. The waiter runs up to him and, not very politely, announces:

"This table is reserved."

"Well so what?" says the customer. "In that case just take it away and bring me another.")

— На́ша ба́бушка ужа́сная труси́ха,—сказа́л мне ма́ленький Ю́рик.

—Почему́ ты так ду́маешь?

—Всегда́, когда́ мы <u>перехо́дим</u> у́липу, она́ хвата́ет меня́ за́ руку.

("Our grandmother is a terrible coward," little Yurik said to me.

"Why do you think so?"

"When we cross the street, she always grabs my hand.")

—Вы по-пре́жнему живёте в той же ти́хой кварти́ре?

—Уже́ нет.

—<u>Перее́хали?</u>

—Нет, моя́ жена́ купи́ла телеви́зор.

("Do you still live in the same quiet apartment?"

"Not anymore."

"Did you move?"

"No, my wife bought a television set.")

Пра́вила у́личного движе́ния

В больши́х города́х, где мно́го тра́нспорта, пешехо́ды должны́ хорошо́ знать пра́вила у́личного движе́ния.

Е́сли вам ну́жно <u>перейти́</u> на другу́ю сто́рону у́лицы, вы должны́ по́мнить, что у нас правосторо́нее движе́ние. Поэ́тому, <u>сойдя́</u> с тротуа́ра, на́до посмотре́ть нале́во. Убеди́вшись в том, что бли́зко маши́н нет, мо́жно <u>переходи́ть</u> у́лицу. <u>Дойдя́</u> до её середи́ны, на́до посмотре́ть напра́во и то́лько пото́м продолжа́ть перехо́д.

На всех больши́х у́лицах, в места́х перехо́да, устано́влены световы́е табло́ для пешехо́дов. Е́сли тра́нспорт остано́вится и перехо́д свобо́ден, зажига́ется зелёное табло́ со сло́вом «<u>ИДИ́ТЕ!</u>» В э́том слу́чае мо́жно споко́йно <u>переходи́ть</u> у́лицу.

Éсли зажигáется крáсное таблó со слóвом «СТÓЙТЕ!» нýжно остáться на тротуáре и ждать, покá <u>пройдёт</u> потóк машúн. <u>Переходúть</u> ýлицу в этот момéнт опáсно. Это знáют все. И однáко нахóдятся пешехóды, котóрые с рúском для жúзни <u>перебегáют</u> ýлицу перед блúзко идýщим трáнспортом.

Для удóбства жúтелей такúх большúх городóв, как Москвá, сдéланы подзéмные перехóды. Здесь пешехóды мóгут спокóйно <u>переходúть</u> через ýлицу.

Traffic Rules

In big cities where there is a lot of public transportation, pedestrians must know the traffic rules well.

If you have to cross to the other side of the street, you must remember that here traffic travels on the right-hand side of the street. Therefore, when you step off the sidewalk, you must look to your left. When you are sure that there are no cars nearby, you can cross the street. When you get to the middle, you have to look to the right and only then continue crossing.

On all major streets at the crosswalks lighted signs have been installed for pedestrians. If traffic stops and the crosswalk is free, a green light with the word *GO!* lights up. Now you can calmly cross the street. If the sign lights up in red with the word *STOP!* you have to stay on the sidewalk and wait until the cars pass. It is dangerous to cross the street at this moment. Everyone knows this. And yet there are pedestrians who, risking their lives, run across the street in front of oncoming traffic.

For the convenience of the residents of large cities such as Moscow, underground crossings have been built. Here pedestrians can calmly get to the other side of the street.

ANSWER KEY

Test for Mastery 1

1. идёшь (now, in one direction)

2. хожý (every day [frequency])

3. идёт (one direction, now)

4. хо́дит (no direction specified)

5. ходи́ть (the activity of walking)

6. хо́дит (the ability to walk)

7. идёт (moving, now, one direction)

8. идёт (rain and snow move in only one direction)

9. хо́дишь (often [frequency])

10. идёт (one direction, one time)

11. иду́т (one direction [to work])

12. хо́дите (in general, every day)

NOTE: Although the subjects of sentences 3 and 7 are vehicles (a bus and a train), the verb for walking is used because they move under their own power.

Test for Mastery 2

1. е́здишь	5. е́здят	9. е́здишь
2. е́зжу	6. е́дете	10. е́дет
3. е́дем	7. е́дем	11. е́дет
4. е́здить	8. е́здила	12. е́здит

Test for Mastery 3

1. переходи́ть	6. ушла́
2. подошла́	7. пришёл
3. перее́хали *or* прие́хали	8. отойди́те
4. вошёл	9. проходи́
5. вы́шел	10. сошла́

16 The Prepositional, Dative, and Instrumental Plural

Предложный, дательный, и творительный падежи множественного числа

Useful Vocabulary—Health and Sickness

Parts of the Body

бок (*pl.* бока́)	side
бровь (*f.*)	brow
висо́к	temple
во́лосы (*gen. pl.* воло́с)	hair
глаз (в глазу́, *pl.* глаза́)	eye
голова́ (*pl.* го́ловы)	head
грудь (в груди́)	chest
губа́	lip
желу́док	stomach
живо́т	abdomen
зуб	tooth
коле́но (*pl.* коле́ни)	knee
ладо́нь (*f.*)	palm
лёгкие	lungs
лоб (на лбу)	forehead
ло́коть (*m.*)	elbow
му́скул	muscle
нога́	foot, arm

но́готь (*m.*)	nail
нос (на носу́)	nose
па́лец (*pl.* па́льцы)	finger[1]
плечо́ (*pl.* пле́чи)	shoulder
подборо́док	chin
ресни́ца	eyelash
рот (во рту́)	mouth
рука́	hand, arm
се́рдце	heart
спина́	back
усы́ (*gen. pl.* усо́в)	mustache
у́хо (*pl.* у́ши)	ear
ше́я	neck
щека́ (*pl.* щёки)	cheek
язы́к	tongue

Diseases and Symptoms

аллерги́я	allergy
аппендици́т	appendicitis
боль (*f.*)	pain
бронхи́т	bronchitis
ветря́нка	chicken pox
воспале́ние лёгких	pneumonia
высо́кое давле́ние	high blood pressure
грипп	flu
инсу́льт	stroke
инфа́ркт	heart attack
ка́шель (*m.*)	cough
корь	measles
на́сморк	head cold
о́бморок	fainting spell
озно́б	chills
просту́да	cold

---

[1] Properly speaking, **па́лец** means *digit*. To translate *finger* or *toe*, say **па́лец на руке́** or **па́лец на ноге́.**

расстро́йство желу́дка	upset stomach
рво́та	vomiting
сви́нка	mumps
тошнота́	nausea
я́зва	ulcer

VOCABULARY PRACTICE 1

Choose the correct word:

1. За́втра де́душка идёт к зубно́му врачу́, потому́ что у него́ боля́т (ресни́цы, зу́бы, лёгкие).

2. Когда́ у меня́ боли́т голова́, я принима́ю (лека́рство от ка́шля, аспири́н).

3. Ва́ню тошни́т. Ему́ (хо́чется, не хо́чется) есть.

4. Вы чу́вствуете стра́шную боль в животе́. Вы бои́тесь, что э́то (на́сморк, аппендици́т, сви́нка).

5. Ка́тя боле́ет гри́ппом. У неё (рво́та, тошнота́, я́зва, температу́ра, озно́б). *(For this sentence choose the word that does not belong.)*

6. Когда́ в груди́ бо́льно, у вас мо́жет бы́ть (бронхи́т, о́бморок).

7. Э́то мне ну́жно как ши́ло (в виске́, в спине́, во рту).[2]

8. Она́ спит на ле́вом (желу́дке, боку́, се́рдце).

9. На́до пойти́ в больни́цу, когда́ у вас (просту́да, ка́шель, воспале́ние лёгких).

10. Подборо́док нахо́дится (на плече́, на голове́, на ноге́).

11. Во рту́ нахо́дится (язы́к, се́рдце, у́ши).

12. (Корь, ка́шель, инсу́льт)—э́то де́тская боле́знь.

13. (На́сморк, сви́нка, высо́кое давле́ние)—э́то боле́знь ста́рости.

14. О́коло гла́за нахо́дятся (пле́чи, ресни́цы, ще́я).

---

[2] *I need this like a hole in the head,* lit. *like an ice pick in the temple.*

VOCABULARY PRACTICE 2

Label the parts of the bunny's head. Use appropriate adjectives.

CONVERSATION PRACTICE

У врача́ в поликли́нике

Врач: На что вы жа́луетесь? Что у вас боли́т?

Пацие́нт: Я уж давно́ боле́ю ларинги́том. У меня́ стра́шно боли́т го́рло. Бо́льно дыша́ть и глота́ть.

В: Во-пе́рвых, дава́йте изме́рим вам температу́ру. Три́дцать семь. У вас есть температу́ра. Сейча́с дава́йте посмо́трим го́рло. Говори́те «А-а-а».

П: «А-а-а».

В: Гмм. А вы принима́ете лека́рство от анги́ны?

П: Да, я принима́ю аспири́н. По две табле́тки, три ра́за в день.

В: Ка́шель у вас есть?

П: Нет, ка́шля нет.

В: Я вы́пишу вам реце́пт на антибио́тики. У вас нет аллерги́й к пеницилли́ну?

П: Нет.

В: А что́ ещё у вас боли́т?

П: Ну, че́стно говоря́, всё боли́т. И го́рло, и голова́, и желу́док, и—как у челове́ка из подпо́лья Достое́вского—пе́чень.

В:	Наве́рное, вы страда́ете стре́ссом. И вы сли́шком мно́го чита́ете!
П:	Да. Во сне я скрежещу́ зуба́ми и днём грызу́ но́гти.
В:	Да, я ви́жу, что вы и сейча́с то́паете нога́ми. По-мо́ему, вам бы лу́чше занима́ться спо́ртом, чем принима́ть снотво́рное и́ли успокои́тельные сре́дства.
П:	Я совсе́м согла́сен с ва́ми. Я ду́маю бе́гать на све́жем во́здухе.
В:	Прекра́сно! Но е́сли го́рло и голова́ и желу́док не переста́нут боле́ть, тогда́ приходи́те к нам неме́дленно.
П:	Обяза́тельно приду́.
В:	И не забу́дьте принима́ть антибио́тики, четы́ре ра́за в день, по две табле́тки.
П:	Я не забу́ду. Скажи́те, пожа́луйста, где апте́ка?
В:	Апте́ка за угло́м, спра́ва.
П:	Спаси́бо, до́ктор.
В:	Выздора́вливайте!
П:	До свида́ния.

At the Doctor's Office in the Clinic

DOCTOR:	What are your chief complaints? What hurts you?
PATIENT:	I have had laryngitis for a long time. I have a bad sore throat. It hurts to breathe and to swallow.
D:	First of all, let's take your temperature. Thirty-seven. You have a fever.[3] Let's take a look at your throat. Say "ah."
P:	"Aaaahhh."
D:	Hmm. Are you taking any medicine for your sore throat?
P:	Yes, I'm taking aspirin. Two tablets, three times a day.
D:	Do you have a cough?
P:	No, I don't.
D:	I'll write you a prescription for antibiotics. You're not allergic to penicillin, are you?
P:	No.
D:	What else hurts?
P:	Well, to be honest, everything hurts. My throat and my head and my stomach and—like Dostoevsky's Underground Man—my liver.
D:	You're probably suffering from stress. And you read too much!

---

[3] Russian body temperature is, interestingly, lower than what Americans consider to be average normal temperature by one degree centigrade.

P: Yes. I grind my teeth in my sleep, and during the day I chew my nails.

D: Yes, I see that even now you're tapping your feet. I think it would be better if you took up sports than take sleeping pills or tranquilizers.

P: I completely agree with you. I'm thinking of taking up jogging in the fresh air.

D: Wonderful! But if your throat and head and stomach don't stop hurting, come back immediately.

P: Of course, I will.

D: And don't forget to take the antibiotics, two tablets four times a day.

P: I won't forget. Could you tell me where the pharmacy is?

D: The pharmacy is around the corner on the right.

P: Thank you, doctor.

D: Get better!

P: Good-bye.

Idioms

На что́ вы жа́луетесь?

Жа́ловаться (на что?) means to complain of or about something. A doctor will ask you this to learn your principal complaints or symptoms. You may also use this verb for complaining in general, plus the preposition **на** plus accusative case:

Он всегда́ жа́луется на всё.	He always complains about everything.
Они́ жа́луются на пого́ду.	They are complaining about the weather.

Что́ у Вас боли́т?

The English expressions *My head hurts* or *I have a headache* are rendered into Russian by a more passive construction. The part of the body that hurts you is the subject of the sentence and governs the choice of singular or plural verb. The person who experiences the pain follows the preposition **у** and takes the genitive case.

У меня́ боли́т у́хо.	My ear hurts./I have an earache.
У ба́бушки боля́т но́ги.	Grandmother's feet hurt.
У сы́на боли́т живо́т.	My son has a stomachache.
У му́жа боли́т спина́.	My husband's back hurts.
У де́душки боли́т зуб.	Grandfather has a toothache.
У неё боля́т лёгкие.	Her lungs hurt.

Note that **Мне бо́льно дыша́ть и глота́ть** (*It hurts me to breathe and swallow*) is an impersonal expression, with the person in pain being in the dative case.

Prepositional, Dative, and Instrumental Plural

The plurals of the prepositional, dative, and instrumental cases are extraordinarily easy to commit to memory. One has only to adjust endings for soft stems and keep in mind fewer than a handful of exceptions in the instrumental case only. You will remember that there is no distinction for gender in the plural of these cases, so there is only one set of endings for all nouns and adjectives.

The endings are as follows:

	Adjectives	**Nouns**
Prepositional	-ых/-их	-ах/-ях
Dative	-ым/-им	-ам/-ям
Instrumental	-ыми/-ими	-ами/-ями

The alternate endings for adjectives allow for both soft adjectives and adjectives where the seven-letter spelling rule applies. Noun endings are adjusted for softness only, since there is no spelling rule for the vowel **a.**

Remember that in order to form the correct plural of these cases you must start with the nominative plural form of the word if there has been any change from the singular. Words such as **бра́тья, сосе́ди,** and **англича́не** have stems that are different from the singular, and these are the stems that appear throughout the plural declension.

The five nouns that are exceptions in the instrumental plural are **людьми́** (people), **детьми́** (children), **дочерьми́** (daughters), **дверьми́** (doors), and **лошадьми́** (horses).[4]

TEST FOR MASTERY

Now is a good time to review verb conjugations as well. Change all the elements, including the verbs, of the following sentences from the singular to the plural:

1. Она́ горди́тся свои́м сы́ном.

2. Я всегда́ ду́маю о моём ста́ром дру́ге.

---

[4] The forms **дочеря́ми, дверя́ми,** and **лошадя́ми** are also occasionally seen.

3. Ка́ждую суббо́ту я пишу́ мое́й сестре́.

4. Он ча́сто хо́дит в кино́ со свои́м зкако́мым.

5. Она́ живёт в э́том до́ме со свои́м бра́том.

6. Лу́чше жить в большо́м го́роде, чем в ма́леньком го́роде.

7. Он заве́дует комите́том по пробле́ме совреме́нной жи́зни.

8. В понеде́льник я е́ду в дере́вню. (*In this sentence you must change the first preposition* в *to* по *and then use the dative plural.*)

9. Она́ о́чень дово́льна свое́й до́черью.

10. Инжене́р е́дет на заво́д на тролле́йбусе.

11. Наш сосе́д ча́сто разгова́ривает с мои́м сы́ном.

12. Ка́ждое воскресе́нье я хожу́ к дру́гу. (*See comment to sentence 8.*)

13. Что́ ты ду́маешь об э́том журна́ле?

14. Э́тому ма́льчику на́до мыть посу́ду.

ANSWER KEY

Vocabulary Practice 1

1. зу́бы

2. аспири́н

3. не хо́чется

4. аппендици́т

5. я́зва

6. бронхи́т

7. в виске́

8. боку́

9. воспале́ние лёгких

10. на голове́

11. язы́к

12. корь

13. высо́кое давле́ние

14. ресни́цы

Test for Mastery

1. Они́ гордя́тся свои́ми сыновья́ми.

2. Мы всегда́ ду́маем о на́ших ста́рых друзья́х.

3. По суббо́там мы пи́шем на́шим сёстрам.

4. Они́ ча́сто хо́дят в кино́ со свои́ми знако́мыми.

5. Они́ живу́т в э́тих дома́х со свои́ми бра́тьями.

6. Лу́чше жить в больши́х города́х, чем в ма́леньких города́х.

7. Они́ заве́дуют комите́тами по пробле́мам совреме́нной жи́зни.

8. По понеде́льникам мы е́здим в дере́вню.

9. Они́ о́чень дово́льны свои́ми дочерьми́.

10. Инжене́ры е́дут на заво́ды на тролле́йбусах.

11. На́ши сосе́ди ча́сто разгова́ривают с мои́ми сыновья́ми.

12. По воскресе́ньям мы хо́дим к друзья́м.

13. Что́ вы ду́маете об э́тих журна́лах?

14. Э́тим ма́льчикам на́до мыть посу́ду.

17 Participles

Причастия

At long last, having acquired a reasonable command of the case system and Russian verbs, students are faced with arguably the most difficult—though not impossible—aspect of Russian grammar: participles. It is for this reason that participles and their cousins, gerunds, are usually left to the last lessons of a textbook. So much of a good understanding of participles depends on the confidence acquired during a review of declension that, if you are shaky in this aspect of Russian, it is better to review the case endings before enmeshing yourself in participles. They are complex, sometimes Byzantine, many times frustrating constructions. In the final analysis, however, participles lend an air of elegance and linguistic sophistication to the written Russian text. It is not possible to read most newspapers, novels, articles, instructions, and more without at least a working knowledge of participles.

With this in mind, and with the awareness of the fact that participles can be fun, especially if you have a particularly analytical mind, let's get down to business.

What Is a Participle?

A participle—also called a verbal adjective—is derived from a verb but behaves like an adjective, modifying or describing an antecedent. There is no comparing Russian and English usage of participles. Whereas English makes use of only present and past participles (*writing, written*), Russian has four kinds (*is writing, was writing, is being written, was written*), not to mention the two gerundive forms (*while writing* and *having written*). Participles express both voice (active and passive) and tense (past and present—but not future).

Active Participles

A participle replaces **кото́рый** plus the verb in a dependent clause. For active participles, **кото́рый** must be in the nominative case. Thus, it is not possible to make an active participle out of the following sentence: **Мы съе́ли все я́блоки, кото́рые О́ля купи́ла сего́дня у́тром.** Despite the fact that at first glance it may look nominative, the **кото́рый** in this sentence is in the accusative case, the direct object of the verb **купи́ла.**[1] Be sure not to confuse the two!

The verb that is governed by **кото́рый** may be present or past tense, but not future. A present-tense verb will form a present active participle, and a past-tense verb, a past active participle.

Present

In order to form a present active participle, **кото́рый** must be in the nominative case and the verb must be present tense. These two criteria lead to numerous exclusions: clauses in which **кото́рый** stands in any other than the nominative case, and verbs that are perfective future (the conjugated form of a perfective verb). As previously mentioned, students may easily mistake the accusative form of **кото́рый** for nominative and may also misperceive the perfective future as the present tense. Care should be taken to avoid these mistakes.

Summary

1. **Кото́рый** must be in the nominative case, that is, the subject of its own (dependent) clause.

2. The verb must be in the present tense; therefore, only imperfective verbs can form present active participles.

---

[1] It is possible, however, to form a past passive participle here. More on that topic later.

3. If they follow the antecedent (the noun that is being described), participial phrases are bordered by commas; if they precede the antecedent, there are no commas.

4. Participial phrases of one word generally precede the object they modify.

Formation

1. Take the third-person plural form of the verb, drop the last letter, and add the consonant **щ** plus the appropriate adjective ending.

2. Stress is the same as in the third-person plural form.

3. The particle **-ся** does not contract with participles.

4. Since a participle behaves like a normal adjective, make sure it agrees with its antecedent in gender, case, and number.

It is important to remember that there are two types of agreement. As previously mentioned, **который** can be only in the nominative case, so the only forms that can be replaced by participles are **который, которая, которое,** and **которые.** Participles, however, will agree completely with their antecedents in every way and therefore may represent all cases, all genders, and both numbers.

Word Order and Punctuation

If a participial phrase follows its antecedent, it will be set off by commas. If the phrase precedes the antecedent, there are no commas. Participial phrases of one word usually stand immediately before the antecedent. This flexibility in the word order of participles allows Russian a wide range of possibilities that are not easily rendered in English. A word-by-word translation of the third set of sentences below will illustrate this fact. The following are examples of pairs of sentences, the first of which uses a participial construction, and the second of which replaces that participial phrase with a **который** clause. Participles will be boldface to make them easier to identify.

Фильм, **демонстрирующийся** в этом зале, создан по роману Тургенева.

Фильм, <u>который демонстрируется</u> в этом зале, создан по роману Тургенева.

The movie that is being shown in this hall is based on a novel by Turgenev.

Электри́ческие провода́ изготовля́ются из хорошо́ **проводя́щих** ток мета́ллов.
(Электри́ческие провода́ изготовля́ются из мета́ллов, хорошо́ **проводя́щих** ток.)
Электри́ческие провода́ изготовля́ются из мета́ллов, <u>кото́рые</u> <u>хорошо́</u> прово́дят ток.
Electrical wires are made from metals that conduct current well (or that are good conductors of current).

Блестя́щие предме́ты отража́ют **па́дающие** на них лучи́ све́та.
Предме́ты, <u>кото́рые блестя́т</u>, отража́ют лучи́ све́та, <u>кото́рые</u> <u>па́дают</u> на них.
Objects that shine reflect the rays of light that fall on them *or* Shining (shiny) objects reflect the rays of light falling on them.

In the first set of examples, the participial phrase follows the antecedent (**фильм**) and is enclosed by commas. In the second set, the participial phrase precedes the antecedent (**мета́ллов**), and the commas are therefore omitted. The two participles in the third set both precede their antecedents (**предме́ты** and **лучи́**), and commas are not used. Note that single-word participial phrases, such as **блестя́щие,** are so commonly used that most native speakers do not recognize them as participles and perceive them primarily (and correctly) as the adjectives they have become. Recall that participles are also known as verbal adjectives.

TEST FOR MASTERY 1

This exercise is a warm-up to the ones that follow. Below you will see phrases or short sentences that contain present active participles. Translate these into English. Remember that the participle precedes its antecedent if there are no commas. Also keep in mind that the word modified by the participle is the performer of the action of the verb from which the participle is formed.

1. говоря́щая ло́шадь

2. ру́сско-говоря́щие студе́нты

3. карандаши́, лежа́щие на столе́

4. семья́, снима́ющая э́тот но́вый дом

5. моя́ сестра́, живу́щая в Петербу́рге

6. ма́льчик, игра́ющий на балала́йке

7. журналист, пишущий статьи об экономике

8. «Спящая красавица»

9. танцующий медведь

10. ведущие учёные

11. недавно приехавшие из России артисты

12. Хорошо занимающиеся студенты сдали все экзамены.

13. Мы едем к бабушке, живущей в маленькой деревне.

14. Вы знаете студента, сидящего в первом ряду?

15. Мы встречались с артистами, выступающими сегодня вечером.

TEST FOR MASTERY 2

Now do the reverse. Form participial phrases from the following:

1. студенты, которые говорят только по-английски

2. женщина, которая идёт по улице

3. новые русские, которые строят себе большие дома

4. дети, которые начинают изучать иностранный язык

5. этот известный критик, который пишет статьи о Толстом

6. У нас нет студентов, которые говорят по-китайски.

7. Вы знаете женщину, которая идёт по улице?

8. Сегодня в Москве много русских, которые строят себе новые дома.

9. Учитель помогает детям, которые начинают изучать иностранный язык.

10. Вы довольны студентом, который пишет дипломную работу о Толстом?

TEST FOR MASTERY 3

Rewrite the following sentences, changing each participle to a **который** clause. To assist in your understanding of the syntax, translations follow each sentence. This exercise is more difficult than the preceding two.

1. Вася купил говорящую лощадь!   (Vasya bought a talking horse!)

2. Студенты, желающие поступить в аспирантуру, должны выполнить эту анкету.   (Students wishing to enter graduate school must fill out this form.)

3. Улыбающиеся нам девочки учатся в третьем классе.   (The girls smiling at us are in the third grade.)

4. Из-за забора мы услышали весёлые голоса детей, играющих на школьном дворе.[2]   (From behind the fence we heard the happy voices of children playing in the schoolyard.)

5. Трава, растущая у самой дороги, стала серой от пыли.   (The grass growing at the edge of the road was gray from dust.)

6. Бывает, что дети неожиданно выходят на дорогу из-за автобуса, стоящего на остановке.   (Sometimes children unexpectedly come out onto the road from behind a bus standing at the bus stop.)

7. Дети, ежедневно делающие зарядку, мало болеют.   (Children who exercise every day rarely get sick.)

8. Я оглядываюсь и вдруг вижу машущего мне рукой приятеля.   (I look around and suddenly see my friend waving (his hand) to me.)

9. Улыбающийся ребёнок всегда красив.   (A smiling child is always beautiful.)

10. Современные учёные создали счётные машины, заменяющие вычислительную работу сотен и тысяч людей.   (Contemporary scientists have created calculators, which replace the work of hundreds and thousands of people.)

11. Входящий в зал человек— знаменитый писатель.   (The man walking into the auditorium is a famous writer.)

---

[2] The use of the present active participle in a past-tense sentence serves to make the action more lively and brings the reader back to that moment of the action. This comment also applies to sentence 12.

12. Стёпа надева́ет вися́щую на
    сту́ле руба́шку.

(Styopa is putting on the shirt that
was hanging on the chair.)

13. Гимна́стика, де́лающая челове́ка
    ло́вким и выно́сливым, должна́
    заня́ть почётное ме́сто
    в шко́ле.

(Gymnastics, which makes a person
agile and hardy, should hold and
honorable place in school.)

14. Радиоста́нция передава́ла
    репорта́ж о слу́хах, не
    име́ющих ничего́ о́бщего
    с фа́ктами.

(The radio broadcast reports on
rumors having nothing to do with
the facts.)

15. Встреча́ющиеся в други́х кни́гах
    по э́тому вопро́су вы́воды не
    соотве́тствуют вы́водам э́того
    а́втора.

(The conclusions encountered in
other books on this question do not
correspond to the conclusions of
this author.)

As Nouns and Adjectives

Some participles have, through long-term use, become well established in the
Russian language and are thought of primarily as nouns and/or adjectives. Many
of these words are restricted to formal or technical usage, in fields such as the
natural sciences, medicine, linguistics, economics, agriculture, military, and so
forth. Some examples of scientific terms include **блужда́ющий** (migratory),
живородя́щий (viviparous), **млекопита́ющее** (mammal, milk-feeding),
яйцекла́дущее (oviparous), and **нержаве́ющий** (noncorrosive, rust-resistant).

The medical field uses such words as **вя́жущий** (astringent),
жаропонижа́ющее (fever-reducing), **плодоизгоня́ющий** (abortifacient),
кровоостана́вливающий (styptic), **отравля́ющий** (asphyxiant, poison),
отха́ркивающее (expectorant), **сосудорасширя́ющий** (vessel-dilating),
успока́ивающее (sedative), and **возбужда́ющее** (stimulant).[3]

In the military, one encounters **военнослу́жащий** (serviceman),
кома́ндующий (commander), **вольнослу́жащий** (a re-enlisted serviceman), and
старослу́жащий (an old soldier, a veteran).

---

[3] Many of these words are neuter in gender because they modify the noun **лека́рство**
(medicine), which has been dropped. This is an extremely productive category, basically
meaning *something that does X*, for instance, something that puts you to sleep, something
that keeps you awake, something that makes you expectorate, and so forth.

Linguistic terminology includes **бу́дущее** (future tense), **настоя́щее** (present tense), **подлежа́щее** (the subject), **свистя́щий** (sibilant), **слогообразу́ющий** (syllable-forming), **шипя́щий** (fricative), **агглютини́рующий** (agglutinative), **а́кающий** (one who pronounces an unstressed **о** as **а**), and **о́кающий** (one who pronounces an unstressed **о** as **о**).

Industry and agriculture use **быстросо́хнущий** (fast-drying), **льносе́ющий** (flax-growing), **тепловыделя́ющий** (fuel, heat-generating), **обраба́тывающий** (manufacturing), **плёнкообразу́ющий** (film-forming), **самовса́сывающий** (self-priming), **свеклосе́ющий** (beet-growing), **угледобыва́ющий** (coal-producing), **хлопкосе́ющий** (cotton-growing), and **электропроводя́щий** (electroconductive).

Nouns from Present Active Participles

The most common examples of participles generally thought of as nouns can be found in the following list. They are widely used in conversational Russian and are declined as adjectives: **басту́ющий** (a worker on strike), **ве́рующий** (a believer, one of the faithful), **военнослу́жащий** (a military serviceman), **говоря́щий** (the speaker), **заве́дующий** (manager, director, head), **игра́ющий** (a player), **напада́ющий** (a forward, in sports), **начина́ющий** (a beginner), **не/куря́щий** (a non/smoker), **не/пью́щий** (a non/drinker), **приезжа́ющий** (arrival; one who is arriving), **самообуча́ющийся** (a self-taught person), **слу́жащий** (white-collar worker), **трудя́щийся** (worker, toiler), **тя́жущийся** (litigant), **уезжа́ющий** (departure; one who is departing), **управля́ющий** (manager, steward), and **уча́ствующий** (participant).

Adjectives from Present Active Participles

Participles commonly used primarily as adjectives have lost most of their connection to the participle form. Among these are words such as **блестя́щий** (shining, shiny). Native speakers of Russian, presented with the task of parsing the following sentence, would nine times out of ten not identify **блестя́щие** as a participle: **Блестя́щие предме́ты отража́ют па́дающие на них лучи́ све́та** (*Shiny objects reflect the rays of light falling on them*). This sentence may be rightly rendered in Russian using **кото́рый** phrases in place of both participles: **Предме́ты, кото́рые блестя́т, отража́ют лучи́ све́та, кото́рые па́дают на них** (*Objects that shine reflect the rays of light that fall on them*). In this particular instance the participial adjective **блестя́щий** is correctly rendered as *that shine,* but the more common use of the word is in its meaning as *brilliant,* as in **блестя́щий студе́нт** or **блестя́щая статья́.**

Among participles primarily used as adjectives are **не/подходя́щий** (in/appropriate), **небью́щийся** (unbreakable), **бодря́щий** (invigorating), **волну́ющий** (troubling), **выдаю́щийся** (outstanding), **зна́чащий** (significant), **зна́ющий** (knowledgeable), **ка́жущийся** (apparent), **любя́щий** (loving), **отдыха́ющий** (vacationer), **пла́чущий** (tearful), **поража́ющий** (astonishing), **потряса́ющий** (tremendous), **предстоя́щий** (impending), **ре́жущий** (cutting), **реша́ющий** (decisive), **сле́дующий** (next), **теку́щий** (current), and **угрожа́ющий** (threatening).

Compound Adjectives from Present Active Participles

Last, there is a large and growing group of compound adjectives based on participles. The first part of the compound adjective is usually a noun form, followed by the participial form of the verb. These may lead to unusually long words in Russian, some approaching ten syllables in length when declined.

Compound Adjective	Noun or Pronoun	Verb	English
саморегистри́рующий	сам	регистри́ровать	self-registering
жизнеутвержда́ющий	жизнь	утвержда́ть	life-affirming
яйцекла́дущий	яйцо́	класть	egg-laying, oviparous
кровоостана́вливающий	кровь	остана́вливать	styptic, "blood-stopping"

Some other common compound adjectives derived from participles are **быстроде́йствующий** (fast-acting), **вперёдсмо́трящий** (forward-looking), **всеви́дящий** (all-seeing), **дорогостоя́щий** (expensive), **звукоизоли́рующий** (soundproofing), **кровососу́щий** (blood-sucking), **огнеды́шащий** (fire-breathing), and **самоуправля́ющий** (self-governing).

One Last Caveat

Not all words that end in **-щий** are participles! There are a handful of adjectives that have no more than a passing resemblance to participles. They may be divided roughly into two groups: (1) those that express a colloquial superlative form of the adjective, using the suffix **-ущий/-ющий** and (2) those that are historical remnants of Old Church Slavonic, the literary language of the Slavs dating to the tenth century.

Participles are, in a way, Old Church Slavonic's gift to the Russian language. Native Russian forms of verbal adjectives take the ending **-чий.** Compare, for instance, the native Russian adjective **жгу́чий** (burning, ardent) with the participle form **жгу́щий** (that which is burning), or **колю́чий** (barbed, as in wire) and **колю́щий** (stabbing, taunting). The word **вя́щий** (very great) is one example of an Old Church Slavonic word that remains in use in Modern Russian on a limited basis but is primarily obsolete or used in a jocular sense. This particular word is used only in certain set expressions: **с вя́щим уваже́нием** (with the utmost respect), **с вя́щим удово́льствием** (with the greatest pleasure).

There are also examples of obsolete participles that are used only in certain set expressions, such as **стра́ждущее челове́чество** (suffering humanity). The correct Modern Russian participle for this verb would be **страда́ющий.**

The following list of commonly used adjectives belongs to the first category mentioned above. They all carry the connotation of *overly* or *more than normal.* In comparison with the simple superlative (**умне́йший**), they are one degree further, although their use is still considered primarily colloquial. The translations provided are meant to suggest some of the colloquial and superlative flavor of their usage in Russian.

Большу́щий (humongous), **гнету́щий** (depressing, dismal), **грязну́щий** (filthy dirty), **длинну́щий** (extremely long), **здорову́щий** (healthy as a horse), **леда́щий** (feeble, puny), **проклятý́щий** (damned), **работя́щий** (industrious, hard-working), **толсту́щий** (fat), **умню́щий** (very smart), **хитрю́щий** (very cunning), and **худу́щий** (emaciated).

One commonly used adjective—**настоя́щий** (real, present) and its negative **ненастоя́щий** (unreal)—has no relation to the present active participle. The word **гуля́щий** (idle, *colloquial*) or its feminine form **гуля́щая** (a streetwalker) are not participial forms. Last, stump your Russian teacher by asking about the colloquial **тьма-тьму́щая** (countless multitudes). Both parts decline.

Past Active Participles

Like present active participles, past active participles are formed from **кото́рый** clauses in which **кото́рый** is in the nominative case. The verb, however, stands in the past tense, which means that nearly all Russian verbs have the potential to form this type of participle, since all Russian verbs occur in the past tense. Thus, both imperfective and perfective verbs can form present active participles.

Formation

To form the past active participle, take the masculine past-tense form of the verb, drop the **-л** and add the consonants **-вш-** plus the appropriate adjective ending.

Verbs whose past tense ends in **-л** but whose conjugated stems end in **-д-** will take **-дший** for the full participle ending. For verbs whose past tense does not end in **-л,** simply add **ш** and the adjective ending.

Note that the particle **-ся** does not contract with participles. Note also that the **ё** in the past-tense form of the verb returns to **е** in the past active participle.

Infinitive	First-Person Singular	Masculine Past	Past Active Participle
говори́ть	говорю́	говори́л	говори́вший
сказа́ть	скажу́	сказа́л	сказа́вший
верну́ться	верну́сь	верну́лся	верну́вшийся
отве́тить	отве́чу	отве́тил	отве́тивший
тре́бовать	тре́бую	тре́бовал	тре́бовавший
приноси́ть	приношу́	приноси́л	приноси́вший
умере́ть	умру́	у́мер	у́мерший
привы́кнуть	привы́кну	привы́к	привы́кший
идти́	иду́	шёл	шедший
перевести́	переведу́	перевёл	переве́дший
боя́ться	бою́сь	боя́лся	боя́вшийся

Since it behaves like a normal adjective, make sure your participle agrees with its antecedent in gender, case, and number.[4]

TEST FOR MASTERY 4

Change the following participial phrases to constructions using **кото́рый.** Keep in mind that they are all fragments rather than sentences. Again, remember that if a participle follows its antecedent, it will be preceded by a comma; if the participle stands before the antecedent, like a normal adjective, there will be no comma. English translations are provided along with the answers, but challenge yourself by trying to do these sentences without referring to the English.

1. студе́нтка, проспа́вшая заня́тия

2. заболе́вшая де́вочка

3. лете́вший над на́ми самолёт

---

[4] Once again, remember that there are two types of agreement. **Кото́рый** can be in the nominative case only, so the only allowable forms that can be replaced by participles are **кото́рый, кото́рая, кото́рое,** and **кото́рые.** Participles, however, agree completely with their antecedents in every way.

4. арти́сты, то́лько что прилете́вшие из Москвы́

5. газе́ты, лежа́вшие на полу́

6. ка́ждый из госпо́д, собра́вшихся в кабине́те

7. упа́вшее на доро́гу де́рево

8. ше́дшая по у́лице стару́ха

9. поги́бшие солда́ты, оста́вшиеся на по́ле сраже́ния

10. подня́вшееся я́ркое со́лнце

11. молоды́е лю́ди, бы́вшие у нас у́тром

12. арти́стка, всегда́ игра́вшая э́ту роль

Make sure you check your answers and feel confident of this section before you proceed to the following set of sentences. Remember, your antecedent will not always be in the nominative case (see sentence 6 above).

Because participles are considered literary or high style, they are likely to be encountered in complex literary texts. The sentences that follow, therefore, may be difficult to grasp at first. An English translation is provided to help you find your way through the syntax to the participles. Any effort you expend in learning participles will pay enormous dividends in the long run, deepening your understanding of Russian syntax and building your confidence in reading Russian literary texts.

TEST FOR MASTERY 5

Rewrite the following sentences, changing each participle to a **кото́рый** clause. This exercise is much more difficult than the preceding ones. If you would like to try them on your own, selected vocabulary follows each Russian sentence.

1. Больно́й ду́мал о врача́х, спа́сших ему́ жизнь. (спасти́ [*to save*])

   (The patient thought about the doctors who had saved his life.)

2. Бы́ло сы́ро от тума́на, поднима́вшегося над реко́й. (сы́ро [*damp*], поднима́ться [*to rise*])

   (It was damp from the fog that was rising over the river.)

3. Мно́го уже́ говори́лось о ро́ли ру́сского наро́да, занима́вшего веду́щее ме́сто в борьбе́ про́тив Ги́тлера. (занима́ть [*to take, hold*])

(Much has been said about the role of the Russian people, who took a leading role in the struggle against Hitler.)

4. Мы услы́шали зва́вший рабо́чих на заво́д гудо́к. (гудо́к [*whistle*])

(We heard the whistle that was calling the workers to the factory.)

5. Останови́вшиеся на о́тдых тури́сты о́чень уста́ли. (останови́ться [*to stop*])

(The tourists who had stopped for a rest were very tired.)

6. Упа́вшее на доро́гу де́рево загороди́ло путь маши́нам. (загороди́ть [*to block*])

(The tree that had fallen on the road blocked the cars' way.)

7. Ме́дленно ше́дшая по у́лице де́вушка вдруг останови́лась.

(The girl slowly walking down the street suddenly stopped.)

8. Он ждал её на ста́нции с нача́вшимся ещё вчера́ ве́чером волне́нием. (волне́ние [*excitement, agitation*])

(He waited for her at the station with a nervousness that had begun already last night.)

9. Потеря́вшие после́дние ли́стья и почерне́вшие от дождя́ дере́вья стона́ли под ветро́м. (*Note that there is no comma, indicating that the participle stands before its antecedent.*) (стона́ть [*to moan*])

(The trees that had lost their last leaves and turned black from the rain moaned in the wind.)

10. Мы напра́вились к До́му культу́ры, находи́вшемуся в це́нтре го́рода.

(We set off for the House of Culture, which was located in the center of town.)

11. Мы приглаша́ем Вас приня́ть уча́стие в конфере́нции и обсуди́ть сложи́вшуюся ситуа́цию в стране́. (обсуди́ть [*to discuss*], сложи́ться [*to grow complicated*])

(We invite you to take part in the conference and to discuss the increasingly complicated situation in the country.)

12. У Николая, встáвшего в пéрвый
раз пóсле болéзни, дрожáли
нóги.

(Having gotten up for the first time
after his illness, Nikolai's legs
shook.)

Adjectives and Nouns from Past Active Participles

There are fewer past active than present active participles used as adjectives and
nouns, but the principle is the same: *someone or something that X-ed*. Some of the
most common are listed here, along with their infinitive form and extended or figurative meanings.

Past Active Participle	Infinitive	English
бы́вший	быть	someone who was; former (adj.)
сумасшéдший	идти с ума	someone who has gone out of his/her mind; mad, insane
нижеподписáвшийся	подписáться нúже	the person who has signed below; the signatory; the undersigned
пострадáвший	пострадáть	the victim (someone who has suffered)
погúбший	погúбнуть	lost, ruined (adj.)
упáвший	упáсть	fallen; weak (from emotion or fear) (adj.)
наболéвший	наболéть	sore, painful (adj.)
потерпéвший	потерпéть	the victim, survivor (someone who has undergone X)
устарéвший	устарéть	obsolete (something that has grown old)
отжúвший	отжúть	obsolete, outmoded (something that has outlived its age)
почúвший	почúть, *rhet.*	the deceased (the one who has passed away)
новоприбы́вший	прибы́ть	newly arrived
обрю́згший	обрю́згнуть	flabby, flaccid; same as обрю́зглый
прошéдший	пройтú	past; прошéдшее—the past
увя́дший	увядáть/увя́нуть	faded, withered (adj. only)
протéкший	протéчь	past, last
истéкший	истéчь	past, preceding
осúпший	осúпнуть	hoarse, husky; same as осúплый

Past Active Participle	Infinitive	English
вы́цветший	вы́цвести	faded
иссо́хший	иссо́хнуть	withered
поту́хший	поту́хнуть	extinct, lifeless
вы́сохший	вы́сохнуть	shriveled, wizened
проту́хший	проту́хнуть	foul, rotten, spoiled

READING

Excerpt from War and Peace

This reading is placed at the end of the lesson for good reason: if you were to attempt to parse it before learning at least the active participles in this lesson, you would, with good reason, throw this book across the room and give up Russian forever. Now, however, with at least a preliminary understanding, you may tackle the passage below and earn a great deal of satisfaction by deciphering it. If you want to peek at our translation, you will find it at the end of the answer key.

Vocabulary

верхово́й	horseman
жгу́чий	burning
копы́то	hoof
повора́чивать	to turn
подня́ться	to rise, climb
по́ле сраже́ния	battlefield
прислу́шиваться	to listen closely
разрыва́ть	to tear, lacerate
раскры́ть	to open
рассма́тривать	to examine
сине́ть	to turn blue
сопу́тствовать	to accompany
страда́ть	to suffer
суди́ть	to judge
то́пот	tramping

[Князь Андре́й] опя́ть почу́вствовал себя́ живы́м и страда́ющим от жгу́чей и разрыва́ющей что-то бо́ли в голове́. . . . Он стал прислу́шиваться и услы́шал зву́ки приближа́ющегоса то́пота лошаде́й и зву́ки голосо́в, говори́вших по-францу́зски. Он раскры́л глаза́. Над ним бы́ло опя́ть всё то же высо́кое не́бо с ещё вы́ше подня́вшимися, плыву́щими облака́ми, сквозь кото́рые видне́лась сине́ющая бесконе́чность. Он не повора́чивал головы́ и не ви́дел тех, кото́рые, судя́[5] по зву́ку копы́т и голосо́в, подъе́хали к нему́ и останови́лись.

Подъе́хавшие верховы́е бы́ли Наполео́н, сопу́тствуемый[6] двумя́ адъюта́нтами. Бонапа́рте . . . рассма́тривал уби́тых и ра́неных[7], оста́вшихся на по́ле сраже́ния.[8]

ANSWER KEY

Test for Mastery 1

1. a talking horse

2. Russian-speaking students

3. the pencils lying on the table

4. the family renting this new house

5. my sister, who lives in Petersburg

6. the boy who plays the balalaika

7. the journalist who writes articles on economics

8. *Sleeping Beauty*

9. a dancing bear

10. leading scientists

11. performers who recently arrived from Russia

12. The students who studied well passed all the exams.

13. We are going to (visit) grandmother, who lives in a little village.

14. Do you know the student who is sitting in the first row?

15. We met the artists who are performing tonight.

---

[5] This is a gerund in form meaning *judging by*.

[6] This is a present passive participle meaning *accompanied by*.

[7] Past passive participles meaning *the dead* and *the wounded*.

[8] Lev Tolstoy, *Voiná i Mir,* vol. 1, part 3, chapter 19.

Test for Mastery 2

1. студе́нты, говоря́щие то́лько по-англи́йски

2. же́нщина, иду́щая по у́лице

3. но́вые ру́сские, стро́ящие себе́ больши́е дома́

4. де́ти, начина́ющие изуча́ть иностра́нный язы́к

5. э́тот изве́стный кри́тик, пи́шущий статьи́ о Толсто́м

6. У нас нет студе́нтов, говоря́щих по-кита́йски.

7. Вы зна́ете же́нщину, иду́щую по у́лице?

8. Сего́дня в Москве́ мно́го ру́сских, стро́ящих себе́ но́вые дома́.

9. Учи́тель помога́ет де́тям, начина́ющим изуча́ть иностра́нный язы́к.

10. Вы дово́льны студе́нтом, пи́шущим дипло́мную рабо́ту о Толсто́м?

Test for Mastery 3

1. Ва́ся купи́л ло́шадь, кото́рая говори́т!

2. Студе́нты, кото́рые жела́ют поступи́ть в аспиранту́ру, должны́ вы́полнить э́ту анке́ту.

3. Де́вочки, кото́рые улыба́ются нам, у́чатся в тре́тьем кла́ссе.

4. Из-за забо́ра мы услы́шали весёлые голоса́ дете́й, кото́рые игра́ют на шко́льном дворе́.

5. Трава́, кото́рая растёт у са́мой доро́ги, ста́ла се́рой от пы́ли.

6. Быва́ет, что де́ти неожи́данно выхо́дят на доро́гу из-за авто́буса, кото́рый стои́т на остано́вке.

7. Де́ти, кото́рые ежедне́вно де́лают заря́дку, ма́ло боле́ют.

8. Я огля́дываюсь и вдруг ви́жу прия́теля, кото́рый ма́шет мне руко́й.

9. Ребёнок, кото́рый улыба́ется, всегда́ краси́в.

10. Совреме́нные учёные со́здали счётные маши́ны, кото́рые заменя́ют вычисли́тельную рабо́ту со́тен и ты́сяч люде́й.

11. Челове́к, кото́рый вхо́дит в зал, знамени́тый писа́тель.

12. Стёпа надева́ет руба́шку, кото́рая виси́т на сту́ле.

13. Гимна́стика, кото́рая де́лает челове́ка ло́вким и выно́сливым, должна́ заня́ть почётное ме́сто в шко́ле.

14. Радиоста́нция передава́ла репорта́ж о слу́хах, кото́рые не име́ли ничего́ о́бщего с фа́ктами.

15. Вы́воды, кото́рые встреча́ются в други́х кни́гах по э́тому вопро́су, не соотве́тствуют вы́водам э́того а́втора.

Test for Mastery 4

1. студе́нтка, кото́рая проспала́ заня́тия (the student who slept through her classes)

2. де́вочка, кото́рая заболе́ла (the girl who got sick)

3. самолёт, кото́рый лете́л над на́ми (the airplane that was flying over us)

4. арти́сты, кото́рые то́лько что прилете́ли из Москвы́ (the performers, who have just arrived from Moscow)

5. газе́ты, кото́рые лежа́ли на полу́ (the newspapers that were lying on the floor)

6. ка́ждый из госпо́д, кото́рые собрали́сь в кабине́те (every one of the gentlemen who had gathered in the study)

7. де́рево, кото́рое упа́ло на доро́гу (the tree that had fallen on the road)

8. стару́ха, кото́рая шла по у́лице (the old woman who was walking down the street)

9. поги́бшие солда́ты, кото́рые оста́лись на по́ле сраже́ния[9] (the dead soldiers who remained on the battlefield)

10. я́ркое со́лнце, кото́рое подняло́сь (the bright sun, which had risen)

11. молоды́е лю́ди, кото́рые бы́ли у нас у́тром (the young people who were visiting us this morning)

12. арти́стка, кото́рая всегда́ игра́ла э́ту роль (the performer who always played this role)

---

[9] **Поги́бшие** is also a past active participle meaning *the soldiers who had perished.*

Test for Mastery 5

1. Больно́й ду́мал о врача́х, кото́рые спасли́ ему́ жизнь.

2. Бы́ло сы́ро от тума́на, кото́рый поднима́лся над реко́й.

3. Мно́го уже́ говори́лось о ро́ли ро́сского наро́да, кото́рый занима́л веду́щее ме́сто в борьбе́ против Ги́тлера.

4. Мы услы́шали гудо́к, кото́рый звал рабо́чих на заво́д.

5. Тури́сты, кото́рые останови́лись на о́тдых, о́чень уста́ли.

6. Де́рево, кото́рое упа́ло на доро́гу, загороди́ло путь маши́нам.

7. Де́вушка, кото́рая ме́дленно шла по у́лице, вдруг останови́лась.

8. Он ждал её на ста́нции с волне́нием, кото́рое начало́сь ещё вчера́ ве́чером.

9. Дере́вья, кото́рые потеря́ли после́дние ли́стья и почерне́ли от дождя́, стона́ли под ветро́м

10. Мы напра́вились к До́му культу́ры, кото́рый находи́лся в це́нтре го́рода.

11. Мы приглаша́ем Вас приня́ть уча́стие в конфере́нции и обсуди́ть ситуа́цию в стране́, кото́рая сложи́лась.

12. У Никола́я, кото́рый встал в пе́рвый раз по́сле боле́зни, дрожа́ли но́ги.

Reading

[Prince Andrew] again felt alive and suffering from a burning pain that was lacerating something in his head. He started to listen and heard the sounds of the approaching tramp of horses and the sounds of voices speaking French. He opened his eyes. Above him yet again was the lofty sky, still the same, with its floating clouds, which had risen even higher and through which could be seen an infinity that was growing blue. He did not turn his head and did not see those who, judging by the sound of hoofs and voices, rode up to him and stopped.

The horsemen who had approached were Napoleon accompanied by two adjutants. Bonaparte . . . was examining the dead and wounded that remained on the battlefield.[10]

---

[10] Leo Tolstoy, *War and Peace,* vol. 1, part 3, chapter 19.

Russian-English Vocabulary

You may assume that verbs ending in **-ать** will be declined like **рабо́тать,** unless otherwise noted.

адвока́т   lawyer
анги́иа   strep throat
апельси́н   orange
апте́ка   drugstore
аспира́нт(ка)   graduate student
аспиранту́ра   graduate school
аудито́рия   classroom (in a university)

ба́бушка   grandmother
бал   ball (party)
бассе́йн   swimming pool
бе́гать / бежа́ть (*see p. 130*)   to run
бе́дный   poor
бе́лый   white
бельё   underwear
бе́рег   shore
беспоко́иться (-ко́юсь, -ко́ишься)   to worry
благодаря́   thanks to
блесте́ть (блещу́, блести́шь)   to shine
блестя́щий   brilliant
ближа́йший   nearest, closest
бога́тство   wealth
бога́тый   rich
бой   battle
бок (*pl.* бока́)   side
боле́ть (боле́ю, боле́ешь) / за-   to be sick
болта́ть   to chat
боль (*f.*)   a pain
больни́ца   hospital
больно́й   a sick person, patient
большо́й   big
боро́ться (борю́сь, бо́решься) за   to struggle for (+ acc.)
боя́ться (бою́сь, бои́шься)   to be afraid of
брат (*pl.* бра́тья)   brother
брать (беру́, берёшь) / взять (возьму́, возьмёшь)   to take
бри́ться (бре́юсь, бре́ешься)   to shave

буди́ть (бужу́, буди́шь) / раз-   to wake someone
бу́дущее   the future
бу́дущий   future
бу́ря   storm
бы́вший   former
бы́стрый   fast, quick

ва́нная   bathroom
ведь   after all
велосипе́д   bicycle
ве́рить (ве́рю, ве́ришь) / по-   to believe
ве́рующий   a believer, congregant
весёлый   happy
весь/всё/вся   all, the whole
ве́чер (*pl.* вечера́)   evening
вечери́нка   party
ве́чером   in the evening
ве́чный   eternal
вещь   thing
вид   view; име́ть в виду́   to have in mind
ви́деть (ви́жу, ви́дишь) / у-   to see
ви́лка   fork
висе́ть (вишу́, виси́шь)   to hang
вишнёвый   cherry (*adj.*)
вку́сный   tasty, good
вла́жный   humid
во́время   on time
во-вторы́х   secondly
води́тель   driver
води́ть (вожу́, во́дишь) / вести́ (веду́, ведёшь) past: вёл, вела́   to lead, conduct
возвраща́ться / верну́ться   to return
во́здух   air
вози́ть (вожу́, во́зишь) / везти́ (везу́, везёшь) past: вёз, везла́   to take by vehicle, transport
вокза́л   train station
волне́ние   agitation
во́лосы   hair

вопро́с   question
воро́та (*pl. only*)   gate(s)
восто́к   east
восто́рг   ecstasy
впереди́   in front
враг   enemy
врач   physician
вре́дный   harmful, noxious
вре́мя   time
все   everyone, all (*pl.*)
всегда́   always
Вселе́нная   the Universe
встава́ть (встаю́, встаёшь) / встать (вста́ну, вста́нешь)   to get up
встреча́ть / встре́тить (-ре́чу, -ре́тишь)   to meet
вся́кий   each, every
вчера́   yesterday
выбира́ть / вы́брать (вы́беру, вы́берешь)   to choose, select, elect
вы́вод   conclusion
вы́глядеть (вы́гляжу, вы́глядишь)   to look
выдаю́щийся   outstanding
выключа́ть / вы́ключить (вы́ключу, вы́ключишь)   to turn off
выноси́ть (*like* носи́ть) / вы́нести (*like* нести́, *but stressed on* вы́-)   to stand, tolerate
выполня́ть / вы́полнить (вы́полню, вы́полнишь)   to fill out
высо́кий (вы́ше)   tall, high
вы́ставка   exhibition

гастроно́м   food store, deli, charcuterie
геро́й / герои́ня   hero; heroine
гла́вный   main, principal
гла́дить (гла́жу, гла́дишь) / по-   to iron
глаз (*pl.* глаза́)   eye
глота́ть   to swallow
глубо́кий (глу́бже)   deep
глу́пый   stupid, silly, dumb
глухо́й   deaf
говоря́щий   the speaker
год   year
голова́   head
го́лод   hunger
го́лос   voice
гора́   mountain
горди́ться (горжу́сь, горди́шься)   to be proud of
го́ре   sorrow, grief
го́род   city

гости́ница   hotel
госуда́рство   state, government
гото́вить (-то́влю, -то́вишь) / при-   to prepare, cook
гро́мкий (гро́мче)   loud
грудь   chest, breast
грузови́к   truck
гря́зный   dirty
гуля́ть / по-   to go out for a walk

дава́ть (даю́, даёшь) / дать (*see p. 130*)   to give
давле́ние   pressure
давно́   long ago
да́нные   data
дари́ть / по-   to give as a present
да́ча   dacha, summer cottage
дверь   door
двор   yard
де́вочка   little girl
де́вушка   girl, young woman
де́душка   grandfather
де́йствие   act, action
де́лать / с-   to do, make
де́ло   affair, business
день рожде́ния   birthday
де́ньги   money
дере́вня   countryside
де́рево (*pl.* дере́вья)   tree
деревя́нный   wooden
детекти́в   a murder mystery
де́тский   children's (*adj.*)
дешёвый   cheap, inexpensive
дли́нный   long
длить (длю, длишь) / про-   to last
днём   in the afternoon
до́брый   good, kindhearted
дово́лен / дово́льна   to be pleased, satisfied
дождь   rain
докла́д   report
до́лжен / -жна́ -жно́, -жны́   must, ought to
дорого́й   expensive, dear
достопримеча́тельность   sight (of a city)
дочь   daughter
дрема́ть (дремлю́, дре́млешь)   to daydream, doze
друг (*pl.* друзья́)   friend
ду́мать   to think
духи́   perfume (*pl. only*)
дыша́ть (дышу́, ды́шишь)   to breathe
дя́дя   uncle

ежедне́вно   daily

е́здить (е́зжу, е́здишь) / е́хать (е́ду, е́дешь)   to go by vehicle

есть / съесть (*see p. 130*)   to eat

ещё   still

жа́ловаться (жа́луюсь, жа́луешься) на   to complain about

жаль   it's too bad, it's a pity

жар   heat

ждать (жду, ждёшь) / подожда́ть   to wait (for)

жела́ние   desire

жела́ть / по-   to desire, wish

желу́док   stomach

жени́ться (женю́сь, же́нишься) на   to marry (said of a man) (+ prep.)

живо́т   abdomen

живо́тное   animal

жизнь   life

жить (живу́, живёшь)   to live

заболе́ть (*see* боле́ть)

забыва́ть / забы́ть (забу́ду, забу́дешь)   to forget

заве́дующий   director, manager

зави́довать (зави́дую, зави́дуешь) / по-   to envy

заво́д   factory

за́втра   tomorrow

за́втракать / по-   to have breakfast

задава́ть / зада́ть (*like* дать)   to ask (a question)

зада́ча   problem, task

закрыва́ть / закры́ть (закро́ю, закро́ешь)   to close

замеча́тельный   remarkable

занима́ть / заня́ть (займу́, займёшь)   to occupy, hold

занима́ться   to study, be engaged in

зану́да   a bore

заня́тия   school, classes

заня́той   busy

за́пад   west

за́пах   smell, odor

запреща́ть / запрети́ть (-прещу́, -прети́шь)   to forbid

заслу́живать / -жи́ть (-служу́, -слу́жишь)   to earn

заходи́ть / зайти́ (*like* ходи́ть, йдти́)   to drop in, by

звезда́   star

зверь   beast, wild animal

звони́ть (звоню́, звони́шь) / по-   to telephone, call

зда́ние   building

здоро́вье   health

здра́вствуй(те)   hello

Земля́   Earth

зима́   winter

змея́   snake

знако́мый   acquaintance

знать   to know

зо́лото   gold

зуб   tooth

зубно́й врач   dentist

игра́ть в   to play (a sport) (+ acc.)

игра́ть на   to play (a musical instrument) (+ prep.)

игру́шка   toy

избега́ть / избежа́ть (*see p. 130*)   to avoid

изве́стный   famous, well known

извини́те   excuse me

измеря́ть / изме́рить (-ме́рю, -ме́ришь)   to measure

изуча́ть / -чи́ть (-учу́, -у́чишь)   to study; master

икра́   caviar

име́ть (име́ю, име́ешь)   to have (with abstract nouns)

и́мя   first name

инсу́льт   stroke (medical)

инфа́ркт   heart attack

иска́ть (ищу́, и́щешь)   to look for

каза́ться (кажу́сь, ка́жешься) / по-   to seem

како́й   which, what kind of

кани́кулы   vacation

ка́пля   drop

каранда́ш   pencil

каса́ться / косну́ться   to concern

касси́р   cashier

кастрю́ля   pan

ката́ться   to go, roll (+ на, + vehicle in prep.)

кача́ть   to shake, nod

ка́шель (*m.*)   cough

кварти́ра   apartment

кинозвезда́   movie star

киносту́дия   movie studio

кла́дбище   cemetery

класть (кладу́, кладёшь) / положи́ть (положу́, поло́жишь)   to put, place

кни́га   book

колбаса́   sausage

колесо́ (*pl.* колёса)   wheel

кольцо́   ring (jewelry)

коне́ц   end

коне́чно   of course

конфе́та   a piece of candy

коньки́   skates

коро́бка box
коро́ль king
коро́ткий (коро́че) short
кото́рый who, which, that
ко́шка cat
край edge
краса́вица a beauty
краси́вый beautiful
кра́сный red
красть (краду́, крадёшь), / у- to steal
кровь blood
круг circle
кру́пный major, important
крыло́ wing
куда́ to where, whence
ку́кла doll
купа́ться to bathe, go swimming
купе́ц merchant
кури́ть (курю́, ку́ришь) to smoke
кусо́к piece
ку́хня kitchen

ла́дно okay, fine
ле́вый left
лёгкий easy, light
лёгкие lungs
лёд ice
лежа́ть (лежу́, лежи́шь) to be lying down
лека́рство medicine
ле́кция lecture
лес woods
лета́ть / лете́ть (лечу́, лети́шь) to fly
ле́то summer
лётчик pilot
лечи́ть (лечу́, ле́чишь) / из- to treat; cure
лицо́ face
лоб forehead
лови́ть (ловлю́, ло́вишь) / пойма́ть (пойму́, поймёшь) to catch
ло́дка boat
ложи́ться (ложу́сь, ложи́шься) / лечь (ля́гу, ля́жешь) to lie down
ло́жка spoon
ло́шадь horse
луг meadow
любо́вь (f.) love

магази́н store
ма́йка undershirt

ма́ленький (меньше) small, little
ма́ло (very) little
ма́льчик boy
ма́рка stamp
ме́бель furniture
мёд honey
медбра́т nurse (male)
медве́дь bear
медсестра́ nurse (female)
ме́лочь change (money)
ме́сто place, spot
ме́сяц month
мех fur
меша́ть / по- to disturb, bother (+ dat.)
ми́шка teddy bear
мла́дший younger (adj.)
Мле́чный путь Milky Way
мне́ние opinion
мно́го much, a lot
мозг brain
молодёжь youth, young people
молодо́й young
молча́ть (молчу́, молчи́шь) / за- to be silent
мо́ре sea
моро́женое ice cream
моро́з frost, freezing weather
мост bridge
мочь (могу́, мо́жешь) / смочь can, to be able
муж (pl. мужья́) husband
мужчи́на man
музе́й museum
мураве́й ant
мыть (мо́ю, мо́ешь) / по- to wash

на́бережная embankment
надева́ть / наде́ть (-де́ну, -де́нешь) to put on
наде́яться (-де́юсь, -де́ешься) на to rely on
на́до must, have to
надоеда́ть / надое́сть (see p. 130) to be sick of, fed up with
назнача́ть / назна́чить (назна́чу, назна́чишь) to name, designate
наконе́ц finally
наро́д the people
насеко́мое insect
настоя́щее the present
находи́ться to be located
начина́ть / нача́ть (начну́, начнёшь) to begin
начина́ющий a beginner

неде́ля   week
не́жный   gentle, loving
нездоро́виться   to not feel well (+ dat.)
нельзя́   not permitted, forbidden
неме́дленно   immediately
немно́го   a little bit
неожи́данный   unexpected
не́рвничать   to be nervous
не́сколько   a few, several
неуже́ли   really?
ни́зкий (ниже)   low
никогда́   never
ничего́   nothing
но́вый   new
нога́ (*pl.* но́ги)   foot, leg
нож   knife
но́жницы   scissors
нос   nose
носи́ть (ношу́, но́сишь) / нести́ (несу́, несёшь) past:
   нёс, несла́   to take, carry
нра́виться (нра́влюсь, нра́вишься) / по-   to like,
   appeal to
ну́жен / нужна́ / ну́жно / нужны́   need
ну́жно   one must

о (об, обо)   about, concerning
обе́дать / по-   to have dinner
обеща́ть / по-   to promise
ого́нь   fire, flame
огоро́д   vegetable garden
одева́ться / оде́ться (оде́нусь, оде́нешься)   to get
   dressed
о́зеро (*pl.* озёра)   lake
озно́б   chills, ague
ока́зываться / -за́ться (окажу́сь, ока́жешься)   to
   turn out to be
окно́   window
опа́здывать / опозда́ть (-зда́ю, -зда́ешь)   to be late
опуска́ть / опусти́ть (опущу́, -стишь)   to drop
о́сень   autumn
основа́ть   to found, base
остано́вка   (bus) stop
о́стров (*pl.* острова́)   island
отвеча́ть / отве́тить(-ве́чу, -ве́тишь)   to answer
отдыха́ть / отдохну́ть   to relax, go on vacation
оте́ц   father
открыва́ть / откры́ть (-кро́ю, -кро́ешь)   to open
откры́тие   discovery
отли́чный   excellent

о́тчество   patronymic
официа́нт/ка   waiter, waitress
оце́нка   evaluation
очеви́дно   obviously, evidently
о́чередь   line, queue
очки́   eyeglasses
ошиба́ться / ошиби́ться (ошиблю́сь, ошиби́шься) в
   to err, make a mistake
оши́бка   a mistake

па́дать / упа́сть (упаду́, упадёшь)   to fall
па́лец   finger or toe
па́мятник   monument
певе́ц / певи́ца   singer
переводи́ть (-вожу́, -води́шь) / перевести́ (-веду́,
   -ведёшь)   to translate
перево́дчик   translator
передава́ть / переда́ть (*like* дава́ть / дать)   to give,
   transmit, broadcast, hand in
переду́мать   to rethink, change one's mind
перехо́д   passage, transition
перо́ (*pl.* пе́рья)   feather; fountain pen
пе́сня   song
петь (пою́, поёшь) / с-   to sing
печь (пеку́, печёшь) past: пёк, пекла́ / ис-   to bake
писа́тель   writer
писа́ть (пишу́, пи́шешь) / на-   to write
письмо́   a letter
пить / вы́-   to drink
пла́вать / плыть (плыву́, плывёшь) / поплыть   to
   swim
пла́кать (пла́чу, пла́чешь) / запла́кать   to cry
плати́ть / за-   to pay (+ за + acc.)
пла́тье   dress
плева́ть (плюю́, плюёшь) / плюну́ть   to spit
плечо́   shoulder
плохо́й   bad
пло́щадь   square, plaza; territory
пляж   beach
по́вар   cook
поведе́ние   behavior
повторя́ть / -ри́ть (-вторю́, -втори́шь)   to repeat
пого́да   weather
пода́рок   a gift, present
подборо́док   chin
поднима́ться / подня́ться (подниму́сь, подни́мешься)
   to go up, be lifted
по́езд   train
пожа́рник   firefighter

позволя́ть / -ли́ть (-во́лю, -во́лишь)   to allow, permit

пока́зывать / -за́ть (-кажу́, -ка́жешь)   to show

покупа́ть / купи́ть (куплю́, ку́пишь)   to buy

по́лдень   noon

по́ле   field

поле́зный   useful

по́лночь   midnight

по́лный   full

полови́на   half

положи́ть   (*see* **класть**)

получа́ть / получи́ть (-учу́, -у́чишь)   to receive

полуша́рие   hemisphere

помеща́ть / помести́ть (помещу́, помести́шь)   to fit

по́мнить (-по́мню, по́мнишь)   to remember

помога́ть / помо́чь (*like* **мочь**)   to help

по́мощь   help (*noun*)

понима́ть / поня́ть (пойму́, поймёшь)   to understand

пора́   it's time (+ dat.)

после́дний   last (in a series)

поступа́ть / поступи́ть (-уплю́, -у́пишь)   to apply; to get in

посу́да   dishes

посыла́ть / посла́ть (пошлю́, пошлёшь)   to send

по́хороны   funeral

по́чта   post office

пра́вило   rule

прави́тельство   administration

пра́вый   right

пра́здник   holiday

пра́здновать   to celebrate

прекра́сный   wonderful

преподава́ть (*like* **дава́ть**)   to teach

привыка́ть / -вы́кнуть   to become used to

приглаша́ть / пригласи́ть (-глашу́, -гласи́шь)   to invite

прие́зда   arrival

принадлежа́ть (-жу́, жи́шь)   to belong (+ dat.)

принима́ть / приня́ть (приму́, при́мешь)   to accept, receive, take

приноси́ть / принести́ (*like* **носи́ть/нести́**)   to bring (carrying)

прича́стие   participle

проводи́ть / провести́ (*like* **води́ть/вести́**)   to pass (time)

продава́ть / прода́ть (*like* **дава́ть/дать**)   to sell

продаве́ц / продавщи́ца   salesperson

продолжа́ть / продо́лжить (-до́лжу, -до́лжишь)   to continue

происходи́ть / произойти́ (-изойду́, -изойдёшь)   to happen, occur

просыпа́ть / -спа́ть (сплю, спишь)   to oversleep

проше́дшее   the past

про́шлый   last (summer, year, etc.)

путеше́ствовать (-ше́ствую, -ше́ствуешь)   to travel

путь   road, way, means

пье́са   play (of literature)

рабо́та   work, a job

равноду́шный   indifferent

рад   happy, glad

разгова́ривать   to converse

раздева́ться / разде́ться   to undress

рассве́т   dawn

рассе́янный   absentminded

рассма́тривать / рассмотре́ть (-трю́, -мо́тришь)   to examine

расти́ (расту́, растёшь) / вы́-   to grow

рво́та   vomit

ребёнок (*pl.* дети)   child

ре́дкий (реже)   rare

режиссёр   director

ре́зать / с-   to cut

река́   river

рекла́ма   advertisement

речь   speech

реша́ть / -ши́ть   solve, decide

рису́нок   drawing

ро́дина   native land

роди́тели   parents

роди́ться   to be born

рома́н   novel

рот   mouth

руби́ть (рублю́, ру́бишь) / с-   to chop

рука́   hand, arm

руководи́тель   guide, leader

ру́чка   pen

ры́ба   fish

ры́нок   market

ряд   row

ря́дом   next to, next door

сад   garden

сади́ться (сажу́сь, сади́шься) / сесть (ся́ду, ся́дешь)   to sit down

самолёт   airplane

са́мый   the most

санато́рий   sanitarium, spa

сва́дьба wedding
све́жий fresh
све́тлый light
свинья́ pig
свобо́да freedom
свобо́дный free
се́вер north
сего́дня today
семья́ family
серди́ться (сержу́сь, се́рдишься) / рас- to get angry
се́рдце heart
серебро́ silver
се́рьги (серёжки) earrings
сиде́ть (сижу́, сиди́шь) to be sitting
си́льный strong
симпати́чный nice, personable, cute
ско́лько how many?
ско́ро soon
ску́чный boring
сла́бый weak
сла́дкий sweet
сле́дующий next, following
сли́вки cream
сли́шком too, excessively
слова́рь dictionary, glossary
сло́во word
сло́жный complex, complicated
слух rumor
слу́чай incident
случа́ться / -чи́ться to happen, take place
слы́шать (слы́шу, слы́шишь) / услы́шать to hear
смерть death
смешно́й funny
смея́ться (смею́сь, смеёшься) to laugh
смотре́ть (смотрю́, смо́тришь) / по- на to look at
снег snow
снима́ть / снять (сниму́, сни́мешь) to take off, to rent, to photograph
снотво́рное sleep-inducing
соба́ка dog
собира́ть / собра́ть (*like* брать) to gather, collect
собира́ться / собра́ться to gather, meet
собра́ние meeting
сове́товать (сове́тую, сове́туешь) / по- to advise
совреме́нный contemporary
согла́сен / -сна in agreement with
согла́сно according to (+ dat.)
со́лнечный sunny
со́лнце sun

соль salt
сомнева́ться в to doubt something
соотве́тствовать to correspond
сосе́д (*pl.* сосе́ди) neighbor
сочине́ние composition
спа́льня bedroom
спаси́бо thank you
спать (сплю, спишь) to sleep
спина́ back (of the body)
спле́тничать to gossip
спо́рить to argue
спортсме́н/ка athlete
спосо́бный competent, able
станови́ться / стать (ста́ну, ста́нешь) to become
ста́нция (subway) station
ста́рший elder
ста́рый old
стира́ть / вы́- to do the laundry
стихи́ verse, poetry
сто́ить to cost (third person only: сто́ит, сто́ят)
столо́вая dining room; cafeteria
сторона́ side
страда́ть / по- to suffer
страна́ country
страни́ца page
стра́шный awful, terrible
стреля́ть / вы́стрелить to shoot
стро́гий strict, stern
стул (*pl.* сту́лья) chair
суд court
судья́ judge
сумасше́дший insane, crazy
су́мка bag, purse
существо́ being
сцена́рий screen play
счастли́вый happy, lucky
сча́стье happiness
счита́ть / со- to count, consider
сын (*pl.* сыновья́) son

танцева́ть (танцу́ю, танцу́ешь) to dance
те́ло body
теря́ть / по- to lose
тетра́дь notebook
тётя aunt
ти́хий quiet
толсте́ть (толсте́ю, толсте́ешь) / по- to gain weight
то́лько only

тосковáть (тоскýю, тоскýешь) to be sad, long for
тошнотá nausea
трéбовать (трéбую, трéбуешь) / по- to demand
треть one third
трóгать / трóнуть to touch
трýдный difficult
тýфля shoe
тьма darkness

убирáть / убрáть (уберý, уберёшь) to clean, tidy up
убóрщик / -щица janitor
уважáть to respect
увéренный self-assured
уверять / увéрить в to assure (someone) of something
ýгол corner
удóбство convenience
удовóльствие pleasure
ужé already
ýжинать / по- to have supper
узнавáть (узнаю́, узнаёшь) / узнáть (узнáю, узнáешь) to recognize
уливляться / -виться (-влюсь, -вишься) to be surprised
ýлица street
улыбáться / улыбнýться to smile (+ dat.)
умирáть / умерéть (умрý, умрёшь) to die
ýмный smart, intelligent
упражнéние exercise
урóдливый ugly
урóк lesson
услóвие condition
успéшный successful
успокóйтельный calming, soothing
ýтром in the morning
ýхо (pl. ýши) ear
учáствовать в to take part in something
учёный scholar, scientist
учи́тель / учи́тельница teacher
учи́ть (учý, ýчишь) / вы́- to learn, memorize
учи́ться to study at
учи́ться на to study to be something (+ acc.)

фéрма farm
фигýргое катáние figure skating
фи́зик physicist
филóсоф philosopher

фи́рма firm, company
хи́мик chemist
ходи́ть (хожý, хóдишь) / идти́ (идý, идёшь) to go (by foot)
холóдный cold
хорóший good
хотéть (*see p. 130*) to want
худéть (худéю, худéешь) / по- to lose weight
худóжник artist

цвет color
цветóк (*pl.* цветы́) flower
цепóчка chain, necklace
цéрковь church
цирк circus

час hour
чáстный private, personal
чáсто often, frequent
человéк (*pl.* лю́ди) person
чёрный black
чéстно говоря́ to be honest, speaking honestly
чини́ть / по- to repair
чи́стить (чи́щу, чи́стишь) / по- to clean
читáть / про- to read
чтóбы in order to
чудóвище monster

шéя neck
широ́кий (ши́ре) wide
шкаф cupboard
шóпотом in a whisper
шýмный noisy
шáхматы chess

щекá cheek

экзáмен major test

юг south
ю́ноша young man
юри́ст lawyer

я́блоко apple
язы́к language, tongue
я́сный clear